THE
ASSEMBLIES
OF GOD

A Chapter in the Story
of American Pentecostalism
Volume 2–Since 1941

Edith L. Blumhofer

Gospel Publishing House
Springfield, Missouri
02–0458

Chapter 6 is adapted from William W. Menzies, *Anointed to Serve* (Springfield, MO: Gospel Publishing House, 1971), chapters 10, 11, 13. Used by permission.

Library of Congress Cataloging-in-Publication Data
(Revised for vol. 2)

Blumhofer, Edith Waldvogel.
  The Assemblies of God.

  Includes bibliographies and indexes.
  Contents: v. 1. To 1941—v. 2. Since 1941.
  1. Assemblies of God—United States. 2. Pentecostal churches— United States. 3. United States—Church history—20th century. I. Title.
BX8765.5.A4B58   1989   289.9'4   88-39626
  ISBN 0-88243-457-8 (v. 1)
  ISBN 0-88243-458-6 (v. 2)

Printed in the United States of America

Table of Contents

Foreword 5

Preface 7

Introduction 9

1. From Isolation to Cooperation: The Assemblies of God and the New Evangelicals 13

2. Fronts for United Action: Cooperation With Evangelicals and Pentecostals 35

3. Dissonance Among Pentecostals: The Assemblies of God Responds 53

4. Ecumenism, Renewal, and Pentecostal Identity 85

5. Education 109

6. Denominational Programs 137

7. The Recent Past 165

Appendices

Administrative and Operational Flow Chart 198

Officers of the General Council: 1914–1987 201

Endnotes 207

Bibliographic Comments 233

Subject Index 235

Foreword

It has been seventy-five years since some three hundred people answered the call to attend a gathering of Pentecostal saints in Hot Springs, Arkansas. Few at that convention could have dreamed the organization they founded—the General Council of the Assemblies of God—would become in so short a time the largest Pentecostal denomination in the world. From those three hundred delegates, the church has grown to encompass over eighteen million members and adherents worldwide.

The story of the Assemblies of God includes testimonies of exceptional commitment by those early leaders as they struggled to forge a strong church even as it underwent the heat and pressure of doctrinal differences, economic crises, and growing pains. But this volume is much more than a story of human efforts. It is most of all the story of divine intervention and guidance as those early believers committed themselves wholly to the Word of God and the leading of the Holy Spirit.

Today, just as seventy-five years ago, we recognize that God's work is accomplished "not by might, nor by power, but by [His] Spirit" (Zechariah 4:6). I commend to you this second of a two-volume history of the Assemblies of God, with the prayer that you will see beyond the record of human efforts and events to the mighty power of God—still at work in His church today.

G. Raymond Carlson
General Superintendent

Preface

My work on *The Assemblies of God—Since 1941* has benefited especially from the comments of Grant Wacker, Jr., Russell Spittler, Cecil M. Robeck, Margaret Poloma, Joel Carpenter, Wayne E. Warner, J. Robert Ashcroft, Adele Dalton, and my father, Edwin H. Waldvogel. I am grateful as well to the Executive Presbytery of the Assemblies of God, and especially to Everett R. Stenhouse, Joseph R. Flower, and R. D. E. Smith for their encouragement throughout this project. With their support, the denomination has allowed me to explore and interpret its history in a way that has not been encouraged in the past. I benefitted as well from conversations with Thomas F. Zimmerman, who commissioned this work in 1985. The staffs of the Assemblies of God Archives and the denomination's Secretariat have been most helpful. My two student assistants at Wheaton College, Teri Kondo and Kristin Helmer, have provided invaluable assistance.

Introduction

In October 1988 a prominent Assemblies of God congregation advertised a seminar entitled "Visions of Loveliness." A promotional flyer encouraged women to attend to gain "poise and confidence as God's representatives." Advertised topics for the six Saturday morning workshops included hair care, nails, diet, makeup and, of course, "inner loveliness." The final activity was a luncheon and fashion show.

Neither promoters nor participants thought the activities incompatible with their Assemblies of God context. That such topics are addressed in church-sponsored groups without reservation, however, illustrates how basically the understanding of the meaning and purpose of Pentecostal experience has shifted within the denomination over the years. A similar schedule dated 1914 and listing sessions with the denomination's founding mothers on the same topics would seem palpably incongruous.

Such events indicate basic differences between the contemporary context of Assemblies of God participant expectations and the denomination's early history. Behavioral norms and the religious and cultural expectations of the faithful tend to evidence the denomination's permeation by the governing assumptions of twentieth-century culture. The changing function of faith (which once excluded, or at least made irrelevant, the claims of the culture) has helped shape a constituency that enjoys popularity and affluence and embraces a growing world-wide membership.[1] By any standard, the denomination's growth, affluence, and energy are impressive. Success, measured by most statistics, seems phenomenal. But popular attitudes, assumptions, and mood have changed, too, and the meaning of such changes for American Pentecostal identity has yet to be assessed.

Recent statistics indicate growth in numbers of Assemblies of God churches, especially in Hispanic districts. The average membership of a local congregation has increased in the past decade from 99.1 to 115.6. Giving in numerous programs has also increased steadily. Average Sunday morning worship attendance at U.S. Assemblies of God churches in 1986 was approaching 1.5 million. Numbers of ministers increase annually, due both to longer lifespans and the credentialing of new workers.[2] At the same time, however, both Sunday school enrollment and average Sunday school attendance are declining. And even as the New Church Evangelism Department reported an average of over 300 new churches per year in the 1980s, the general secretary's office noted the closing of 215 Assemblies of God churches in 1985 and 1986.[3] The denomination intends to address and reverse such decline in its Decade of Harvest, an evangelistic focus for the 1990s.

The story of growth, influence, and changing expectations that helped transform a small denomination into a large and thriving one begins in the 1940s. The following chapters explore basic issues in the Pentecostal subculture since World War II, with a focus on their importance for the Assemblies of God.

The World War II era accelerated social change in America. Population shifts and the draft loosened family ties; technological developments and the demands of wartime production contributed to prosperity after prolonged depression; new roles for women and blacks weakened long-established cultural patterns. After the war, the GI Bill made higher education a reality for hundreds of thousands of men and women. America emerged from the war a world power, committed by treaty to maintaining freedoms abroad, her culture more extensive than ever before.

American religion, influenced by cultural changes, seemed more popular than ever at the close of the war.[4] As measured by Sunday school and church attendance, religion was increasingly important to Americans through the 1950s. But the postwar surge of interest in religion was a revival with a difference. Of its popular spokespersons, only Billy Graham echoed the rhetoric of earlier revivals. At one level, other expressions of renewed religious strength dismayed American Pentecostals: a burgeoning ecumenical movement, the growing influence of Catholicism and of individual Catholics like Fulton Sheen, the best-selling religious versions of self-help manuals (Norman Vincent Peale's *The Power of Positive Thinking,* for example). At another level, of course, these were palpable and optimistic "signs of the times," and events in the Pentecostal subculture seemed to suggest that a new Pentecostal effusion was likely.

The newly visible religiosity was closely linked to patriotic pride in America. The defeat of fascism, the ongoing cold war, the Berlin airlift; the Korean War—all kept the threat of totalitarianism, especially communism, vivid. Being religious was one way of affirming patriotic indignation with "godless communism." Religiosity also tended to include affirming longstanding American values. But it endorsed new values as well, as a value system endorsing America's indulgence of growing materialistic appetites emerged.

Like other religious institutions, the Assemblies of God was deeply influenced by rapid cultural change. Each of the broad topics considered in this book must be understood in the context of the times. Until the 1960s, at one level, a benign religiosity seemed, to some, to characterize much of the nation. At another level, of course, unrest in such forms as the civil rights movement threatened equanimity. Americans, more mobile than ever, faced social change amid loosened family and neighborhood ties. This, too, posed a challenge for the churches. And in the background was the constant threat of nuclear annihilation, more appalling than even the grim memories of Hiroshima and Nagasaki.

A survey of the *Pentecostal Evangel* during the war years indicates that Assemblies of God leaders and lay people tended to support World War II more than they had World War I. Like most Americans, they seem to have conceded that the evil of war was preferable to the greater evil of a fascist victory. War raised the question of chaplains in evangelical ranks. For Pentecostals, chaplaincy training became an issue that ultimately influenced the course of denominational education. Ecumenism, and the purported cultural force it brought to mainline denominations, became a rallying point for evangelicals who felt both threatened and excluded. Mobilizing against a common enemy brought the Assemblies of God into the ranks of an early evangelical coalition: the National Association of Evangelicals. The ecumenical movement, however, helped revive an earlier definition of Pentecostalism that had understood its function as reviving all churches. The activities of David du Plessis symbolize the resurgence of interest among some Pentecostals and mainliners in discovering what the Pentecostal movement had to say to older denominations. In the religiously attuned atmosphere of the late 1940s, vigorous Pentecostal efforts to evangelize America commingled as the salvation/healing revival. Meanwhile, as the Assemblies of God sought to meet contemporary challenges, an uncompromising call to an earlier definition of Pentecostalism as the "latter rain" attempted to reassert forgotten rhetoric and to renew experience in a generation of adherents more staid than the last.

At the same time, of course, the Assemblies of God sought to organize a growing constituency and to keep alive a heritage that valued experience as well as doctrine. Influenced by church growth ideas as taught, for example, at Fuller Theological Seminary, the denomination attempted to balance its older rhetoric of reliance on the Holy Spirit with a systematic, goal-oriented approach to growth. It is easy to cite the statistics of growth; it has proven more difficult to assess its quality.

1. From Isolation to Cooperation: The Assemblies of God and the New Evangelicals

Early in April 1942, Ernest S. Williams, general superintendent of the Assemblies of God, J. Roswell Flower, general secretary, Noel Perkin, foreign missions secretary, and Ralph Riggs, superintendent of the Southern Missouri District, boarded a St. Louis-bound train in Springfield, Missouri. Their destination was the Coronado Hotel, where they had been invited to consult with other conservative Protestant leaders about the prospects and possibilities of united evangelical action. They had accepted the invitation gratefully, without apparent misgivings.[1] For the Assemblies of God, the trip became the first stage of a journey from isolation to cooperation.

Isolation of Early Pentecostals

Until the 1940s, American Pentecostalism was relatively isolated from traditional Protestantism. In general, its adherents purposely rejected both institutional affiliation and practical cooperation with non-Pentecostals. (For that matter, Pentecostal groups had extremely little contact with one another.) Several factors made such aloofness seem both necessary and attractive.

First, Pentecostals ardently believed that their movement had a more accurate perception of New Testament Christianity than any other Christian group: They spurned the "cold," "dead" denominational churches, which (because they rejected certain worship styles or spiritual gifts) presumably lacked sensitivity to the Holy Spirit.

Second, an important ingredient in the early Pentecostal psyche had been the cultivation of a sense of being alienated

13

from the culture.[2] Sermons, songs, and published admonitions reminded Pentecostals that they lived in perpetual conflict: The enemy, real or imagined, played an important role in defining their attitude toward culture. If physical persecution waned, spiritual conflict continued. And nowhere was that conflict more intense than with "unbelievers" in the church at large. Modernists, fundamentalists, holiness advocates, ordinary members of traditional churches, had many dissimilarities, but they all opposed Pentecostalism. At any given time, one or all of them fulfilled the role of enemies against whom Pentecostals tested their own spiritual vitality.

Third, the splintering of Pentecostalism complicated the picture, giving the impression of internal disarray. In its opposition to centralized institutional authority, Pentecostalism had nurtured a strong individualism; in its appeal to the authority of the Holy Spirit as Revealer and Illuminator, it had assured the persistence of new insights that often shattered old loyalties and spawned new sects.

In spite of frequently reiterated claims that Pentecostals were forced by the ill will of longer-established denominations to develop on their own, clearly in the beginning Pentecostals found that such rejection by other religious groups confirmed for them the truth of their message. Once they formed denominations, Pentecostals often felt neither an inclination nor a need to associate with one another or with other Christians. Isolation was not entirely imposed on them: It was by some carefully cultivated and served an important social function.

Pentecostal denominations evolved on their own, without reference to one another. At least since 1916, the Assemblies of God had exhibited tendencies that separated it from other Pentecostal denominations. Well-defined requirements for credentialing differentiated insiders and outsiders. To be sure, probably a majority of Assemblies of God members continued to affirm the restorationist intentions of early Pentecostalism. However, their behavior often belied such affirmations.

After they disowned Oneness advocates in 1916,[3] Assemblies of God leaders opted for courses of action that distanced the denomination in important ways from what others regarded as the essence of Pentecostalism: The Assemblies of God became increasingly organized; it quickly developed educational institutions to train its ministers, encouraged affiliated churches to utilize various techniques for Christian education, developed an aggressive missionary program, implemented programs, and devised statistical measures of success. (A subtle but profoundly significant change in assumptions about success would contribute to the tendency to equate growth with divine approval.) By 1925, a remnant of early Pentecostal leaders looked askance at this denomination, which, they admitted, sponsored excellent programs but which, they charged, was most emphatically no longer Pentecostal.[4]

The Assemblies of God was by far the largest and most widely dispersed Pentecostal denomination. As it mushroomed it shed its early restorationist and premillennialist fervor and became more like longer-established denominations. A few Assemblies of God leaders believed that by cooperative efforts they could both strengthen their movement and contribute support to causes they sympathized with. Some Assemblies of God ministries (like Raymond T. Richey's) already cooperated extensively with other evangelistic efforts. The causes espoused by fundamentalists seemed to coincide in meaningful ways with Assemblies of God denominational interests and to offer as well an opportunity for expressing Pentecostal sympathies with doctrinal "fundamentals."

The question of whether they were fundamentalists did not preoccupy early Assemblies of God leaders; they simply assumed they were. The question had significant implications, however, for some cherished Pentecostal assumptions as well as for non-Pentecostal definitions of "fundamentalist" and "evangelical": Were Pentecostal distinctives optional or did they constitute an essential part of Christian experience? Many Pentecostals (though not necessarily Assemblies of God adherents) maintained that Pentecostal views were essential to full Christian experience, whereas promoters of united action seemed to hold that such views were optional. On the part of fundamentalists, could they properly embrace those who upheld the importance of experiences the dispensationalist hermeneutic deemed impossible? During the 1940s new answers to such questions were proposed. They had profound meaning for the future of the Assemblies of God.

The Assemblies of God and Fundamentalism

When the delegation from Springfield arrived in St. Louis for consultations beginning April 7, 1942, they mingled with a group of men from many denominations who were convinced of the need to rethink how to state who they were. Some were persuaded that the term "fundamentalist" had outlived its usefulness—that it connoted thoroughgoing dispensationalism, separatism, anti-intellectualism, and bitter confrontations. They had already decided to avoid founding a "council," since both liberals and militant fundamentalists had appropriated that word. Instead, they chose to try to renew the force of an old word: "evangelical."

Throughout most of the nineteenth century, American evangelicals, strongly influenced by European pietism, had advocated a stress on religious experience, reverence for the Bible, and commitment to moral action as basic ingredients of American Protestantism. Evangelicals held positions of importance in major denominations and exerted considerable cultural authority.[5] During the years that Pentecostalism emerged, however, evangelicalism had suffered declining cultural prestige as secularism, modernism, and immigrant faiths gained visibility and influence. In response to modernism, conservative evangelicals (some of whom later came to be known as fundamentalists) determined to define and defend right belief.[6]

Several studies of fundamentalism have given new precision to the definition of this elusive term. In his pivotal study *The Roots of Fundamentalism*, Ernest Sandeen defined fundamentalism as a premillenarian movement whose advocates joined forces with Princeton Calvinists—inerrantists—to uphold orthodoxy.[7] More recently, in the authoritative *Fundamentalism and American Culture*, historian George Marsden assigned the movement broader origins, including D. L. Moody's revivalism, the Keswick movement, premillennialism, and Common Sense philosophy.[8] An interdenominational phenomenon, fundamentalism centered in Bible institutes, publications, and conferences, sponsored first by some to whom Pentecostals also traced their roots: D. L. Moody, A. J. Gordon, R. A. Torrey. The denominational supporters of such efforts were usually Baptists, Presbyterians, and Congregationalists. They came to be known as fundamentalists only after World War I, when they took the offensive against modernism.[9]

Fundamentalists controlled few denominations (generally only those they created), but they mobilized their supporters through various voluntary associations. Although many of these associations were technically unrelated, they often shared directors and benefactors.

Pentecostals had not sought—nor had they been offered—affiliation in these agencies. Confrontations with modernists kept fundamentalists' sensitivity to theological "error" keen and made toleration of Pentecostal aberrations from traditional views unlikely. Assemblies of God adherents nonetheless identified with conservative evangelical views on the verbal inspiration of Scripture, and especially with the fundamentalism represented by Bible institutes and Bible conferences. They shared the prophetic fascination[10] for current events as well as the premillennial dispensationalism of popular fundamentalist pastors and Bible teachers (though admittedly Pentecostal dispensationalism was "dispensationalism with a difference").

In 1928, however, when the wrangling among American Protestants was intense, the Assemblies of God found itself (with modernism) the target of the World's Christian Fundamentals Association, one of the agencies through which dispensationalist fundamentalists offered one another support:

> Be it Resolved, That this convention go on record as unreservedly opposed to Modern Pentecostalism, including the speaking in unknown tongues, and the fanatical healing known as general healing in the atonement, and the perpetuation of the miraculous sign-healing of Jesus and His apostles, wherein they claim the only reason the church cannot perform these miracles is because of unbelief.[11]

Pentecostal Evangel editor Stanley Frodsham reported this action in the *Evangel* under the heading "Disfellowshipped!" (They had never been "fellowshipped.") Claiming that the resolution "disfellowshipped a great company of us who believe in all the fundamentals of the faith as much as they themselves do," Frodsham exhorted Assemblies of God adherents to "love these Fundamentalists."[12] "We are Fundamentalists to a man," the *Evangel* had declared earlier.

Frodsham's list of the "fundamentals" Assemblies of God adherents subscribed to coincided with similar lists authored by non-Pentecostals: the Bible's verbal inspiration, the miraculous virgin birth of Christ, His deity and humanity, His vicarious death and bodily resurrection, His ascension and His "session" at God's right hand, His return and eternal Lordship.[13]

Furthermore—putting aside the theological distinctives that especially distanced Pentecostals from the militant wing of dispensationalist separatistic fundamentalists (like those who formed the World's Christian Fundamentals Association in 1919)—Assemblies of God adherents shared the antipathy toward modernism and much of the view of history that motivated fundamentalists. And they took comfort in the realization that, despite appearances, rejection by members of the World's Christian Fundamentals Association was not complete: Association promoter John Roach Straton, pastor of New York City's independent Calvary Baptist Church, had staunchly defended the ministry of teenage evangelist Uldine Utley during the 1920s. (Utley's services had a definite Pentecostal cast.)[14] And Frodsham noted that R. A. Torrey and some of his colleagues professed belief in physical healing.

Separatism in Fundamentalism

Such points of agreement with Pentecostals heightened awareness of the disagreements among those commonly known as fundamentalists. During the 1930s, one issue, separatism, took on greater proportions in the growing fundamentalist debate about the appropriate response to liberal control of denominations. Since the 1920s, the Northern (later American) Baptist Convention and the Presbyterian Church in the U.S.A. had been embroiled in controversy as fundamentalists strove to gain influence and to force doctrinal fidelity. They failed, however, and modernism was tolerated in both groups. Separatistic fundamentalists countered by forming their own "pure" churches and denominations. Cultural hope waned, for they seemed to be losing on many fronts. Anticipation of Christ's return increasingly became their cultural solution and personal solace.

Independent churches proliferated as aggressive leaders called the faithful out of unholy alliances. Although fundamentalists often failed to exert extensive denominational influence, they found ways to influence extra-denominational Protestantism. Periodicals, Bible institutes, Bible conferences and camps, and revival campaigns all served the fundamentalist cause. In these settings dispensationalism, with its emphasis on prophecy and the end-times calendar, flourished. From this perspective (which, as noted, the Assemblies of God shared in a slightly modified form), especially from the separatist vantage point, evil would increase as the final cataclysm neared. Like cultural changes, then, modernism could be regarded as a "sign of the times." The faithful remnant could never transform culture, nor could they win worldly approval; they could do little more than pray for Christ's speedy return. Though some sought to save the nation by advocating temperance, anticommunism, patriotism, or anti-Catholicism, most knew the battle would not be won.[15]

By the late 1930s, a growing split over separatism revealed deep tensions within fundamentalism. An emerging generation of leaders recognized as well that internal disagreements accounted in part for the movement's lack of cultural force. Because they believed deeply that the fundamentalist disarray did not express "the inherent genius of the great evangelical tradition," they determined not to abandon fundamentalism, but to recover its dynamic.[16]

George Marsden has pointed out that this group of young emerging fundamentalist leaders disliked both separatism and "the doctrinal and cultural implications of thoroughgoing dispensationalism."[17] Led by men like Harold John Ockenga and J. Elwin Wright, they were also influenced by conservative Presbyterian theology as represented at Princeton Theological Seminary by men like J. Gresham Machen. Their historical roots were not in "Old School" confessionalism, however, but rather in eighteenth and nineteenth century "New Light" and "New School" revivalism.[18] They thus represented a heritage with deep cultural roots that helped their cause appeal to Baptists, Presbyterians, and moderate dispensationalists.[19]

Marsden has also described a fundamentalist paradox: Sometimes fundamentalists regarded themselves as the defenders, or conservators, of true Christianity; sometimes they saw themselves as outsiders.[20] In viewing themselves as defenders, fundamentalists often overlooked traditions that shared their view of Scripture but not their evangelical, Calvinistic heritage.[21] Lutherans, Disciples of Christ, Wesleyans, and Pentecostals, for example, held convictions about Scripture and doctrine that made them sympathetic with many fundamentalist goals; they formed a growing segment of the American evangelical mosaic. But they were not accepted as fundamentalists by fundamentalists. In short, fundamentalists were evangelicals, but all evangelicals were not fundamentalists.

Efforts to Unite Evangelicals

In 1940 several concerned, young fundamentalist men decided to act on plans they had contemplated for some time. Primarily pastors and editors, they also tended to be associated with one or another of the nondenominational voluntary associations through which fundamentalism exerted a wide—though often ignored—influence on the American scene. Most importantly, the majority of them shared a background in the evangelical Calvinism that helped shape fundamentalism. J. Elwin Wright became an important facilitator for their goals.

As leader of the New England Fellowship, Wright had toured the country extensively during the 1930s, building a wide base of support among conservative evangelicals, fundamentalists, and others for his growing interdenominational efforts. From

1939, he used such opportunities explicitly to encourage evangelical cooperation through a national evangelical front. His friend Ralph Davis of the Africa Inland Mission followed up such contacts with correspondence. Late in 1940 Davis probed the attitudes of several leading fundamentalist Bible school presidents. J. Davis Adams of the Philadelphia School of the Bible, Howard Ferrin of Providence Bible Institute, Will Houghton of Moody Bible Institute, and Louis Talbot of the Bible Institute of Los Angeles responded favorably to his suggestions about rallying conservatives for united action.[22]

In lectures, sermons, and correspondence during 1940 and 1941, Wright and Davis shared with evangelicals around the country their fears about liberal Protestant encroachments on fundamentalist liberties. "Insidious forces are at work against us," Davis wrote, "and we question whether we are awake to the probable consequences of their activities." For them, modernism had assumed a specific, threatening institutional form, which made a visible target: the Federal Council of Churches of Christ. This agency, founded in 1908 to promote cooperation among America's Protestant denominations, had become, fundamentalists charged, nothing less than a front for those conspiring to subvert fundamentalists' civil and religious liberties.

Davis's correspondence alleged that the majority of America's Protestants deplored the theology of the Federal Council's leaders; he specifically objected to the cultural influence the Council exerted as the "voice" of American Protestantism. He warned his contacts that as long as evangelicals remained "divided into so many larger and smaller groups with but little point of contact," they could not hope to counter Federal Council influence.

Assured of the support of some key Bible institute presidents, Ralph Davis, J. Elwin Wright, and Harold John Ockenga (energetic pastor of Boston's historic Park Street Church) invited others who shared their vision to convene at Moody Bible Institute in Chicago. The meeting in October 1941, chaired by Moody's president, Will Houghton, had the endorsement of some of the most popular, nationally-known conservative evangelicals: V. Raymond Edman, president of nearby Wheaton College; Walter Maier, radio preacher on the *Lutheran Hour*, Lewis Sperry Chafer, president of Dallas Theological Seminary; Charles Fuller, founder of a popular radio broadcast, the *Old Fashioned Revival Hour*. Present with them were Carl McIntire, H. McAllister Griffiths, and Harold Laird, separatist Presbyterians who represented the Bible Presbyterian Church. Like Davis, Wright, and Ockenga, they dreamed of uniting fundamentalists. They had, in fact, already begun. One month earlier, they had launched the American Council of Christian Churches (ACCC).[23]

The formation of the American Council immediately prior to the Chicago meeting raised doubts in some minds about the proper course to pursue: Should those gathered in Chicago urge others to unite with this organization, or should they pursue plans to explore possibilities further?[24] It soon became apparent that prudence mandated the latter. McIntire had arrived in Chicago prepared to join forces on his terms: Whereas most participants intended to discuss strategies for cooperation, he brought non-negotiable battle plans.

The immediate issue focused on the Federal Council of Churches. McIntire called for an all-out attack on the Federal Council and insisted that congregations desiring affiliation with a united evangelical front should repudiate all ties to denominations represented by the Federal Council.[25] The majority, however, disavowed confrontation and opted rather to offer simply to represent those who did not wish the Federal Council to speak for them. Participants also decided to avoid terms like "modernist" and "fundamentalist"; they would soon adopt the label "new evangelicals."[26]

Outvoted on these basic issues, McIntire vowed to proceed on his own. He understood this to involve delineating clearly the "pagan evils" of the Federal Council, insisting on doctrinal orthodoxy, and upholding separation as a critical test of faith.[27] Each issue of his periodical, the *Christian Beacon*, faithfully exposed the "heresies" of the new evangelicals.

Accounts of what happened at the Chicago meeting vary, but it is clear that McIntire and Ockenga—both as individuals and as representatives of opposing views about fundamentalism and American religious institutions—came to a parting of the ways. From 1941 Ockenga probably best represented those who disavowed separatism and called for united evangelical action; McIntire headed an increasingly vocal separatistic council that made requisite for membership antipathy not only toward the Federal Council but also toward non-separatist conservatives. Ironically, a bitter argument about separatism fostered this separation.

McIntire's formation of the American Council had already elicited prompt responses from several fronts. While the editor of *The Lutheran Witness* (Lutheran Church, Missouri Synod) cheered McIntire on, *The Christian Century* labeled his charges against the Federal Council "unprovable and preposterous."[28] "It takes more than a desire to capture free radio time to divide the churches or to start the great revival which the sponsors of this movement declare they want," the editor noted.[29] *The Church Times* agreed: "The sickening news that a group of little men who have been notorious disturbers of the peace and unity in the Christian churches have set up a so-called American Council of Churches" would "make the enemies of religion rejoice."[30] From McIntire's perspective, such comments both proved him right and fueled his determination.

Meanwhile, those who stayed at the Chicago planning meeting formed a temporary committee, named Ralph Davis chairman, and issued a call to another planning session for April 1942 in St. Louis.

A Forum for United Action

The call for another planning session of the new evangelicals described the dream of cooperation that had been partially implemented in J. Elwin Wright's New England Fellowship (the Congo Protestant Council, an interdenominational council of missions in the Belgian Congo, also served as an institutional model). The new evangelicals proposed to create a voluntary association that would uphold the "traditionally accepted evangelical position."[31] They envisioned as potential "fields for cooperative endeavor" issues covering the separation of church and state, religious radio broadcasting, public relations, evangelism, foreign missions, Christian education, and local evangelical cooperation. The Assemblies of God, the Church of God (Cleveland, Tennessee), and several holiness denominations were invited to participate. Assemblies of God General Secretary J. Roswell Flower was one of 147 religious leaders who in 1941 accepted the invitation to sign the call to St. Louis.

In these early steps to implement their plans for united action, these new evangelicals revealed some important facts about their understanding of fundamentalism. Extending an invitation to holiness and Pentecostal groups recognized what Assemblies of God leaders had known all along: Fundamentalist ideas permeated these constituencies. In fact, many Assemblies of God leaders traced their spiritual heritage to the people George Marsden has identified as the precursors of fundamentalism. The fundamentalists who envisioned what would finally become the National Association of Evangelicals (NAE) thus broadened their scope sufficiently to enable new cooperation among those whose histories overlapped. They ultimately failed, however, to create a forum for evangelicals who expressed, or interpreted, their faith differently (like Missouri Synod Lutherans).[32]

The Temporary Committee for United Action Among Evangelicals had met several times during the winter of 1941–1942 to prepare for the St. Louis gathering. J. Elwin Wright had reported to the committee a widening positive response to overtures from the committee. Southern Presbyterians were "pleased," he noted, and he considered Southern Baptists (after a conversation with the secretary of the Home Missions Board of the Southern Baptist Convention) "cautious but friendly."[33] Conversations with spokesmen for the Disciples of Christ appeared promising.

Some 150 religious leaders gathered in St. Louis on April 7, 1942. Williams, Perkin, and Flower composed the Assemblies of God delegation. Riggs and several other district officials and Assemblies of God pastors (including Thomas F. Zimmerman, future president of the emerging organization) observed the proceedings.

As J. Elwin Wright stood before the group to deliver his opening remarks, he had cause for satisfaction. The prospects seemed good for unprecedented cooperation among a broader fundamentalist constituency. In his audience sat delegates from denominations that had purposely avoided one another for decades. Wright urged them to "speak out with courage against apostasy and apostate movements," at the same time being "wise and gracious enough to recognize that there are differences of doctrine among Bible believing members of the church of Jesus Christ upon which there is little hope that we will see eye to eye."[34] Pentecostal "distinctives," it followed, were nonessential "differences of doctrine." This was a major acknowledgment indeed, one which neither side would have made earlier and which many on both sides resented (the anti-Pentecostal position being considered equally significant doctrinally by those who held it).

During the next two days, the delegates discussed the benefits and details of cooperation and elected Harold John Ockenga president of a newly constituted evangelical agency: the National Association of Evangelicals for United Action. More basically, as one participant described it, they learned (to the surprise of some) that fears that "I, only I remain a prophet" were groundless.[35] Pledges of financial support came from congregations, denominations, voluntary associations, and individuals. (A constitutional convention would complete the organizational process in May 1943.) When the Assemblies of God delegation returned to Springfield on April 9, 1942, they had embraced the vision of strength through unity.

Implementing United Action

Several concerns predominated during the first years of attempted cooperation. First, organizers hoped to broaden the base of support. Early hopes that independent institutions like Bible institutes and voluntary associations as well as major denominations would commit themselves to NAE objectives were soon frustrated. Especially disappointing was the failure to attract major southern denominations. Although many Baptist and independent congregations affiliated, the larger co-operating denominations tended to be of holiness or Pentecostal origin: the Free Methodist Church, Church of God (Cleveland), the Assemblies of God. Bible institute leaders, some voluntary fundamentalist associations, and independent religious publishers, though initially cooperative, soon largely faded from the scene. They probably could not afford to align themselves closely with one side in the ongoing dispute over separatism and compromise.[36]

A second concern centered in the recognition that this attempt to foster united evangelical action had revealed how deeply divided conservatives were. McIntire was not alone in stridently opposing the NAE: William Bell Riley (whom NAE organizers later honored as the "grand old man" of fundamentalism) responded bitterly to the St. Louis meeting. In an article entitled "The Fatal Weakness of Fundamentalism," Riley charged both Ockenga and McIntire with promoting division to slake their thirst for power. "So it goes," he bemoaned. "The army of the Lord has not enough regiments to make room for would-be officers. I saw that years ago and joined the privates. . . . Fundamentalism would prosper more if fighters increased and officials diminished."[37]

The *Sunday School Times* also joined the attack on the NAE.[38] Ernest Gordon, son of Baptist pastor and editor A. J. Gordon, commended McIntire's attacks on the Federal Council, calling it "the extensive approximation to Unitarianism which goes under the name of Modernism." Gordon's descriptions of the council were nearly as charged as McIntire's. "A little knot of clerical politicians who issue manifestos as from 'we the Christians of America' " managed the Federal Council, he alleged.[39]

An overview of the literature of the rival conservative associations reveals several significant facts about the widening fundamentalist rift. In spite of widely aired disagreements, the similarities between the American Council of Christian Churches and the National Association of Evangelicals were more striking than the differences: The agencies shared fully an understanding of the nature and function of the Federal Council of Churches, which motivated their actions (and which

Federal Council spokesmen claimed were "misunderstandings").[40] There was no discernible difference. When the NAE began to publish *United Evangelical Action,* it regularly carried articles criticizing the Federal Council of Churches, including an eight-part incendiary series by Ernest Gordon entitled "Ecclesiastical Octopus."[41] The two conservative groups also shared deeply rooted anti-Catholic prejudices, strong anticommunism, and reverent patriotism (features evident among liberal Protestants of the period as well).[42] Their disagreement over the Federal Council was one of theoretical approach rather than of substance; nevertheless, McIntire exploited it. In Field Secretary J. Elwin Wright's report to the NAE Board of Administration in 1943, he noted sadly (expressing sentiments he would reiterate often): "The American Council of Christian Churches is working against us in every way they can. They are a foe that is wily, astute, and will do everything they can to wreck the movement."[43]

Differences in conservative theological priorities became apparent as well. Not surprisingly, some who shared Ockenga's fundamentalist heritage found cooperation with Arminian holiness and Pentecostal denominations distasteful. During the first year, serious disagreements jeopardized the association's existence. And it rather quickly became apparent that, in McIntire's view, separation from any form of doctrinal "error"—modernist or Pentecostal—had become essential. The NAE was wrong, not only because it apparently tolerated the Federal Council but also because it embraced Pentecostal and holiness congregations and denominations.

Although the participation of Pentecostals did not prompt debate among NAE founders (Wright had solicited Pentecostal participation in his New England Fellowship and invited it in the NAE), it troubled both some fundamentalists and some Pentecostals.[44] In 1944, for example, Donald Grey Barnhouse, pastor of Philadelphia's Tenth Street Presbyterian Church (and, at the time, an NAE supporter), called on the annual NAE convention to solicit old-line denominational participation to counterbalance Pentecostal influence. Barnhouse unequivocally declared that the NAE could not be a meaningful force unless it was controlled by well-established denominations. (He suggested Southern Presbyterians, Southern Baptists, and United Presbyterians.) If they failed to gain control within five years, he warned, the NAE would be just "one more movement to bury." Leadership by "the little fringes on the fringe" simply would not work.[45]

Ockenga publicly repudiated Barnhouse's views. McIntire, meanwhile, approved: Calling NAE executives "Federal Council denominational men" because they refused to enjoin separatism, he accused them of paternalism toward a predominantly holiness and Pentecostal constituency that presumably was too "simple" and "humble" to assert leadership. For their acquiescence, McIntire alleged, holiness and Pentecostal groups gained recognition as evangelicals; and Ockenga, Wright, and their associates discovered an opportunity to exercise power.[46]

Although Ockenga personally had little empathy with Pentecostals, he did insist that they be recognized as fellow evangelicals.[47] And he argued for his convictions with special eloquence when McIntire was his antagonist. McIntire grouped holiness and Pentecostal advocates together and insisted their theology was "a subtle, disruptive, pernicious thing" and that their movement "was a work of darkness whose disorder is known to all."[48] He declared his readiness to affiliate his organization with the NAE if it met two conditions: took an "organizational position" against the Federal Council and "got rid of the radical Holiness, tongues groups."[49] His offer spurned on both counts, he continued his attacks on the NAE.

Criticisms of Pentecostal participation, however, were not exclusively from non-Pentecostals. Not all Pentecostals regarded the NAE as either a vehicle for their own legitimation or a means of extending their influence: Some of them declared Assemblies of God involvement a fundamental betrayal of their own identity. Robert Brown, influential pastor of New York City's Glad Tidings Tabernacle, for example, spoke out directly. He believed Pentecostalism (or any religious movement) could thrive only if it distanced itself from organized religion. Commenting on the NAE he declared:

> This association is not Pentecostal and many of their speakers who are listed for a convention . . . not only do not favor Pentecost, but speak against it. This [cooperating with the NAE] is what I call putting the grave clothes again on Lazarus, while the Scripture says: "Come out from among them, and be ye separate, saith the Lord, and touch not the unclean thing; and I will receive you and will be a Father unto you, and ye shall be my sons and daughters, saith the Lord Almighty."[50]

Such disharmony seemed at times to jeopardize the ambitious tasks new evangelical leaders had placed on their agenda. They hoped to appoint evangelical chaplains and to clarify the evangelicals' rights to radio time. They supported the efforts of other voluntary associations (like the National Fellowship for Spiritual Awakening, which sought to promote revival, and the National Commission for Christian Leadership, which mobilized lay people through breakfast groups and campus ministries) and they worked to alert Americans to court decisions relating to such church/state issues as released time for religious instruction and public subsidies for Catholic schools.

The NAE and American Culture

All of this was woven together in Harold John Ockenga's grand vision for American culture. It combined his ardent anti-Catholicism and his hope for a Christian (i.e., Protestant) America as the basic components of a renewed Christian culture. Ockenga warned conservative Christians (who shared his general views about Catholics and America's lost evangelical past) of the growing political menace of a "Roman Catholic machine." Americans, he maintained, were blissfully unaware of the dangerous philosophy promulgated by Monsignor Fulton J. Sheen, popular speaker on *The Catholic Hour.* Sheen's views, he warned, might well "involve a change in American culture almost as fundamental as that of Joseph Stalin."[51] He challenged American evangelicals to respond by "reaffirming the Reformation." He called his constituency to battle, but assured them that the warfare was defensive: Enemies (Catholicism, communism, modernism) were marching. Charging growing political interference by the Catholic church, he claimed to note deference toward Catholicism in such varied settings as the entertainment industry and pamphlets distributed to the military.[52]

In his NAE leadership role, Ockenga sought to imbue his followers with a broad sense of American destiny, which had deep roots in his Presbyterian heritage—he also expressed their own sentiments for them. It is hardly coincidence that Assemblies of God views on war and country changed significantly at about the same time the denomination affiliated with the NAE. In many ways, Ockenga both expressed and influenced Assemblies of God opinions about American culture. After all, some Assemblies of God leaders had considered America a chosen nation all along, and in the grim days after Pearl Harbor, a call to patriotic destiny offered meaning in suffering. In a presidential address to the NAE Constitutional Convention in 1943, Ockenga challenged:

> I believe that the United States of America has been assigned a destiny comparable to that of ancient Israel which was favored, preserved, endowed, guided and used by God. Historically, God has prepared this nation with a vast and united country, with a population drawn from innumerable blood streams, with a wealth which is unequaled, with an ideological strength drawn from the traditions of classical and radical philosophy but with a government held accountable to law, as no government except Israel has ever been, and with an enlightenment in the minds of the average citizen which is the climax of social development.[53]

The nation, Ockenga continued, was at a crossroads: The "kingdom of hell" was "at hand." If evangelical religion were not revived, a return to the "Dark Ages of heathendom" threatened. In fact, the force of "heathendom" was powerfully at work in America, he warned. Yet he offered more hope than did separatistic dispensationalists. After America's chastening in World War II, it would emerge with renewed seriousness about government, religion, and morals; the "present indifference to God" would yield to the triumph of evangelical faith if only his hearers would dedicate themselves to the realization of their historic American evangelical heritage.[54]

Such sentiments coincided neatly with Assemblies of God leaders' confidence in America's destiny under God. Confrontations between Catholics and Protestants in South America (particularly in Colombia) as well as events at home also seemed to lend credence to Ockenga's anti-Catholicism.[55]

Ockenga called for Christians to become intellectual leaders. The church, he declared, had to produce "thinkers" who "stood for Christ" to lead a new generation. He urged as well that Christians assume prominent places in business and, above all, that they commit themselves to discovering a "new power in personal life."[56]

Many of the 613 delegates, among them numerous Assemblies of God participants, responded favorably. Southern California District Superintendent Ben Hardin (who admitted coming with "many questions and mental reservations") was surprised that no one "shed a wild gourd into the pottage on doctrinal matters." Evangelist Raymond Richey found the sessions "deeply spiritual and constructive."[57] More importantly, J. Roswell Flower gained a place on the executive committee (as did J. H. Walker, general overseer of the Church of God [Cleveland]).

Conclusion

In the complex evangelical network, then, the Assemblies of God gained acceptance from an important group of emerging leaders who became known as new evangelicals. Like many Assemblies of God leaders, they were white males with a fundamentalist heritage informed by Keswick piety. This shared piety enabled men like Flower, Williams, Ockenga, and Wright to build a congenial working relationship. After all, Flower and Williams believed that Pentecostalism was simply evangelical Christianity enhanced by a vital experience with the Holy Spirit. The Christ-centered quest for full salvation united people whose preferences for religious experiences varied greatly.

Although Assemblies of God leaders sympathized with NAE objectives, they could not formally affiliate with the NAE without General Council action. In September 1943, the General Council authorized both denominational application for membership in, and financial support of, the National Association of Evangelicals.[58] The application received favorable action by the NAE later the same month.[59] The Assemblies of God had officially become part of an evangelical coalition dedicated to assuring evangelicals a voice in the public arena.

Thomas F. Zimmerman

The five men on these two pages represented the Assemblies of God in meeting with other conservative Protestants in 1942 about the possibilities of united evangelical action.

Ralph Riggs

Noel Perkin

J. Roswell Flower

Ernest S. Williams

2. Fronts for United Action: Cooperation With Evangelicals and Pentecostals

The Assemblies of God and the National Association of Evangelicals

Although the National Association of Evangelicals and its affiliated agencies never achieved the degree of evangelical unity its founders had envisioned, they did at first comprise a large diverse segment of American evangelicals. Even after some denominations, voluntary societies, and institutions failed to follow through on early tentative support, the composition of the NAE helped demonstrate a difference between new evangelicals and fundamentalists. Perhaps the new evangelicals had overestimated either the percentage of committed conservatives in American denominations or their impatience with the Federal Council of Churches. Most likely many ordinary lay people had little experience with the issues fundamentalist and new evangelical leaders targeted. Some lay people undoubtedly concurred with Federal Council leaders who maintained that the attack on the Federal Council was rooted in a basic misunderstanding of its position. In general, Federal Council representatives refused to be drawn into controversy. "We have," noted Samuel Cavert, Federal Council general secretary, "too weighty a responsibility to justify our dissipating our energies in argument with other Christians."[1] And occasional contacts of NAE representatives with Federal Council personnel in fact tended to demonstrate the shared commitment of both groups to evangelism.

Certainly NAE organizers had exposed the fierce individualism that thrived in fundamentalism. Strong, independent leaders like John R. Rice and Bob Jones cooperated for a while, then chose separatism. Many fundamentalists not only failed to join, they maintained a steady barrage of criticism. As an association, the NAE failed in its primary goal: It never directly won the support of the millions of evangelicals it maintained constituted the majority of American Protestants.

But the NAE created a new coalition and recognized a larger evangelical network than most fundamentalists had previously acknowledged. In antagonizing Carl McIntire, NAE leaders both helped reveal deep tensions within fundamentalism and occasioned permanent division, evident in part in the way advocates of each side chose, in the future, to network.

Radio

Much of the National Association of Evangelicals' impatience with the Federal Council of Churches revolved around issues pertaining to radio broadcasting. During the 1940s several radio networks offered free time to Protestants, Catholics, and Jews. Network managers looked to the Federal Council of Churches (as the most prominent voice of Protestantism, including over twenty-five denominations and claiming to speak for some thirty-six million Protestants) to provide Protestant programs.

Harry Emerson Fosdick, speaker on *The National Vespers Hour,* was probably the Federal Council's best-known radio voice. Fosdick's magnetic personality, his confident message—assuring his generation that scientific advances did not destroy Christianity's timeless truth—his wistful hope for moral progress, and his yearning for certainties amid changing realities evoked widespread response.[2] He addressed the felt needs of millions of Americans.

To fundamentalists, however, Fosdick represented a perspective many of them dismissed without effort to understand. Like the Federal Council, Fosdick (pastor, author, professor at Union Theological Seminary, as well as radio speaker) had become a symbol of what most conservative evangelicals considered wrong with American Protestantism. Even the more irenic among them could not admit without reservation that

Fosdick was, in fact, a Christian. Yet he was probably America's most popular Protestant preacher, and he was closely identified with the Federal Council of Churches.[3] His participation seemed to conservatives to validate J. Elwin Wright's contention that the Federal Council was "hopelessly heretical" and "committed to the destruction of the evangelical faith."[4]

Organizers of the National Association of Evangelicals felt especially threatened by two situations. The first was that powerful American agencies assumed that the Federal Council—and thus Fosdick—adequately represented a majority of American Protestants. Given long-held fundamentalist expectations of an end-times world church, the Federal Council, like the emerging World Council of Churches, seemed especially threatening.[5] Although this had implications for other matters (like the appointment of military and institutional chaplains), its most immediate threat seemed to be to evangelical broadcasting rights.

Leaders of both the American Council of Christian Churches and the National Association of Evangelicals repeatedly challenged the Federal Council's right to be the voice of Protestantism, claiming that their statistics were misleading and that at least half of America's Protestants (many of whom were members of denominations affiliated in the Federal Council of Churches) were evangelicals. They countered the official statistics, compiled in religious censuses, with their own numbers—which sometimes varied by several million in the heated exchanges. "Fundamentalists," William Bell Riley insisted, "constitute not less than five-sixths of the Evangelical Church membership. The Federal Council's claim of 20,000,000 associates in unfaith is an egregious lie; and they know it."[6] Conservatives quarreled among themselves about numbers too: McIntire asserted in 1944 that his American Council spoke for some 750,000. The NAE countered that he had no more than 150,000 followers.[7]

When NAE leaders asked the networks about free air time, they learned that organizations representing constituencies of four to five million could anticipate free time slots. Meanwhile, they accused McIntire, who gained free time on the Blue network (ABC) late in 1943, of grossly misrepresenting his constituency to do so.[8]

The question of free time raised immediate but less serious problems than did more specific patterns of local behavior. Free time could be obtained once evangelicals truly united (lack of free time seemed intolerable mostly because it was based on the assumption that spokesmen of the Federal Council of Churches adequately represented American Protestants). Keeping paid broadcasts on the air posed the more serious challenge.

Free time came from local stations, and NAE publicists exploited it in desperate attempts to help raise their budget. The Federal Council, they believed, had helped persuade the CBS and NBC radio networks to exclude paid religious broadcasts and to grant free time to the major faiths. Since denominations affiliated with the Federal Council represented a majority of American Protestants, Federal Council leaders had successfully argued their right to the Protestant segment of free air time. By 1941 the Federal Council was part of an interfaith coalition lobbying both the Mutual Broadcasting System and the National Association of Broadcasters to adopt a similar policy.

NAE publicity urged pastors to support the association in order to protect their congregations from the alleged hostility of local mainline churches. Mainline Protestants (abetted by the Federal Council), the NAE warned, might well complain to station managers about evangelical church-sponsored local programming. Station managers would most likely respond by putting fundamentalists off the air.[9] NAE publications also alleged that liberal Protestants and Catholics would be likely to conspire with local authorities against conservative congregations seeking building permits.

Some of the earliest conveners of the NAE were radio broadcasters. Among the most outspoken was William Ward Ayer, pastor of New York City's Calvary Baptist Church. Ayer had a dual concern: He wanted first to pressure the Federal Communications Commission to encourage stations to air local religious programs and to find ways to assure the rights of broadcasters to purchase time. He found unacceptable the common practice of stations granting several free slots and then refusing to sell time for additional religious broadcasts. Ayer's second dream was to formulate ethical standards for religious broadcasters.[10]

These were, in fact, timely concerns. Much of what Ayer wanted in a code of ethics resembled recommendations circulated to religious radio broadcasters by the National Conference of Christians and Jews. That agency encouraged broadcasters not to attack other faiths but rather to affirm their own, not to appeal for funds on the air or to charge for religious objects, not to address broadcasts to a selected group but to a cross section of the potential audience. Liberals and conservatives agreed that the World War was stimulating a "reawakening" of religious interests, and advocates of the major religious traditions, liberal as well as conservative, hoped to use radio time to kindle a national revival.[11]

Although the Assemblies of God had authorized radio outreach in 1933, the denomination as yet had no radio broadcast. Many of its local churches, however, purchased radio time.[12] Thomas F. Zimmerman, who later became the first head of the Assemblies of God Radio Department, for example, participated in evangelistic radio broadcasts sponsored by a coalition of local churches during his pastorate in Granite City, Illinois. Glad Tidings Tabernacle in New York City also broadcast weekly.

Just as the Assemblies of God was becoming a part of the NAE, a General Presbytery committee began to consider national network broadcasting. A radio department was organized at the headquarters in 1945, and in 1946 the denomination began releasing a fifteen-minute broadcast, *Sermons in Song*. The general superintendent, E. S. Williams, was the speaker; Thomas F. Zimmerman narrated the program. The name was changed to *Revivaltime* in 1950, when General Superintendent Wesley Steelberg became the speaker. After Steelberg's untimely death in 1952, Bartlett Peterson and Wilfred Brown filled the vacancy. The 1953 Executive Presbytery appointed a full-time speaker, C. M. Ward (the son of Pentecostal pioneer evangelist A. G. Ward), for a half hour paid broadcast over the

ABC network. (The *Revivaltime* broadcast, since January 1979 under the leadership of Pastor/Evangelist Dan Betzer, remains a vital denominational outreach. It is carried on more than 550 stations in more than 100 countries.)

Assemblies of God adherents tended to share evangelical suspicions of a Federal Council engineered conspiracy to deprive them of a hearing, and—as they organized their own radio outreach—they readily cooperated with NAE efforts to address the situation. Some 150 religious broadcasters met during the second annual NAE convention in April 1944 and organized the National Religious Broadcasters (NRB). Later that year the new voluntary association adopted a constitution, developed a code of ethics, and elected officers. Thomas F. Zimmerman, then pastor in Granite City, Illinois, served on the first executive committee.[13]

Meanwhile, as the NAE gained visibility, it was occasionally offered free time on one or another of the networks.[14] In June 1944 the Blue network sponsored NAE weekly broadcasts over which Ayer, Donald Barnhouse, and Stephen Paine, president of Houghton College, spoke. Through the National Religious Broadcasters, as well as in other ways, evangelicals monitored congressional bills that affected religious broadcasting. For example, in 1944, at the suggestion of Walter Maier of the *Lutheran Hour,* they lobbied to assure that the Communications Act then under consideration would subject religious broadcasters only to such restrictions as applied to all broadcasters.[15] Believing as they did that "broadcasting the gospel [was] an evangelical duty," they considered themselves engaged in a vital task.[16]

Within a few years the situation changed. Free time for religious broadcasting became a thing of the past, their access to paid air time seemed assured, and other issues absorbed the NRB's energies. The timing, evangelicals believed, was no coincidence: Their efforts had succeeded. In radio's first few years, to those evangelicals supportive of the NAE and the NRB, it seemed that they had taken long strides toward effecting their desired ends. They no longer felt powerless: They had begun the campaign to recapture cultural influence.

Sunday School

Another NAE concern that coincided with contemporary Assemblies of God interests was Sunday school promotion. Conservatives had long objected to the lessons prepared by the International Council of Religious Education primarily because the council was dominated by liberal Protestants. So NAE executives discussed providing an evangelical alternative.

The issue of lesson preparation was complicated at first by the rivalry between the American Council of Christian Churches and the National Association of Evangelicals; independent, conservative publishers like David C. Cook feared alienating either side, and finding lesson writers acceptable to both associations proved impossible. The Assemblies of God had substituted its own lesson preparation for the lessons of the International Council of Religious Education in 1937, and NAE leaders gratefully accepted an offer of counsel from Flower (whom NAE officers described as "a wise, cautious, devout Christian leader").[17]

Throughout the 1930s, Assemblies of God leaders had, in fact, worked systematically to generate more interest in Sunday schools. Marcus Grable, a layman from Springfield, Missouri, joined the staff of Gospel Publishing House in 1935 and accepted responsibility for promoting Sunday schools. Throughout the 1940s and early 1950s, the Assemblies of God sponsored ever larger Sunday school conventions. After 1953, regional conferences replaced the earlier national meetings, which had become too large for Springfield's limited conference facilities. Such conventions attracted an interdenominational response.

During the same years, the NAE organized the National Sunday School Association, an agency dedicated to promoting evangelical Sunday schools. During the 1940s their huge Sunday school conventions also generated enthusiasm, and work toward lesson plans acceptable to evangelicals progressed. Assemblies of God personnel found places of leadership in the National Sunday School Association: Ralph Riggs, for example, (later general superintendent of the Assemblies of God) served on its original executive committee.

Youth

Leaders in the evangelical resurgence naturally targeted youth. Among the supporters of the NAE were some who like Torrey Johnson were prominently identified with Youth for Christ. The National Committee for Christian Leadership and InterVarsity also sponsored campus outreaches. In recognition of the proliferation of both denominational and independent youth ministries, the NAE sponsored a National Youth Conference in 1945 with several goals: stimulating interest in youth work, preventing overlapping efforts, and creating a directory of evangelicals active in youth work. Ralph Harris, an Assemblies of God minister, figured prominently in NAE-sponsored youth activities in the mid-1940s.

Harris, a Michigan native, was closely identified as well with youth-oriented Assemblies of God programs. He had moved from a pastorate in Clio, Michigan, to Springfield, Missouri, in 1943 to head the newly created Christ's Ambassadors Department. "Christ's Ambassadors" (based on 2 Corinthians 5:20) had been chosen as the name for the denomination's youth program after Carl Hatch, youth director at Bethel Temple in Los Angeles, had used it for Bethel Temple's youth group. Hatch had begun a publication for youth in the Southern California District called *The Christ's Ambassadors Herald.* Several other California pastors shared Hatch's dream of a strong youth program: Wesley Steelberg and A. G. Osterberg were both prominently associated with large youth gatherings in the state.

The idea proved timely. By 1937, with the increasing numbers of organized Assemblies of God youth groups across the country, the Assemblies of God headquarters agreed to assume responsibility for the publication of Hatch's district paper. Robert Cunningham was named editor, and in January 1938 the *C.A. Herald* began publication.

At about the same time that NAE leaders decided to encourage youth ministries by sponsoring national conferences,

Assemblies of God participants discovered increasing enthusiasm for extending their own youth efforts. From 1940 until 1944, annual national youth conferences (patterned after a North Carolina Southern Baptist youth conference some headquarters employees had visited) conducted in Springfield, Missouri, brought several hundred Assemblies of God youth together. Contact with Youth for Christ leaders and other evangelical youth ministries tended both to reassure Pentecostals about evangelicals and to make some local Assemblies of God leaders willing to cooperate with non-Pentecostal evangelical efforts among youth.

Missions

Another arm of the NAE, the Evangelical Foreign Missions Association, also served Assemblies of God needs. Since 1919 the Assemblies of God had occasionally worked with the Foreign Missions Conference of North America. This mainline Protestant agency had assisted Assemblies of God missions personnel as necessary to expedite business affairs related to missionary outreach. Those evangelicals who united to form the NAE shared the alarm of many conservative Protestants over the practical implications of liberal theology for mainline Protestant missionary work, and in 1943 the NAE set up a Department of Home and Foreign Missions in Washington, D.C. Clyde Taylor headed the office while NAE executives decided precisely how a permanent missions agency should be constituted.

In May 1945, leaders representing some seventy-five mission boards met in Chicago and created the Evangelical Foreign Missions Association. Assemblies of God Foreign Missions Secretary Noel Perkin cooperated from the start with NAE efforts, and he served (as has his successor, J. Philip Hogan) on the executive board of the missions association. The association, through its Washington office, expedited the acquisition of visas and kept the needs of evangelical missionaries prominent. Coordinated action made possible Assemblies of God involvement in projects that would have been difficult on a smaller scale. Throughout the 1940s, for example, the NAE provided both guidelines and coordination for evangelical relief work in Europe.

The Assemblies of God—one of the NAE's key financial contributors—formally reevaluated its commitment to the NAE during the late 1940s. Some pastors, citing tension on the local level, tried to discourage continued denominational participation.[18] Strong feelings that Pentecostals necessarily compromised their distinctives whenever they cooperated with non-Pentecostals continued to agitate the Assemblies of God for the next several decades. Considerable confusion (aided by McIntire's allegations) about NAE-affiliated congregations belonging to denominations represented by the Federal Council of Churches prompted misunderstanding that nourished the dissent. An Illinois pastor wrote to the headquarters for clarification: "Some of my people are unduly alarmed, inasmuch as they think we as the General Council of the Assemblies of God have joined the Federal Council of Churches. Some of our folk are converted Lutherans and utterly opposed to that organization and threaten to leave the Council if we have joined."[19]

In spite of such misgivings, cooperation on the national level proved far simpler than jointly-sponsored local evangelism, which tended to reawaken deeply rooted tensions. Several times during the 1940s, officers of the NAE attended Assemblies of God General Councils to promote the benefits of cooperation. In the end they won their point, and Assemblies of God personnel gained increasing prominence in NAE-related activities.

Undoubtedly some Assemblies of God pastors had dubious motives in supporting the NAE. Some clearly hoped to persuade NAE adherents to accept Pentecostalism. Carl McIntire bluntly accused them of being "hopeful" that the gift of tongues would "come on all."[20] And McIntire was partly right, as a sampling of correspondence between Assemblies of God ministers and the denomination's general secretary indicates. An enthusiastic description of an NAE regional meeting in Baltimore in 1942, for example, began with the following: "Dr. Gordon

Brownville of Tremont Temple sounds Pentecostal. I heard him say, 'Praise the Lord, Amen.' "[21]

Reconsiderations about cooperation with new evangelicals were part of a broader unsettlement in the Assemblies of God during the late 1940s. For some, denominational loyalty took apparent precedence over the common experience of opposition to modernism. In a period of transition, they clung to the past. But with increasing frequency those who were committed to cooperation gained national office and built on the foundation J. Roswell Flower (who had accepted appointment to NAE leadership committees) had ably laid.

On the other side, things were also changing. Most conspicuously, the immediate "enemy," the Federal Council of Churches, was superseded by the National Council of Churches of Christ, and the World Council of Churches was formed. The National Council, composed of denominational agencies rather than denominations, could not be assumed to represent Protestants in the same way that the Federal Council had. In fact, NAE representatives had hoped that in the transition from the Federal Council to the National Council "a more Biblical viewpoint, a more evangelistic program, a more democratic organizational structure and a united front for Christianity in America might emerge."[22] Disappointed when Federal Council members failed to invite their participation or to call union prayer meetings, conservatives castigated the National Council as a "superchurch" that threatened to destroy "individual freedom of thought and action."[23]

As noted, NAE-affiliated congregations and denominations not only affirmed several "fundamentals," they also shared some basic convictions about America. Their perception of history and culture united them perhaps as strongly as their theological views. A sense of having been forced to surrender cultural leadership to an unacceptable party, or of having been arbitrarily excluded from such leadership, haunted them and made some evangelicals willing to minimize issues that historically had been divisive.

Although the Federal Council of Churches and the Roman Catholic Church were the primary institutional targets of evangelical criticism, cultural patterns also alarmed the new evangelicals. America needed to return to its roots; these evangelicals echoed their ancestors in calling for a Christian America. They urged the return to a "Christian Sabbath" and called for educational and moral reform (the latter included the removal—by Executive order—of beer from army camps "to preserve the moral fiber of the cream of America's manhood").[24] Educators, they warned, were "poisoning America with communistic teaching." In response they proposed a Christian university and called for evangelical intellectuals who could produce a "new literature," a "new Bible history abreast of recent archeology," a monthly magazine, evangelical "reading rooms," and an evangelical apologetic.[25]

"The main attack on Christianity has begun," they declared. The World War was but a prelude. "Hosts of antichristian armies and powers are in motion. Whole nations are again on the march towards heathendom and idolatry."[26]

Cataclysmic events did not mean despair. The horrors of war raised evangelicals' expectations of revival. They had hope, confidence in the moral fiber of a nation that needed purging but would emerge strong. The NAE organized local chapters through which it sponsored evangelistic outreaches. It identified, too, with other agencies working toward revival: the National Fellowship for Spiritual Awakening, formed in 1946 to coordinate prayer and efforts for revival in Washington, D.C. (which its promoters were convinced would spread around the world); Christ for America, led by Horace F. Dean, an early supporter of the NAE; the National Commission for Christian Leadership (which had begun in 1935 in Seattle). At the same time, Americans in general became more interested in religion. Through its participation in the NAE, then, the Assemblies of God recommitted itself to revitalize America and evangelize the world. When, in 1949, the new evangelicals discovered in Billy Graham a prophet for the anticipated national revival, they dared to believe the awakening had begun.[27]

The Pentecostal Fellowship of North America

The experience of a few Pentecostal denominations in the

National Association of Evangelicals encouraged them to attempt a forum for American Pentecostals, who remained badly fragmented. In May 1948, representatives of eight white Trinitarian Pentecostal denominations met in Chicago after the annual NAE convention to discuss ongoing association. As in the NAE, the Church of God (Cleveland) and the Assemblies of God provided leadership. J. Roswell Flower served the meeting as secretary.

In August the group met again, this time with representatives of four more Pentecostal denominations. They appointed a committee, chaired by Flower, to frame a constitution for a convention they scheduled for Des Moines, Iowa, in October. When nearly two hundred delegates assembled on October 26, they proceeded quickly and amicably through their business and gave structure to the Pentecostal Fellowship of North America (PFNA). J. R. Flower was chosen their first secretary.

The PFNA resembled the NAE in both its statement of faith and its constitution. Its purposes were to coordinate common efforts, to express the fundamental unity of "Spirit-baptized believers," and to facilitate evangelization.

Assemblies of God leaders responded favorably to the PFNA, and the 1949 General Council approved Assemblies of God membership. Serious misgivings soon surfaced, however, revealing the persistence of sharp divisions among Pentecostals over holiness, sanctification, and worldliness. Some Assemblies of God ministers believed that smaller Pentecostal denominations should merge with the Assemblies of God. Objection arose in the General Presbytery over plans for cooperation among local Pentecostals in evangelistic outreaches. Opening Assemblies of God pulpits to non-Assemblies of God ministers—or permitting Assemblies of God ministers to preach in non-Council churches—had the potential, warned a committee appointed to explore the subject, to "create confusion rather than promote unity among Pentecostal believers."[28]

Promoters of the PFNA won their case, however, and the Assemblies of God over the years has made substantial contributions to it. Even so, the PFNA has not succeeded in effecting full classical Pentecostal cooperation. Affiliated denominations remain white and Trinitarian, while large segments of American Pentecostalism are black, Hispanic, and/or non-Trinitarian.

The World Pentecostal Fellowship

Whereas American Pentecostal denominations developed with little reference to one another, European Pentecostals shared contact from the beginning. Regular conferences contributed to the solidarity and growth of independent movements in several northern European countries until World War I. In 1921, contact through occasional conferences resumed. Several men, notably England's Donald Gee and Sweden's Lewi Pethrus, enjoyed popularity in the movement as a whole. (Both were also well-known in the United States.)

After World War II, European and American Pentecostals gathered in Zurich in May 1947 and organized the World Pentecostal Conference. Misgivings among Pentecostals with strong congregationalist sympathies (especially Scandinavian Pentecostals) at first jeopardized the experiment. At the second meeting, in Paris in 1949, however, delegates were persuaded that the conference would respect member groups' autonomy and organizational preferences. Since 1949, conferences have met triennially and have included a growing number of participants. They continue, however, to retain a Trinitarian Pentecostal cast.

The first World Pentecostal Conference authorized a publication and appointed Donald Gee editor. The quarterly journal *Pentecost* served not only as a dispenser of news and reports, but also as a forum for Gee to admonish the worldwide movement on timely issues. A remarkable man, noted for wrestling thoughtfully with troublesome and controversial issues, Gee was widely revered as a Pentecostal statesman and was arguably the most astute spokesman the movement had yet produced.

The Assemblies of God participated from the beginning in the World Pentecostal Conferences. J. R. Flower, Ernest Williams, and especially Thomas Zimmerman decisively influenced the course of the worldwide movement.

Conclusion

By 1950, then, the Assemblies of God had not only discovered advantages in cooperation, it had also assumed leadership roles in each of the three cooperative associations it had helped organize. Over time, each of them helped reassure Assemblies of God adherents about other Pentecostals and evangelicals. Through the judicious efforts of men like Flower and Zimmerman, others gained confidence in the Assemblies of God as well.

The name of *Sermons in Song* was changed to *Revivaltime* in 1950 and has been under the leadership of Dan Betzer since January 1979.

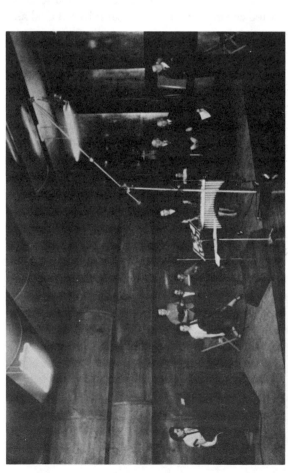

A recording session of *Sermons in Song*, the Assemblies of God radio broadcast, in the 1940s. Gwen Jones is at the organ. The three men at the right are W. I. Evans, E. S. Williams (general superintendent and speaker of the broadcast until 1950), and T. F. Zimmerman (narrator of the program).

Leaders of Pentecostal Fellowship of North America looking over the "Spiritual Marshall Plan" in 1948. Front (l–r): W. L. Chesser, E. S. Williams, David du Plessis, Rolf McPherson, Ray Hughes. Back (l–r): Demos Shakarian, Wesley Steelberg, C. E. Britton, R. D. Heard, Howard Rusthoi.

Meeting of World Pentecostal Conference at Trafalgar Square, London, 1952. Gayle F. Lewis at the microphone.

National Sunday School Convention in Springfield, Missouri, 1948

3. Dissonance Among Pentecostals: The Assemblies of God Responds

During the 1940s and 1950s, the Assemblies of God responded to dissonant voices raised within Pentecostalism. Pentecostals cherished spiritual gifts and independence, though many, recognizing a need for structure, had affiliated with Pentecostal denominations. Individuals who challenged authority readily found a following, however, and often their messages appealed to latent hopes and dreams that seemed consonant with early Pentecostal expectations.

Two movements which did precisely that also gave new visibility to the thousands of Pentecostals who rejected denominational structures and clung to a rhetoric that equated denominations with spiritual "coldness" and death. (The power of that imagery was evident in the Assemblies of God, too, when adherents referred routinely to the "dead denominational churches.") These movements were the New Order of the Latter Rain and the salvation/healing revival. Both identified themselves (in relation to the turn-of-the-century Pentecostal revival) as forward movements. Because such claims had validity and because both movements nurtured rhetoric and practice that would deeply influence the emerging charismatic renewal, they help illumine parts of Assemblies of God history. They reveal the reasons for initial Assemblies of God hesitations about the charismatic movement, to which the salvation/healing movements were linked, as well as the differences between organized Pentecostalism and the large varied non-organized movement.

On February 13, 1949, nearly five thousand people crammed the facilities of Bethesda Missionary Temple, an Assemblies of

God church in Detroit. Some seventeen hundred more were turned away. The occasion was the dedication of the congregation's new three-thousand-seat auditorium. But the event was much more than ceremony; the crowd was charged with expectation, convinced that "the restoration" was in progress, intent on "receiving their portion from God."[1] The word was out: Revival had begun—a revival with a difference. The "latter rain" had begun to fall, and the New Testament faith was being fully restored. A participant exclaimed: "At last it is here! Had I not seen it with my own eyes and felt the witness in my own heart, I might have been skeptical, but it's real! Hallelujah! What am I talking about?—THE LATTER RAIN OUTPOURING! We've dreamed about it, prayed about it and hoped to see it. Now the showers are falling and spreading rapidly."[2]

Some of the same people had said precisely the same things forty years earlier; the language evoked American Pentecostalism's earliest history. Nearly five decades after Charles Parham launched the Apostolic Faith Movement, second and third generation Pentecostals yearned anew for tangible evidence that they were God's end-times people. Discouraged by waning spiritual fervor and the relentless institutionalization and professionalization of North American Pentecostalism, they viewed their early history as having merely set the stage for a greater event and opted once again to believe that in their day, the full restoration of apostolic power would be realized.

They discovered—as their ancestors had—that renewed emphasis on the latter rain and restoration involved implicit and explicit indictment of their fellow believers. And it revived themes, language, and expectations of experiences that had long since faded from the general Pentecostal milieu. Since theirs was the *full* restoration, it followed that early Pentecostalism had been a partial restoration. Those who preached and defended the latter rain in the 1940s differed from early North American Pentecostals in at least one basic way: They focused on New Testament offices and sought to restore the authority of those offices in contemporary Pentecostalism.

It is significant that the Latter Rain movement of the late 1940s directed its criticisms of the status quo almost exclusively at fellow Pentecostals. Unlike the first generation of Pentecostals who hoped to influence Protestantism generally, latter rain advocates felt it necessary to demonstrate why claims that the latter rain and the restoration should be dated to the first decade of the twentieth century were false. Theirs was a remnant mentality. They knew they were outsiders, even in relationship to other outsiders, and they consciously cultivated that recognition. Though they occasionally hinted that their message would some day engage the larger religious world, for the moment they focused on their own movement.

Bethesda Missionary Temple attracted many who hoped for a dynamic realization of divine intrusion in their lives. Its popular pastor, Myrtle Beall, was recognized as a leader among those who believed that the turn-of-the-century Pentecostal revival had been the "early rain" and that in the 1940s the true "latter rain" was falling. But Beall had accepted such views from others. The events that made her congregation a center of latter rain expectations had been set in motion in a small village in Saskatchewan late in the fall of 1947.

The Restoration and the Latter Rain

George and Ernest Hawtin and Percy Hunt had fallen into disrepute with their denomination, the Pentecostal Assemblies of Canada (the Canadian counterpart of the Assemblies of God), in 1947. They had left under pressure and launched an independent Bible school in North Battleford, Saskatchewan. The Bible school was an extension of the efforts that Herrick Holt, a minister of the International Church of the Foursquare Gospel, had already begun in the town. Some of the students from the Pentecostal Assemblies of Canada's Bible school in Saskatoon (which George Hawtin had founded twelve years earlier) had joined the men to form the nucleus of the student body.

The school routine resembled that of early Pentecostal Bible schools. Students and staff spent much time in prayer, setting aside prolonged periods for fasting, until by early February 1948 they believed they had entered a "new order" of spiritual experience. Ushered in by prophetic announcement, this "new order" focused on prophecy, spiritual gifts, and the rhetoric of early Pentecostalism. Surveying the organized Pentecostal movement from the vantage point of disinherited participants, Hawtin, Hunt, and Holt found departures from early Pentecostal practice and expectations rampant. They launched a stern critique of organized Pentecostalism, announced a new and more powerful revival, and reemphasized the supernatural.

Although their personal problems with Pentecostal denominational leaders undoubtedly influenced them, they were not alone in perceiving a fundamental shift in the direction of North American Pentecostalism, a shift they attributed largely to organization. Others had expressed similar reservations over the years. Much of what was declared by the New Order of the Latter Rain advocates had basic similarities to teaching at Ivan Spencer's Elim in Hornell, New York; it also shared in significant ways the emphases of Max Wood Moorhead[3] and Seeley Kinney, longtime independent Pentecostal evangelists and writers who, by the 1930s, were prominently associated with Elim. Its antidenominationalism (evolving into advocacy of radical congregationalism) was identical to that of the Scandinavian Pentecostals who organized the Independent Assemblies of God in Chicago. Spokesmen for the Scandinavians included Joseph Mattsson-Boze and A. W. Rasmussen; their role model was Stockholm pastor Lewi Pethrus, one of the best-known Pentecostals in the world.

If the Hawtins' predispositions could be traced among other Pentecostals, the continuity of their message with the rhetoric of early Pentecostals assured them both a hearing and opposition. Advocates of the New Order rediscovered William Durham, whose name remained familiar as the precipitator of one of the most divisive controversies in Pentecostal history, namely, the timing of sanctification. Pentecostals who agreed with Durham's views on sanctification had read him selectively. They had usually disregarded his uncompromising hostility toward organization and education. Durham's views on these and other subjects indicted the course North American Pentecostalism in general, and the Assemblies of God in particular, had taken.

Advocates of the New Order found Durham's most dire predictions fulfilled in the Pentecostal denominations they attacked.

Some first-generation Pentecostals had begun within a decade to bemoan their movement's waning power and had pointed to future, more copious showers of the latter rain. Consequently, there was even precedent for the eschatological innovation by the New Order advocates. Daniel Kerr, for example, noting a declining focus on healing as early as 1914, had heralded a coming dispensation in which healing would have the prominence accorded to tongues at the turn of the century. As Pentecostal groups had organized and charismatic fervor had waned in some places—or was largely confined to revival campaigns and campmeetings—voices had been raised asserting that the turn-of-the-century Apostolic Faith Movement had seen only the beginning of a revival whose more copious latter rains were yet to come.

Some bewailed the movement's declension then, regularly reminding adherents of the characteristics of the early revival. Others, on a more positive note, encouraged believers not to look back but to expect more miracles and more fervor in the future. Thus while many Pentecostals looked contentedly on their growing, stabilizing movement, a few here and there, uncomfortable with acculturation, sought to fill a prophetic role. In so doing, they recalled a radically separatist part of their Pentecostal heritage most Pentecostals had gladly neglected. As outsiders calling a movement to task, however, they helped reveal dimensions of Pentecostal self-understanding that had seldom been so clearly targeted.

The New Order Message

Those who participated in the meetings at North Battleford, in which apostolic ministries were purportedly restored to the church, described in glowing terms the intense, highly-charged context in which the end-times church was set in order. Through tongues, interpretations of tongues, and prophecies, prophets instructed individuals to fill designated offices in the church.

The laying on of hands figured largely as an act of initiation. Reports of new dimensions of worship, including "spiritual singing," as well as gifts of healing, slayings in the Spirit, and calls to a "deeper" life struck responsive chords in the hearts of thousands of Pentecostals in western Canada and then in the United States. The yearning for a contemporary recurrence of apostolic power was intense; and, like forty years earlier, some Pentecostals seemed fascinated by the rhetoric and display of the miraculous and the claimed restoration of primitive Christianity. Like their Pentecostal forebearers, they dreaded "missing God."

As in early Pentecostalism, a wide range of teaching and practice emerged in the ranks of New Order advocates. While some views (like transubstantiation, or "rightly discerning the Lord's body") were admittedly extreme and not widely disseminated, both doctrine and polity were reconsidered from the perspective of the "deeper" spirituality that was promoted. Two basic issues loomed especially large as the Hawtins and Hunt disseminated news of the restoration, one focusing on church government, the other on spiritual gifts.

Since radical restorationists led the discussion, it was filled with appeals to the New Testament. Advocates of the New Order insisted that the New Testament mandated strict congregationalism as a form of church government. To prove that this affirmation had respectable Pentecostal antecedents, they invoked William Durham's long-ignored tract entitled *Organization*. Their rejection of organization became one of the main points of controversy with the existing Pentecostal movement, most of which was by then clearly divided into numerous denominations.

New Order spokespersons found themselves in agreement as well with several articles that Joseph Mattsson-Boze had published in the June 1944 issue of *Herald of Faith,* the official publication of a largely Scandinavian denomination known as the Independent Assemblies of God. The articles asserted that the "biblical way" called for sovereign local congregations "founded on the Word of God" and "filled with His Spirit."[4] But "people [were] not aware that God was able to take care of His own business." Consequently, Pentecostal denominations were rooted not in faith but in unbelief. For "like Uzzah of old, they stretched forth their own hands to help God and like Israel of old they cried for a king, to be like the rest of the people. God never wanted it that way."[5]

Pentecostal denominations—and the Assemblies of God in particular—had emerged either because no wise "'master-builder' (1 Corinthians 3:10)" had been available or because his advice was ignored. The articles in *Herald of Faith* drew a response from J. R. Flower, which in turn generated a defense from Mattsson-Boze. Clearly the strong anti-organizational sentiments even such bitter antagonists as Durham and Parham had agreed on survived; and time would prove that many Pentecostals were susceptible to the argument (which had a familiar ring to the old-timers) that denominations necessarily quenched the Spirit. It allowed them to shift responsibility for their self-diagnosed spiritual languor from themselves to someone (or something) else.

By 1949 the controversy had intensified on several fronts, and George Hawtin found it advisable to publish his thoughts on the church. In a book entitled *Church Government,* he maintained that "all sects and denominations from Paul's day till now exist because of Man's carnality." Rooted in humankind's "unscriptural fence building," denominations effectively excluded "new wine" and "greater light." They stagnated—and then actively opposed a "true work of God."[6]

Hawtin and his colleagues maintained that much of the problem was rooted in unwillingness to recognize the validity of the ministry of apostles and prophets. If each congregation adopted full congregational sovereignty and did so with spiritual rather than ambitious intentions, true unity among "full gospel" believers would inevitably follow. Local churches (whose members presumably included apostles, prophets, teachers, evangelists, and pastors) should set apart their own workers, commission their own missionaries, and discipline their own members, at the same time maintaining a cooperative attitude toward other local congregations.[7] They should be accountable only to God. To Hawtin this not only made sense, it was compelling because it conformed to the biblical model.

The emphasis on congregational responsibilities and the accompanying attack on organization often seemed directed at the Assemblies of God. The Assemblies of God in Canada and the United States was the largest, most affluent, most powerful, and most visible Pentecostal group. It was also the denomination that many of the prophets and apostles of the revival had once identified with.

A second primary focus of the New Order of the Latter Rain was on spiritual gifts. At first, this consisted of discovering within local congregations those who could exercise the nine spiritual gifts listed in 1 Corinthians. Before long, however, other gifts were added to the list, and people found themselves singled out as recipients of such purported gifts as journalism, cartooning, mercy, giving, etc.[8]

The act of discerning gifts was simple. One participant described how it was exercised daily during a week of prayer at Detroit's Bethesda Missionary Temple: "During the day men of God, who have been called to various offices by the Lord, as they feel led by the Spirit, call out of the congregation folks whose hearts have been made ready, lay hands upon them and set them apart for God. This laying on of hands is accompanied by various prophecies relative to their ministry and gifts of the Spirit that God has bestowed upon them."[9] In practical terms, this seemed to discount Assemblies of God ordination by local presbyteries because such laying on of hands involved no prophetic designation of the ministry and gifts the ordained should exercise. Those people—lay or ordained—whose gifts had been prophetically assured exercised them as local circumstances warranted and constituted a potentially arrogant higher order within local congregations.

The elevation of prophets and apostles obviously made way for strong individuals to exercise and abuse authority. And it allowed some to give the "Spoken Word" equality with Scripture. "There could be no greater error," denominational leaders warned. "Such prophets commence by saying, 'I, the Lord thy God, say unto thee.' "[10] "Predictive prophecy," Assemblies of

God General Secretary J. Roswell Flower cautioned, had "resulted in untold disaster wherever it had been given free course."[11] Flower was well-versed in the history of Pentecostalism and recalled numerous prophecies that had come to nothing. The New Order of the Latter Rain in fact taught nothing new, he claimed. The ground had been covered before, with lessons learned through costly mistakes. Now a new generation seemed to want to repeat it all.

In fact, some New Order advocates seemed intent on outdoing the earlier generation. They led some gullible candidates to believe that they would be spirited into Russia, or other "closed" countries, for example, where they would be supernaturally enabled to preach the gospel in local dialects before being spirited back to safety.[12] A couple in their mid-fifties had been instructed through prophecy to embark for China. As soon as their feet touched Chinese soil, they were promised, they would both gain ability to speak in "all the Chinese dialects," and the wife's total deafness would be healed.[13]

The list could go on. Canadian evangelist R. E. McAlister reported that a pastor's wife had been given a gift of administration, and her husband had been granted the gift of obedience. "He was to ask his wife what he should preach, and do accordingly."[14] More significant than the variations on the prophetic theme (all of which had occurred frequently in early Pentecostalism), however, was probably the restatement of another "deep truth," which had preoccupied some Pentecostals for decades: "the manifestation of the sons of God."

Derived from a phrase in Romans 8:18–23, the "manifestation of the sons of God" focused on the notion that a privileged few, whom New Order advocates designated "overcomers," would receive "redemption bodies" in this life. "Eternal life" really meant eternal *physical* life (a thought that had intrigued Charles Parham early in his ministry). Those who "pressed through" to receive it, the "manifest" sons of God, would never die.[15] They, accordingly, constituted a select group within the Church.

Max Wood Moorhead, Seeley Kinney, and Ivan Spencer all thought they were "manifest sons of God." Moorhead preached frequently and fervently on "victory over death." However, when he died on May 2, 1937, Spencer could hail him only as one who had "embraced the truth," not as one who had experienced it.[16] The restoration, Spencer noted, came "by stages"; he believed the "manifest sons of God" were part of God's final stage. In 1970 Spencer, in deteriorating health, was forced to admit that "translation" had eluded him too; he was deeply agitated. Reminded of his own admonition on Moorhead's death, however, he found comfort. "Standing for the truth as you see it," his daughter reminded him, "is as acceptable to Him as the act of your translation."[17] The deaths of these and other prominent advocates of the "manifest sons of God" have further marginalized (but not eliminated) the teaching.

A rereading of the New Testament with a stress on contemporary restoration, therefore, led to a harsh indictment of contemporary Pentecostalism and to an emphasis on congregational polity, spiritual gifts, and supernatural phenomena. The movement called for days of prayer and fasting, and even its detractors admitted that New Order services often had "a very fine spiritual atmosphere."[18] It is not surprising that some thought the New Order a powerful manifestation and continuation of early Pentecostal power. New Order churches tended to operate on schedules that most Pentecostal congregations had long abandoned, though once typical of the movement at large. A weekly schedule including nightly meetings, days of prayer, morning Bible studies, and three Sunday services was not uncommon. Nor is it surprising that these two streams within Pentecostalism collided: New Order themes had been latent throughout Pentecostal history, and they clashed—as they always had—with dominant views. Pentecostals in organized denominations naturally took offense at what they regarded as the primary effort of New Order advocates, "the dividing and breaking up of organized work."[19] And they were probably correct. The New Order considered the denominations the symbol, if not the cause, of the spiritual stagnation they claimed was rife in Pentecostalism.

The New Order of the Latter Rain in the United States

Bethesda Missionary Temple in Detroit became a center of

New Order teaching after Myrtle Beall traveled to Vancouver, British Columbia, to encounter the message firsthand. Beall, a high school graduate with seven years of experience in evangelistic efforts before she received Assemblies of God credentials in 1937, maintained a grueling schedule and built a sizable congregation in Detroit before she identified with the restoration movement. In addition to shepherding her congregation of more than thirteen hundred members, she extended her influence via three daily radio broadcasts.[20]

Beall claimed to disavow the more extreme teachings of the New Order movement, while maintaining, "This is the hour of Restoration."[21] Her facilities became a center for days of prayer, the exercise of spiritual gifts, and the setting apart of Christian workers. Beall identified readily with others who shared her interests, many of whom had no relationship to the General Council of the Assemblies of God. New Order sympathies generated new networks that transcended prior loyalties. Beall's sermons were printed in *The Elim Pentecostal Herald,* the organ of the Elim Missionary Assemblies in Hornell, New York, for example, as well as in *The Voice of Faith,* a latter rain publication from Memphis, Tennessee.

The Latter Rain Messenger, a publication issued from Oklahoma City, featured in its January 1, 1951, issue an article it billed as a prophecy, "Waiting Daily at His Gates." The "prophet" was a prominent Assemblies of God leader, former *Pentecostal Evangel* editor Stanley Frodsham. Frodsham had traveled to Beall's church, where his prophetic gift had been publicly proclaimed. His sympathy for aspects of the New Order dismayed Assemblies of God general presbyters; he resigned his office and broke his official ties to the General Council.[22] He represents many who looked with hope to the promise of revival. Frodsham, undoubtedly the single most prominent Assemblies of God member to identify with the New Order, soon discovered alarming extremes and abandoned the restoration.

The New Order leaders in Canada designated three apostles for the United States and encouraged inquirers to contact them for understanding "the fundamentals" of the latter rain outpouring. They were A. W. Rasmussen (Tacoma, Washington) of the Independent Assemblies of God and two Assemblies of God ministers, D. Bruzelius (Monroe, Wisconsin) and Elvar Blomberg (Hibbing, Minnesota).[23]

The Assemblies of God and the New Order

Many factors helped form the Assemblies of God response to the restoration teaching. Not least was the New Order's explicit indictment of the "old Pentecost"—which had shaped the Assemblies of God movement. "This is not the old whoop, shout, and jump Pentecost," New Order advocates boasted of their revival, "but a fresh revelation of God's Word and an entirely different moving of God's Spirit. Don't try to make this outpouring fit in with preconceived ideas of what the LATTER RAIN OUTPOURING should be like. Other denominations tried to do that with Pentecost in 1906 and missed the 'day of His visitation.' "[24]

Assemblies of God leaders were also deeply concerned about the growing emphasis on prophecy and the laying on of hands. They believed that these practices were being unduly emphasized and would promote confusion and failure. They readily cited experiences from Pentecostal history to support their case. Advocates of the New Order agreed that the emphasis characterized them; they maintained that prophecy and the laying on of hands filled a comparable role in their ranks to that of tongues speech in Pentecostal denominations.

In the spring of 1949, Assemblies of God General Superintendent Ernest Williams resolved to meet the growing demand for teaching on issues raised by the revival by writing two articles for the *Pentecostal Evangel*, "Are We Pentecostal?" and "Spiritual Gifts." They appeared in the April 9 and 16 issues. On April 20, the denomination sent out a special edition of its ministers' letter, outlining the disagreements between the denomination and the New Order and explaining the denomination's stance on prophecy. These actions were a response to a growing number of letters that questioned views promulgated from several cities, all informally linked to Detroit and Canada. Strong centers of New Order teaching had been formed in Detroit, St. Louis, Memphis, Oklahoma City, Beaumont (Texas), Tacoma (Washington), and Portland (Oregon), and the movement had outspoken leaders in many small towns, especially in the upper Midwest.

Assemblies of God leaders noted with growing concern the stress on the word "deliverance." They deplored the New Order tendency to urge deliverances from a wide variety of sinful habits, diseases, and fears. Proponents of the New Order referred readily to the "keys of the kingdom of heaven" as the source of their deliverance ministries, and some reportedly went so far as to claim power to forgive or retain sins.[25] The deliverance/healing ministries that shaped the emerging healing revival during the same years in Canada and the United States occasionally had links to New Order ministries and expectations.[26]

More basically, the Executive Presbytery stressed a subtle difference between "true gifts" and their perversions. They noticed among New Order advocates an "inflationary" tendency to "exalt the human spirit into an ecstasy" with messages announcing power, prominence, success, and spiritual gifts. "It is no wonder," they noted, that those involved "feel a spirit of exaltation and blessing."[27]

Because 1949 was a General Council year, the General Presbytery convened immediately before the Council gathering in Seattle. A committee report on the New Order recommended the preparation of a resolution for General Council consideration. It specifically disapproved three practices: (1) imparting, identifying, bestowing or confirming gifts by the laying on of hands and prophecy; (2) the teaching that the Church was built on the foundation of present-day apostles and prophets; (3) advocacy of confessing sins and problems to people who then pronounced deliverance or absolution.[28]

The Council convened late in September amid increasing controversy over the New Order. Assemblies of God executives had been warned in July that the Hawtins and other New Order advocates planned to use various tactics to disrupt the Council[29] and were cautioned to expect demonic opposition: "They [the Hawtins] attract every Sodomite, degenerate, prostitute and whoremonger whose immorality is hidden in songs and signs and pains and groans from Hell. Their meetings are like a spiritualistic seance, and the demon powers are surely in command."[30] On the other hand, there were letters supporting the Hawtins. "You have fallen asleep," wrote one H. F. Gambill. "You carol yourselves to sleep with that same sectarian lullaby that your mother the Great Harlot sang so sweetly before you. . . . You speak of being a movement, having an end-times message. But did you know that your message should have ended when first you started your Backward Movement into the weak and beggarly elements of this present world?"[31]

In spite of such sharp divisions in sentiment, the executive report to the General Presbytery indicated that no ministers had been disfellowshipped solely for accepting New Order views. Some had resigned voluntarily; others had been disciplined for such schismatic activities as encouraging congregations to withdraw from the Assemblies of God to form "Latter Rain" churches. In the end, the New Order did not present a major threat to the Assemblies of God. Its adherents' acceptance of radical congregationalism made continued participation in the denomination distasteful to them, and they withdrew accordingly.

The issues raised by the New Order of the Latter Rain did not disappear, however. Some of them were incorporated into the emerging healing revival, which shared the New Order stress on deliverance ministries. The emphasis on deliverance differed in significant ways from what most Assemblies of God leaders had concluded about spiritual self-discipline. Some of the healing revivalists had direct links to New Order leaders. Both William Branham and William Freeman, for example, participated enthusiastically in Latter Rain efforts.[32] And the deliverance ministries, as well as significant parts of the New Order message and the expectations it generated also energized the later charismatic movement in important ways.[33]

During the late 1940s, then, the felt needs of large numbers of Pentecostals for spiritual vitality made them receptive to a modified form of the early Pentecostal message. Presented as God's "restoring early Church power to the last minute Church," the New Order of the Latter Rain promised power and blessing. Often criticized by the Assemblies of God for fostering a "martyr spirit" and nurturing spiritual arrogance and exclusiveness, the New Order nonetheless survived and influenced the course of other movements the Assemblies of God, and other classical Pentecostals, have interacted with in the past forty years. The two most prominent of these have been the salvation/healing revival and the charismatic movement.

The Salvation/Healing Revival

In 1955 Assemblies of God evangelist Asa Alonzo Allen announced an ambitious plan, the Billion Souls Crusade. The "miracle ministries" of Allen, T. L. Osborn (an independent), and two other Assemblies of God ministers, Velmer Gardner and Gordon Lindsay, were poised, Allen reported, to conduct a "great crusade" that would "bring JESUS BACK." Not surprisingly, they billed it as "the greatest thing that has ever been announced."[34]

"A billion souls for Christ," Gordon Lindsay mused. "There are a billion souls in this world ready to hear the Gospel if it is preached with the signs following."[35] The "signs" would surely make the difference. Lindsay appealed for support for a series of crusades designed to "take the secrets that God has given us and move forward in the only plan that will save the world from . . . horrible catastrophe."[36]

A man gripped by an audacious vision, Lindsay, with his colleagues, played a central role in channeling a growing, popular religious fascination for the miraculous. Besides these men and women appealing to people within Pentecostal denominations, their activities helped reveal the dimensions of the nondenominational Pentecostal movement (as well as the durability of anti-organizational rhetoric in the denominations) and contributed to the growth and visibility of independent Pentecostalism. Convinced that their message of the spiritual and physical benefits of faith offered the world its final opportunity for redemption, salvation/healing revivalists (many holding Assemblies of God credentials) gained visibility by preaching simple, emotion-packed sermons to the huge audiences that crowded into their tents to hear prophecies and witness miracles. The setting encouraged ignoring the customs observed by most Americans in their worship. Warmth, rhythm, and shouts pervaded the atmosphere, which was also hospitable to spiritual gifts. Crowds identified with the overstatements and the exaggerated criticisms that punctuated the messages. But the highlight of such gatherings was usually the time allotted for prayer for the sick. In a faith-charged setting, charismatic leaders who had won the confidence of their audiences claimed to exercise gifts that brought physical—and sometimes material—benefits to believers.

William Branham and Oral Roberts were two of the most prominent spokesmen of this revival, but scores of lesser known men and women also carried its message.[37] That message was shaped by Pentecostal expectations and found ample response among members of various Pentecostal denominations. But the effort was part of a much broader hope that revival would sweep America: The late 1940s and early 1950s saw the proliferation of evangelistic outreaches across America, including such efforts as Youth for Christ rallies, Billy Graham crusades, and religious radio broadcasts, seeking to promote religious awakening.

Although the Billion Souls Crusade faded from the headlines of its promoters' papers as they became sidetracked by other matters, it initially conveyed admirably what a growing group of Pentecostal evangelists was trying to accomplish. Convinced that miracles would attract the masses and that Pentecostal experience was "enduement with power," they set out to preach the present possibility of deliverance from sin and sickness. Their message was cast in end-times rhetoric and generally stressed increasingly miraculous claims. Tending to charge that the Pentecostal movement had strayed from its heritage, they played on memories of the "good old days," which evoked response among Pentecostal people who were often bewildered by their movement's changing character.

In general, promoters of the salvation/healing movement spoke the language of the people and identified with the physical and economic hardship experienced by many in their audiences. Once they had established a support network, they often made increasingly radical claims.[38] For example, late in the fall of 1955, A. A. Allen pitched his tent in Los Angeles. He gave a glowing description of the meetings that followed:

> Many had declared that never before had they seen the Spirit of God manifested in such a miraculous way. People had received healing while sitting in their seats. . . . Tumors disappeared as those so afflicted stood before [Allen]. Blind eyes came open at the touch of his hand, even without prayer. Scores of people had already leaped from wheel chairs. People who had been carried in on their death beds had arisen from their beds and carried them out of the meeting. There was no question that the miracle working power of God had been in operation from the start.[39]

As the excitement mounted, a woman stood to prophesy. The hushed crowd heard her convey the message that God would do "a new thing" within three days. (The promise of a "new thing" was historically well calculated to capture Pentecostal attention; it was evidence, needed by some, of God's immediacy and reassurance of participation in His present plan.) All who believed would see "miracle oil" flowing from their hands. This "anointing" would bring responsibility. Believers were charged with laying their oil-exuding hands on the sick and promised that the blind, deaf, and lame would be healed.[40]

The next day, participants began to claim that oil flowed from their hands, and the afflicted came themselves or sent handkerchieves in expectation of healing. The meetings continued for weeks. Allen drew up a statement attesting the appearance of the oil; twenty-four ministers (some representing local Assemblies of God churches) signed it.[41] Countless varieties of such claims surfaced in other ministries too.

Although the revivalists welcomed such signs as impressive and conclusive evidence of God's activity through them, their interests also included a more typical premillennialist fascination for current events and signs in the heavens. In April 1954, *The Voice of Healing* magazine, organ of the largest association of salvation/healing revivalists, published a cover story entitled "The Mystery of the Flying Saucers in the Light of the Bible." Testimonies to many varieties of divine intervention in commonplace circumstances vied for space in such magazines with glowing reports of the revival's progress, testimonies of healings, and explanations of current events. As time passed, some of the publications made increasingly radical claims and attacked the movement's enemies.

In an effort to make the revival more credible by promoting accountability, Gordon Lindsay, a young Assemblies of God minister, became its promoter. Lindsay had been influenced in his youth by people who had participated in the earliest history of American Pentecostalism (F. E. Yoakum, John Lake, and Charles Parham, for example) and although he had affiliated with the Assemblies of God, he had imbibed their fascination for contemporary miracles as well as their independence. Lindsay made an enormous contribution to the revival. He proved adept at working with people of various religious affiliations and contributed his business sense and literary skills to the progress of the movement.

In April 1948, while working as campaign manager for healing revivalist William Branham, Lindsay began publishing The Voice of Healing, a monthly magazine promoting the revival. When Branham withdrew temporarily from ministry, Lindsay's magazine featured the meetings of William Freeman, an evangelist linked to the New Order of the Latter Rain. At the end of one year, Lindsay had a circulation of thirty thousand and it was rapidly growing.

In December 1949, Lindsay organized a convention of healing revivalists, which met in Dallas. It featured two men whose ministries dated from early Assemblies of God history, F. F. Bosworth and Raymond T. Richey. After leaving the Assemblies of God in 1918, Bosworth had affiliated briefly with the Christian and Missionary Alliance. He had later opted to minister independently, conducted healing campaigns and a Chicago-based radio broadcast (which brought in over two hundred fifty thousand letters per year), and published a monthly magazine until his retirement to Florida. Richey had been active from his youth in the Assemblies of God. He had organized the

Richey Evangelistic Association, based in Houston, Texas, and was widely known among Pentecostals for his salvation/healing crusades. In addition to these mentors of the new generation, Lindsay featured several with emerging ministries, some of whom were Assemblies of God evangelists: O. L. Jaggers, Gayle Jackson, Velmer Gardner, Clifton Erickson.[42]

The next year some one thousand evangelists gathered at the Voice of Healing Convention. The movement was growing rapidly. From a risky venture that had absorbed most of Lindsay's personal savings, it had become an impressive, popular religious movement. In Lindsay's mind, it seems, the Voice of Healing was two things: a loose, voluntary association of salvation/healing revivalists (male and female) who agreed to abide by certain regulations and a monthly magazine that featured publicity about upcoming meetings and testimonies of their results. Being listed in *The Voice of Healing* implied that evangelist's willingness to follow the association's rules; the magazine advertised evangelists with "proven" ministries.[43] The conventions helped demonstrate both the movement's magnitude and its diversity. They offered inspirational rallies and small workshops, and participation on the program was a coveted honor.

Lindsay encouraged healing evangelists to avoid attacking denominations. He sought unsuccessfully to discourage their creating rival publications and making claims to bizarre miracles and was criticized by some who thought he deferred to the Assemblies of God. During the early 1950s, five Assemblies of God evangelists and T. L. Osborn functioned as the nucleus of the Voice of Healing association.

The activities of the healing evangelists received considerable press coverage, which brought with it notoriety. Among the most popular of the evangelists was the Assemblies of God's Jack Coe. Ordained to the ministry in 1944, Coe renounced a rough life-style to travel the revival circuit. Crowds loved his blunt, forthright language, his defiance of ministerial dignity, his bold faith. Always ready for the "hardest" cases, he seemed to court publicity. Outspoken in his opposition to medicine, Coe insisted on the supreme adequacy of faith.

In February 1956 Coe was in Miami in the midst of a forty-four-day campaign (which from the first drew capacity crowds of six thousand) when he was charged with practicing medicine without a license. The trial drew to Florida some of the most prominent leaders of the revival, all of whom testified in Coe's defense. Charges were dismissed.[44] Early the next year, Coe's death at forty-seven in a hospital shocked his following; he had denounced the use of medicine by his followers, but his family had turned to physicians when he was fatally stricken with polio. The various institutions through which he had conducted his ministry continued, but without him, their visibility faded.

During his heyday, Jack Coe had been dismissed by the Texas District Council of the Assemblies of God. A contentious man, he had failed to honor Lindsay's guidelines and had confronted district leaders bitterly and publicly. Fiercely independent and naturally zealous for his own efforts, he not only had failed to cooperate with the Assemblies of God, but also had consciously sought to undermine the denomination's credibility among those who participated in the revival. Coe's brief leadership has obscured his popularity. During the early 1950s, he was a force others had to reckon with, especially as he rapidly gained the popular support necessary to withdraw from Lindsay's umbrella organization.

Another member of the original nucleus of the Voice of Healing, A. A. Allen, also held Assemblies of God credentials. Late in 1955, Allen was arrested in Knoxville for driving while intoxicated. The evidence gathered by Knoxville police was conclusive. Allen chose to label the incident "persecution," became incensed that others would believe the incident had occurred, and refused to abide by a recommendation that, until the matter was settled, he refrain from preaching.[45] He lost his credentials in 1956.

Both the Coe and Allen cases brought the Assemblies of God unprecedented media attention. Not only the secular press, but also the magazines spawned by the revival (which circulated by the scores of thousands, Coe's *Herald of Healing,* for example, having a circulation of three hundred thousand in 1958) aired the controversies between the evangelists and their denomination. When Assemblies of God publications refused to carry word of their meetings, the evangelists attacked national and district Assemblies of God leaders by name.[46]

The Coe and Allen cases were the most publicized of several that demanded denominational attention during the height of the salvation/healing revival in the 1950s. They forced the Assemblies of God to respond to issues raised by the revival. In a sense, the conduct of some healing evangelists seemed to validate the denomination's decision not to endorse a movement even though some of its own ministers were a prominent part of it. Both Coe and Allen were major personages among the evangelists, holding forth in large tents (Coe claimed his was the world's largest) and on a growing number of radio stations. They published their own monthly magazines and built sizable organizations. They lived in a world in which miracles and intense spiritual experiences were commonplace, in which prophecies and conflicts with evil forces were part of everyday life. It is no wonder that, from their viewpoint, average churches were "dead" and denominational organizations were hopelessly politicized.

Already in the late 1940s, Assemblies of God executives disallowed testimonies of healings in the salvation/healing crusades in the *Pentecostal Evangel*.[47] Since a sizable percentage of healing evangelists endorsed by *The Voice of Healing* magazine held Assemblies of God credentials, this policy generated considerable discussion. Executive leaders succeeded in convincing the General Presbytery that many testimonies emerging from the revival were unverifiable and sensationalist and would ultimately damage the healing message. They encouraged, instead, the submission of testimonies of healings occurring in local congregations and carrying the endorsement of denominationally accountable pastors.

Discussion in the General Presbytery in September 1953 revealed some of the matters that troubled local Assemblies of God congregations. Leaders expressed concern about the revival's varied fund-raising techniques, its exaggerated claims and bitter criticisms, and the growing tendency of some healing evangelists to claim ability to diagnose diseases. This last item, the presbyters agreed, "bordered on the occult" and should be discouraged.[48]

A lengthy discussion resulted in the adoption of several motions. They recommended a renewed emphasis on the teaching and practice of "scriptural truths" of healing and "deliverance from sin, sickness and satanic forces." They disapproved fundraising methods and reports of attendance and healing that were open to challenge. They further endorsed the preparation of a series of articles for the *Pentecostal Evangel* on divine healing, the baptism in the Holy Spirit, and prophecy.[49] They noted with concern that the excitement and extravagance of salvation/healing crusades tended to make people dissatisfied with local congregations and pastors. By this time, complaints and questions about specific Assemblies of God evangelists who identified with the healing movement had been received.

During the early 1950s, as Lindsay's influence as coordinator and promoter of the revival waned, the restraint he had promoted through the Voice of Healing virtually disappeared. Open confrontations between district officials and independent-minded Assemblies of God evangelists publicized bitter recriminations. The Texas District, in which some of the more controversial healing evangelists held credentials, was especially hard pressed. Its well-respected veteran superintendent, James O. Savell, became the target of some of Jack Coe's most vehement criticisms. No longer needing to accept Lindsay's restrictions in order to achieve their legitimacy, evangelists who set up their own organizations increasingly defied Assemblies of God precedent and structure.

Although many denominational leaders had reservations about the healing revival, large numbers of adherents did not. Their willingness to financially support the projects of the revivalists made the movement possible at the same time that it took support from denominational projects and local church programs.

During the 1950s, some of the healing evangelists undertook large-scale overseas efforts. Gordon Lindsay claimed divine inspiration for his use of salvation/healing campaigns in overseas evangelism. Issues of *The Voice of Healing* as well as magazines representing individual ministries regularly carried reports of immense crusades abroad. Some evangelists enjoyed considerably more success abroad than at home, notably T. L. Osborn and Tommy Hicks (whose 1954 crusade in Argentina is described by David Edwin Harrell in *All Things Are Possible* as "perhaps the most famous single meeting in the history of the revival"[50]). In 1967, Lindsay symbolized his shift by changing *The Voice of Healing* to *Christ for the Nations*. Just as The Voice of Healing was much more than a publication, so Christ for the Nations came to describe a growing network of efforts, including a large charismatic Bible school in Dallas that continues to operate under that name.

Although Pentecostal missionaries at first welcomed the mass meetings, the fund-raising practices of the healing evangelists (compounded by their general lack of financial accountability) and their promotion of financial support for national workers soon complicated the picture. Concerns about related issues supported the definite trend among executive leaders to distance the Assemblies of God from the salvation/healing revival.

In 1965, fund-raising techniques related to institutions and causes spawned by the salvation/healing revival resulted in the General Council's adoption of "Criteria for Independent Corporations." These criteria ultimately forced Gordon Lindsay (who had remained an Assemblies of God minister in good standing throughout the tumultuous years of the revival) to choose between the Assemblies of God and the various independent efforts he had devoted most of his life to. Not surprisingly, he withdrew from the denomination. His Dallas-based efforts did not suffer. With his talented wife, Freda, he identified increasingly with neo-Pentecostalism; expanded his native church program, his production of native literature, his teaching tapes (some two thousand of which he supplied to charismatic prayer groups monthly); and devoted himself to the operation of his school and thirty-acre headquarters complex in Dallas. When he died suddenly on April 1, 1973, Lindsay had gained widespread recognition for his varied abilities. Perhaps most significantly, he left a sizable body of literature that chronicled and explained the revival. His passing marked the end of an era: His experience had reached through denominational affiliation back to participation with some of Pentecostalism's earliest leaders and forward into charismatic settings. He had known the revival's founders and their successors. Although he had failed to contain their ministries, he had succeeded in retaining his own reputation for balance and wisdom.

Another man with a reputation among Pentecostals for wisdom and balance who sought to influence independent and denominational Pentecostal perceptions of the revival was Granville H. Montgomery, a long-time Pentecostal Holiness Church leader. Montgomery worked closely with Oral Roberts before joining Juanita Coe in her Dallas-based ministries in 1962. That year he published a series of articles that criticized both sides.

Montgomery's familiarity with both classical, organized Pentecostalism and the salvation/healing revival lent credence to his observations. They continue to have relevance whenever questions about financial and moral accountability surface. In many ways the problems the denomination has faced in the 1980s are not new.

Montgomery castigated the evangelists for the personal independence they preserved, he alleged, by creating family-dominated institutions. This practice, he cautioned, "opened the door to many dangers." Because each evangelist was "a law unto himself," each tended to use other people as "tools," rather than "as the children of God with brains, gifts and callings as clear and distinct as his own."[51]

Montgomery gave vent to his disgust with the evangelists' preferences for this world's luxuries: "Men who preach the meek and lowly Nazarene to a lost and dying world, and yet live in palatial homes built on money contributed by God's poor people, cannot call themselves followers of Jesus."[52] By 1962 Allen's weakness for alcohol had already been revealed. Montgomery alleged that others, too, used alcohol and drugs, abused their spouses, associated with prostitutes, and were subject to blackmail.[53]

Consequently, not only were the evangelists' spiritual claims incredible, their life-styles and morality failed Christian expectations. Montgomery brought the weight of a participant's testimony to bear in charging that miraculous claims were often fraudulent. He assembled a list of twenty-three products the evangelists hawked and claimed miraculous powers for.

He reserved his bitterest complaints for the subject of finances, storming about funds diverted from the purposes they were solicited for and devoted instead to the evangelists. He had harsh words for Pentecostal denominations too, claiming that their failure to nurture the revival and to control its spokespersons had tended to encourage the inclinations of some participants toward extreme claims and unaccountable independence.

By the time Montgomery wrote, the revival was no longer so prominent. Its character had changed somewhat, as leaders aged and died and tent evangelism slowly gave way to televangelism. In a sense, deliverance evangelism never died; rather, it remade itself into the electronic church. During the 1960s, deliverance evangelism still had thousands of followers, but for a time, as it regrouped, the issues it raised did not directly affect the larger Pentecostal denominations.[54]

The boundaries of the post-World War II salvation/healing revival are difficult to fix, for the revival overlapped in significant ways other movements in American evangelicalism. And it served multiple purposes. Not only did it reveal the persistence of fiercely independent, prophetic leadership within Pentecostalism, it also demonstrated that hundreds of thousands of Americans willingly identified with charismatic figures accountable to no one. Perhaps it did challenge an increasingly institutionalized movement to renew its stress on the miraculous. Certainly it proved that the rhetoric and claims of the first-generation Pentecostal revival still struck responsive chords in many hearts.

The salvation/healing movement thrived at least in part because the claims of its leaders made sense to their audiences. Many Protestants anticipated revival and believed that the horrors of war had inclined people toward religion. Americans were proving responsive to the assurance of people like Norman Vincent Peale, whose book *The Power of Positive Thinking* became a best-seller in 1952. The seeds of "positive confession" teaching were clearly evident among some of the healers. Kenneth Hagin, whose charismatic leadership and Rhema Bible Institute (Tulsa, Oklahoma) have become symbolic of the view that a Christian commitment should effect health and prosperity, was an Assemblies of God minister who identified prominently with the salvation/healing revival from its inception. The evolution of such thought (including its implications for fund-raising) is most readily traceable in the ministry of Oral Roberts.[55]

During a time that science and modernity seemed to pose a new threat to evangelical faith, the salvation/healing revival was a call to "old-time religion" under old-fashioned gospel tents. In an era of a cold war that added patriotic overtones to religious commitment, the revival was presented as essentially American—opposing "godless communism" (linked through some of its personalities, as a matter of fact, to right-wing politics). It also unashamedly avowed the presence of the supernatural to transform human existence. Further, the revival made thousands of people aware of Pentecostal worship and spiritual gifts. Out of it came associations, like the Full Gospel Business Men's Fellowship International, that both promoted and influenced the emerging charismatic movement.

In reemphasizing experience, the salvation/healing revival downplayed doctrinal differences, first among Pentecostals, then among Christians. By the 1970s, for example, revivalist Kathryn Kuhlman had become a well-known charismatic leader whose ministry readily embraced Catholics and Protestants of all varieties. Especially after it became apparent that no Pentecostal denomination would identify with the revival, many salvation/healing evangelists forsook Pentecostal denominations (either willingly or under pressure) and stressed the essential unity of all who shared charismatic experience. Links among the various healing ministries, especially in support of specific associations or gatherings, were not uncommon.

Independent Pentecostals who had historically rejected organization of their movement and charismatics who forsook denominations they no longer felt at home in (or who chose to remain in denominations and to identify as well with parachurch efforts) together constituted an increasingly visible and vocal segment of American Pentecostalism. Some who had been alienated from Pentecostal denominations over the New Order of the Latter Rain readily accepted the premises about faith and miracles that salvation/healing revivalists preached and identified with nondenominational Pentecostalism.

The salvation/healing revival, then, gave rise to many of the assumptions that operated later in charismatic circles. It contributed, as well, to the reservations Pentecostal denominational leaders expressed about the charismatic movement. The connections are most visible in the careers of men and women like Oral Roberts, Gordon and Freda Lindsay, and Kathryn Kuhlman.

Conclusion

Taken together, the New Order of the Latter Rain and the salvation/healing revival revealed the dimensions of a large segment of Pentecostalism that had opted historically for nonorganization. They demonstrated as well the continuing appeal of restorationist and end-times concepts and the extent of the feeling among Pentecostals that denominations had betrayed the movement.

These movements are important. They were not aberrations. Instead, they revealed the continuing hospitality among American Pentecostals to themes that dominated Pentecostalism's early history. They serve further as reminders of the inadequacy of definitions of American Pentecostalism that focus on its denominations and ignore the vitality and direction of its independent segment.

Myrtle Beall, pastor of the large Bethesda Missionary Temple in Detroit, brought the New Order of the Latter Rain into the United States after a trip to Vancouver, British Columbia.

Herrick Holt, Percy G. Hunt, and George Hawtin at the groundbreaking for Sharon School, a New Order of the Latter Rain school, 1948 (sign for the school below)

A. A. Allen, Assemblies of God evangelist, announced the Billion Souls Crusade in 1955.

Jack Coe holding his daughter in a Miami courtroom after he was accused of practicing medicine without a license, 1956

Gordon Lindsay at the pulpit during one of William Branham's healing campaigns, 1950.

This General Council was held in the midst of the controversy over the New Order of the Latter Rain (1949, Seattle, Washington). Executives had been warned that New Order advocates would try to disrupt the meetings.

Joseph Mattsson-Boze was a spokesman for the Scandinavian Independent Assemblies of God, which held strong antiorganizational ideals.

4. Ecumenism, Renewal, and Pentecostal Identity

When Dennis Bennett, rector of St. Mark's Church in Van Nuys, California, resigned his parish under pressure early in 1960, his predicament attracted media attention. That summer, *Newsweek* carried a story about the controversial rector's spiritual pilgrimage.[1] It focused on tongues speech and other "gifts of the Spirit" that had surfaced in his experience and among his congregation. Considered "proper" for Pentecostals, such speech proved "strange and troublesome indeed" for a well-educated, upper-middle-class, suburban Protestant Episcopal parish.[2] And what occurred was not an isolated incident: Bennett and seventy members of his congregation were part of a growing network of local ministers and laypeople in the diocese who had spoken in tongues since late in 1959. But it was Bennett who had emerged as the acknowledged leader of this enthusiastic group that had determined to nurture a Pentecostal witness from within the historic denomination.[3]

When Bennett had tried to explain and defend the practice of tongues speech to his people, one of his curates took off his vestments and resigned between services, and church officers, in turn, demanded Bennett resign. Bennett complied, but at the same time he refused to renounce the priesthood and exhorted his supporters to remain in the church. A few months later, he accepted reassignment to a struggling, nearly bankrupt parish, St. Luke's in Seattle, Washington. Within a year, nearly one hundred communicants of St. Luke's had spoken in tongues, and the congregation had outgrown its building. By the mid-1970s, some two thousand people worshipped weekly

85

at St. Luke's, and Bennett had become the symbol of a movement that had spread throughout the Christian world.[4]

Classical Pentecostal Bridges to Charismatic Renewal

Stories in *Newsweek* and *Time* played an important role in giving national visibility to a general growing interest in the Holy Spirit. The interest manifested itself in two separate but interrelated series of events: the charismatic renewal (in some mainstream Protestant denominations and Roman Catholicism) and the ecumenical movement. The episodes the media covered in 1960 helped mark a new phase in American religious awareness of charismatic Christianity. And the episodes themselves ultimately joined the stream of events that made Pentecostalism the largest twentieth-century Christian movement.

While scholars may debate whether the charismatic movement was spawned primarily by classical Pentecostalism or developed indigenously in mainstream Protestantism and Catholicism, it is evident that several trends within classical Pentecostalism helped forge ties between the two movements. For over a decade, at least three developments within classical Pentecostalism had generated expectations, events, and institutions that helped make some Pentecostals hospitable to the emergence of Pentecostal distinctives in non-Pentecostal churches.

First, the Latter Rain movement, despite its elitist message, energized expectations that helped mold the perceptions of some who later became charismatic leaders. Second, the salvation/healing revival both introduced masses of non-Pentecostals to Pentecostal expectations and created a variety of nondenominational agencies and institutions that helped sustain and channel interest in charismatic worship and spiritual gifts. Third, the remarkable activities of David du Plessis, an Assemblies of God pastor and international Pentecostal leader, gave Pentecostalism greater visibility, first among ecumenical leaders of mainstream denominations and then among Roman Catholics.

Each of these developments created substantial friction within Pentecostal denominations like the Assemblies of God. Each thrived, however, partly because it claimed to recapture something that had been central to early Pentecostal perceptions about the movement's meaning and mission. Each insisted that Pentecostalism was essentially a renewal movement that should not be confined to specific denominations: Its purpose, rather, was to empower the entire Church, to enable the Church to realize its essential unity in Christ.

Each of the three developments also emphasized the conviction that the extent and intensity of Pentecostal witness should constantly increase. Resisting the tendency to locate Pentecostalism's golden age in the past, they maintained that it was in the present and future. Latter Rain leader George Hawtin described a "wonderful deliverance from the terrible bondage of the Babylon of the denominational system" as he substituted "present truth" for "past truth."[5] Healing evangelist A. A. Allen used the slogan Miracles Today; he and his Voice of Healing colleagues proclaimed a worldwide revival.[6] They emphasized divine activity in their day rather than wistful hopes for a return to prior power. In so doing, they legitimated their ministries by placing themselves at the center of God's end-times plan. Jack Coe, despite his feisty reputation, sincerely expressed a hope many healing evangelists shared: "I'm only interested in bringing the body of Christ into the unity of the Spirit, with love in their hearts for one another."[7]

Most prominent healing evangelists had broken their ties to denominations by the mid-1950s, some willingly, others unwillingly. Their interdenominational appeal clearly targeted a broad audience without calling for new denominational loyalties. "Doctrine," Coe insisted, "is not the basis of fellowship among Christians. The basis of fellowship is the blood of the Lord Jesus Christ."[8] Coe foresaw a day when Pentecostal phenomena would sweep through the Christian church without respect to denomination or creed: "Soon the wilderness is going to be made rivers of water and the desert places are going to spring forth . . . and you old 'dry hides' are going to get into this thing too!"[9]

Salvation/healing evangelists and advocates of the Latter Rain explicitly coveted early Christian fervor and power. Although they found more evidence of such fervor in American Pentecostal history than in their time, they believed they were heralds of "God's second call," a call that would find readier response among traditional Protestants than among Pentecostals.[10] Circumstances contributed to such convictions, of course. Criticized by Pentecostal denominational leaders, the Pentecostal spokesmen of God's contemporary "new move" were forced to develop an emphasis on Christian unity in order to build and expand independent ministries.

Themes of unity resonated as well in a growing trend among Pentecostal denominations toward associational agencies like the National Association of Evangelicals (NAE) and the Pentecostal World Conference. British Pentecostal editor Donald Gee noted that such associations eased friction and strengthened common testimony. Gee observed, however, that Pentecostals who rejected denominational organization for independent ministries only superficially imitated primitive Christians.[11] Rather, they evaded "the stern necessity of serving our own generation."[12] A similar concern "to serve the present age" had motivated denominational federations like the Federal Council of Churches of Christ. Gee's vision for unity was remarkably similar to that of both the Federal Council and the World Council of Churches: He preached "unity of obedience to Christ as Lord," unity that he described as a "personal matter." "My ultimate unity," Gee maintained, "is with my brother, irrespective of whether we belong to the same or different, outward communions. We do not come together to 'make' unity, for it already exists by the grace of God. . . . Its test is mutual acceptance of the Lordship of Jesus Christ."[13]

Although many Assemblies of God adherents agreed in theory, in practice denominational organization and popular triumphalist rhetoric made it difficult to realize the unity their talk envisioned. Two prominent Pentecostals, Oral Roberts and Demos Shakarian, a wealthy California dairyman, sought to give it institutional expression in 1951 in the Full Gospel Business Men's Fellowship International (FGBMFI). Focusing on business and professional men, the new organization offered men from many denominations opportunities for fellowship. It was widely influential in cultivating a grass-roots ecumenical outlook. Local chapters organized social meetings where those interested in Pentecostal experience, as well as tongues-speaking members of non-Pentecostal denominations, mingled with adherents of Pentecostal churches. Offering neutral ground, such meetings provided more respectable settings than did humble Pentecostal churches. Since the FGBMFI was not controlled by a Pentecostal denomination, its programs promoted no specific church affiliation. Beginning in 1953, it extended its influence with a monthly publication, *Full Gospel Business Men's Voice.* Filled with accounts of members of mainline denominations who had spoken in tongues, the magazine was widely distributed outside Pentecostal denominations.

Many Assemblies of God adherents shared the excitement and vision that prompted efforts like the FGBMFI. Although some welcomed efforts to extend a Pentecostal witness in mainline denominations, others were deeply concerned. Some local pastors disliked the time and money their well-to-do business members devoted to the FGBMFI. And the organization ultimately conflicted as well with the Assemblies of God's Men's Fellowship Department, which was, on the whole, denominationally focused. Puzzled by apparent inconsistencies, Pentecostals struggled with the meaning and extent of the term "unity." By the 1950s, Pentecostal denominations typically emphasized specific doctrines and practices as biblical requisites for Spirit baptism. Assemblies of God adherents, for example, generally believed that Spirit baptism evidenced by tongues would follow a crisis conversion experience and baptism by immersion. Although the events might occasionally be ordered differently, adherents were encouraged to expect all three. When people who claimed Pentecostal, or charismatic, experiences failed to leave denominations that stressed liturgy, infant baptism, sacramental theologies, or other such "unacceptable" expressions of faith and when they failed to renounce life-styles that embraced long-held Pentecostal taboos—e.g., dancing, smoking, drinking—this raised uncomfortable questions. Was sharing an experience of the Holy Spirit a sufficient basis for unity? Or would true unity necessarily begin with doctrinal agreement?

Ecumenism and David du Plessis

For members of the Assemblies of God, this question about the basis of unity was raised most forcefully by a South African immigrant, David J. du Plessis, in whose career the two issues of renewal and ecumenism became inextricably intertwined.[14] A veteran Pentecostal, having joined the Pentecostal movement in 1918, Du Plessis had been secretary of his denomination, the Apostolic Faith Movement (South Africa). Like Donald Gee, he promoted communication among isolated Pentecostal groups throughout the 1930s and helped run the first Pentecostal World Conference in 1947. As secretary of the Pentecostal World Conference, Du Plessis was widely recognized for his gentle, persuasive spirit. Late in the 1940s, he and his wife, Anna, migrated to the United States, where he soon obtained Assemblies of God credentials and accepted a small congregation, Stamford Gospel Tabernacle, in Stamford, Connecticut. He continued to serve the Pentecostal World Conference and to exert influence well beyond his congregation.

Du Plessis shared with Donald Gee the persuasion that true Christian unity came through acknowledgment of Christ as Lord. When the ongoing, broader Protestant quest for unity in submission to the Lordship of Christ resulted in the formation of the World Council of Churches in 1948, a deluge of Pentecostal and evangelical protests followed—drawing on prophetic images of "superchurches" and "the beast." Du Plessis, however, resisted the logic. In typical Pentecostal fashion, he later recalled, he "began to pray earnestly about His purposes."[15]

Before long, he claimed being divinely instructed to visit World Council leaders and witness to his Pentecostal faith. Arriving at the council's New York City offices unannounced, Du Plessis did not know what to expect. To his surprise, he was warmly welcomed and spent the entire day in conversation with staff, explaining "things that I thought they did not want to hear."[16] His visit began a lifelong association with mainline denominational leaders marked by mutual respect.

In 1952 Du Plessis accepted an invitation to participate in the International Missionary Council's extended sessions in Willingen, West Germany. The meetings brought together some two hundred representatives (many of them prominent in the growing ecumenical movement) from forty-five countries to consider the church's missionary obligation; as a group, they strongly endorsed a basic Christian commitment to evangelistic witness.[17] During the ten-day conference, Du Plessis responded to several questions in plenary sessions and to requests for personal interviews from over half the delegates.[18]

By 1954, when the World Council of Churches met for its second assembly in Evanston, Illinois, Du Plessis was a familiar figure in ecumenical ranks. Prominent leaders like John Mackay, president of Princeton Theological Seminary, and Visser 't Hooft, secretary of the World Council of Churches, urged him to mingle freely with delegates, talking about Pentecostal experience. Du Plessis was elated when he discovered widespread interest in his testimony among church leaders and academics.[19] But he soon learned as well that "a prophet is without honor in his own country."

Like their fellow evangelicals in the NAE, most Assemblies of God adherents both misunderstood and disliked the ecumenical movement.[20] Many in the denomination had long been fascinated with predictive prophecy. Major religious and political developments invariably invited their prophetic speculation. This prepossession for making current events fit the prophecies of Ezekiel and Daniel—heightened in the 1940s by both events in Israel and a world war's roster of candidates for the Antichrist—found expression in such common evangelistic tools as dispensational charts. Assigning ecumenism prophetic import, then, proponents of prophecy believed it heralded the prophesied world church; they also rejected ecumenism's stress on unity as predicated on false assumptions. It is important to note, however, that leading American proponents of the ecumenical movement during the 1950s specifically disavowed an attempt to unite denominations: "The idea of a world church ecclesiastically united has not found explicit or even vague expression in this movement," editor Charles Clayton Morrison wrote in *The Christian Century* in 1954.[21] Nonetheless, evangelicals generally preferred to believe that the prophesied world church would soon emerge through the World Council of Churches. Thus Du Plessis's involvement represented a fundamental betrayal of Pentecostal principle because he associated with heralds of the "scarlet woman" and compromised truth in favor of experience.

Du Plessis understood this attitude: He had once shared it fully. Recounting his growing ecumenical involvement during the 1950s, he reminisced: "I could remember days when I had wished I could have set my eyes upon such men to denounce their theology and pray the judgment of God upon them for what I considered their heresies and false doctrines."[22] Du Plessis claimed his attitude had been transformed by "a warm glow" of the Holy Spirit that filled him with love for the mainstream church leaders distrusted by so many of his fellow Pentecostals.

Not only did Du Plessis engage in suspect ecumenical activities, he also joined those Pentecostals who voiced concern from within about the waning vitality of American Pentecostalism. During the 1940s, the *Pentecostal Evangel* had published articles alleging that despite its growth, much of the movement had departed from its early practices.[23] Du Plessis heartily concurred and prescribed a remedy in a widely distributed tract, *God Has No Grandsons.*

Noting that "today the sons and grandsons of Pentecostal pioneers are teaching in Sunday Schools and holding all kinds of offices in the local churches without ever having had a real baptism in the Spirit," Du Plessis warned that "the waves of Pentecostal power and revival are receding fast. There is danger that in another generation we may have a Pentecostal Movement without Pentecost—that is, without the experience, just like other revivals which still emphasize some or other truth but never experience it. Revivals crystalize into societies and establish churches when the 'grandsons' take over. But *God has no grandsons.*"[24] From Du Plessis's perspective, only a divinely inspired renewal could reverse the situation. His restorationist hope anticipated God's activity rather than human success to recover apostolic power. "God," he maintained, "wants to repeat what He did in the first Christian Church in every generation."[25]

Objections to Ecumenism

Du Plessis, consequently, challenged Pentecostal denominations on at least two fronts: He raised questions of identity that were rooted in long-nurtured suppositions, and he deplored the movement's status quo. His activities helped force the Assemblies of God to make explicit some long-held assumptions about the burgeoning ecumenical movement. As noted, by 1948 when the World Council of Churches was formed in Amsterdam, most Assemblies of God leaders had fully identified with the new evangelicalism of the NAE. Like others in that association, they transferred their dislike of the Federal Council of Churches to the World Council, and later to the National Council of Churches, reserving their deepest disdain for American proponents of ecumenism.

From time to time the *Pentecostal Evangel,* like *United Evangelical Action* and other evangelical periodicals, noted the progress of worldwide ecumenism. The World Council for the most part, the *Evangel* alleged, represented denominations that were "spiritually cold and formal."[26] In pursuing unity among Christians, moreover, they were going after something they would never gain, something that should not be sought, but maintained, since "all true Christians" already possessed it.[27] Those who identified with ecumenism, it followed, could not be described as "true" Christians.

Such views underscored the more basic contention that ecumenical leaders sought to create a "superchurch," a concept that evoked both horror and excitement in evangelical minds. (In the postwar period this was fed, as well, by general American fears of rising communism.) Dire predictions of end-times judgment accompanied warnings about religious unity. "The fact that so many churches may be in a mood to unite may be one of the most significant signs of the times," the *Evangel* noted. "Could it be that the steps now being taken are leading to the unholy and illegitimate pseudo-church which we believe is mentioned in Bible prophecy?"[28] Such observations, however, encouraged the faithful to await with renewed expectancy the soon return of Christ.

Pentecostals also disliked the "catholic type" church they thought ecumenism promoted. Disregarding the possibility that all denominations (including their own) might well have sinners as well as saints, they deplored any ecclesiastical structure in which regenerate and unregenerate mingled. Such settings, they noted, had historically been "the enemy of the prophetic type of Christianity."[29] Assemblies of God spokesmen charged that the same liberals and modernists who had dominated the Federal Council of Churches had emerged as the American presence in the World Council and insisted that the new organization would inevitably mean a "watering-down of the gospel testimony and a compromise with worldliness."[30] But it was not only theological liberalism that repelled them: They foresaw, as well, the ultimate unfolding of a new religion focusing in the worship of Antichrist. The *Evangel* quoted with approval the words of prominent evangelical leader Wilbur Smith: "Christians need well beware of all this talk about a world church. A world church . . . will become a perfect agency for the accomplishment of Antichrist's purpose."[31]

When in 1948 the World Council of Churches issued a statement of Christian faith that evangelicals had to acknowledge was "sound" (the statement forcefully affirmed the Virgin Birth, substitutionary atonement, physical resurrection, and future return of Christ), the intensity of evangelical antipathy toward the ecumenical movement was laid bare. Nothing the mainstream denominations did, it seemed, could be right in the eyes of separatistic evangelical and fundamentalist constituencies. The voices of the Assemblies of God and the NAE blended on this point: J. Elwin Wright was quoted in the *Evangel* when he said of those who signed the World Council statement of faith: "We know the infidelity and heresies of its most prominent leaders," the *Evangel* adding, "it seems to reveal . . . the hypocrisy our Lord foretold" about wolves in sheep's clothing.[32]

Pentecostal concern about a "superchurch" was part of a broader rejection of federation as a "sign of the times": They assumed that consolidation would mark every aspect of human organization in the end times. At midcentury, the *Pentecostal Evangel* editorialized about the "weeds" that were being "gathered and bundled" in contemporary America: "In industry, a corporations bundle; in labor, a trade-unions bundle; in international politics, NATO and the United Nations; and in religion, ecumenical federations." "Our Lord," the *Evangel* solemnly warned, "said that the bundling would be for the burning."[33]

Such reflections marked the grim years of Soviet aggression in Eastern Europe and conflict in Korea. The "signs of the times" seemed evident everywhere, and considerable speculation about the end times characterized evangelicals who awaited judgment as they worked for revival and anticipated their own release in Christ's triumphant return.

Occurring amid such prophetic speculation, Du Plessis's activities were suspect from the start. In the same years that the *Pentecostal Evangel* warned readers against the ecumenical movement, Du Plessis won the confidence of growing numbers of ecumenical stalwarts—who came to relish their contact with an insider when official relations with Pentecostal denominations were impossible. Since Du Plessis was an acknowledged leader in the worldwide Pentecostal community, it is not surprising that some on both sides as well as in the secular media thought that he acted in an official capacity in his dealings with ecumenical organizations. Especially after Dennis Bennett's activities captured media attention in 1960, the press tended to identify Du Plessis as "a leader of 10 million Pentecostal church members throughout the world."[34]

Carl McIntire predictably entered the fray, leading with an article in his *Christian Beacon* entitled "Are the Pentecostalists Also To Be Duped?"[35] Calling Du Plessis a "world leader of the Pentecostal churches," McIntire vehemently denounced the "ecumenical apostasy" he claimed Du Plessis sought to associate Pentecostalism with. McIntire vented his wrath on the movement as a whole. He charged that the most recent

World Pentecostal Conference (which had met in Jerusalem in May 1961) had failed to denounce three (third-world) Pentecostal denominations that had affiliated with the World Council of Churches—noting at the same time that Assemblies of God General Superintendent Thomas F. Zimmerman, featured speaker on Pentecost Sunday, was also president of the NAE. Zimmerman's presence symbolized for McIntire the NAE's inexcusable compromise on ecumenism. In failing to repudiate those third-world Pentecostals having ecumenical sympathies, McIntire charged, Pentecostals assisted "the church of the Antichrist, the one great world church, the coming ecumenical Babylon."[36]

Meanwhile, complaints from Assemblies of God pastors and adherents resulted in denominational action against Du Plessis. Although denominational leaders readily admitted that they had no quarrel with Du Plessis's "testimony for Pentecost," they cited criticisms of his advocacy of the ecumenical movement and objected to the use of the influence and name of the Assemblies of God "as tools for compromise."[37] The Executive Presbytery requested that Du Plessis make three promises (which revealed much about contemporary Assemblies of God attitudes toward the religious culture). Given the perspectives of the men in leadership and the prophetic fascinations of their constituency, the requests seemed reasonable. However, they would have ended Du Plessis's decade-long involvement in a movement that would soon grow rapidly as charismatic experience erupted in Roman Catholicism.

First, Du Plessis was requested to avoid "making disparaging remarks or reflecting on the position of the Assemblies of God" in his discussions with World Council leaders. Second, he was asked not to "pose, officially or unofficially, as spokesman for the Assemblies of God." Third, he was asked not to invite others to accompany him to National Council or World Council meetings.[38] Not surprisingly, Du Plessis and the Presbytery failed to reach agreement, and Du Plessis was invited to withdraw from the denomination.[39] His departure was indisputably under pressure. As his influence in the ecumenical movement increased, Du Plessis remained a member of an Assemblies of

God congregation in Oakland, California. Shortly after Du Plessis lost his credentials, the rapid expansion of the charismatic movement shifted the focus of the Assemblies of God from ecumenical issues to charismatic phenomena. For the next two decades, the Assemblies of God wrestled with issues raised by the charismatic movement, many of them having roots in independent Pentecostalism and the ecumenical movement. The restoration of Du Plessis's credentials in 1980 signaled the mellowing of some attitudes that had ostracized Du Plessis even as he had gained wide acclaim outside the constituency.

Also in 1962, after Du Plessis surrendered his credentials to the Assemblies of God, the General Presbytery formalized the denomination's longstanding opposition to ecumenism. (This action was, in part at least, a response to issues raised by Du Plessis.) Noting that the ecumenical movement was both a "sign of the times" and "contrary to the real Biblical doctrine of spiritual unity in the Church of Jesus Christ," the presbyters opposed "ecumenicity based on organic and organizational unity" and the formation of a "World Superchurch," which, they said, would "probably culminate in the Scarlet Woman or Religious Babylon of Revelation."[40] They recommended that Assemblies of God ministers and congregations refrain from promoting the ecumenical movement or any of its organizations. An amendment permitting Assemblies of God ministers to participate on a local level in interdenominational activities and to offer "Pentecostal witness" freely was added to the original resolution, perhaps indicating a measure of support for Du Plessis's accomplishments. It was also a tacit acknowledgment that many Assemblies of God ministers already participated in such local interdenominational forums through ministerial alliances.

Ecumenism and the Holy Spirit

Meanwhile, Du Plessis continued to cultivate both ecumenical and charismatic contacts. His close friendship with two Presbyterians, the president of Princeton Theological Seminary, John MacKay, and the president of Union Theological

Seminary (New York City), Henry Pitney Van Dusen, brought him numerous invitations from around the world. In April 1959 MacKay expressed the conviction that God had "raised up [Du Plessis] to play a very special role in the ecumenical movement of our time."[41] Before MacKay and Van Dusen had met Du Plessis, they had become convinced that American Protestants often neglected the Holy Spirit and that an emphasis on the Holy Spirit would make a vital ecumenical movement both plausible and possible. They saw in the common neglect of the Spirit the basic source of Christian disunity.

Their interest in the Holy Spirit included a strong focus on Christ. Van Dusen elaborated on the historic problem of dealing with the Holy Spirit's activity in the Church in his study *Spirit, Son and Father:*

> Each fresh outpouring of the Spirit has been fraught with perils and has bequeathed problems.... The perplexities ... created for the guardians of tradition and good order have led them to two alternative expedients in dealing with their troublesome disturber. Some ... have ignored the Spirit altogether.... But the more usual method of handling this innovator and upsetter of the status quo has been to bring it under their own direction and control—either by making its Voice subservient to ecclesiastical interpretation or by limiting its authentic speech to the recorded writings of the past.
>
> The right and true solution of the "problem of the Spirit" lies in none of these directions. It lies in bringing men's claims of inspiration or possession of the Holy Spirit into subjection to Christ. It lies in taking with utmost seriousness and fullest acceptance the noblest insight of the greatest interpreter of this as of so many other truths of Christian Faith—the Apostle Paul—that "the Lord is that Spirit," for the Spirit which is the Holy Spirit which is the Spirit of God is—THE SPIRIT OF CHRIST.[42]

Du Plessis, too, consciously stressed the Christocentric aspect of Spirit baptism. He claimed, for example, that he eliminated the behavioral "excesses" that often stereotyped Pentecostals by confronting those who sought Spirit baptism with seeking Christ, "the BAPTIZER rather than the Baptism." This distinction, he believed, accounted for the absence from his services of "the excesses of noise, shaking, trembling, jerking" that seemed frequently to occur as people pursued Pentecostal experience.[43] Those who "met the Baptizer" (rather than sought the baptism) typically manifested no "physical demonstration" beyond tongues speech. Such speech, Du Plessis maintained, was also qualitatively different: It was not ecstatic utterance, but reverent, tender, loving "speaking to GOD."[44] Since a "fruit of the Spirit" was love, Du Plessis counseled people "NEVER to think of resigning or 'coming out' " of their denominations to join a Pentecostal church.[45] The Spirit, he insisted, would bind rather than divide. Noting with satisfaction that those who truly experienced Spirit baptism served their denominations "better than ever," Du Plessis emphasized the Spirit as the Source of unity and power. Those who truly experienced Him, in any Christian denomination, must, he insisted, recognize, cherish, and cultivate their fundamental unity.

The Problem of Pentecostal Identity

Du Plessis's plight in his denomination symbolized, at least in part, the persistence of two opposing perceptions of Pentecostal identity. By 1961, Assemblies of God leaders were firmly committed to the evangelical consensus of the NAE. They shared fully the anti-communism, anti-Catholicism, and anti-ecumenism of their fellow NAE members. Disturbed by cultural trends toward federation and international organizations, they shared with the junior (Republican) senator from Wisconsin, Joseph McCarthy, an absorption with communist conspiracy. When Methodist Bishop G. Bromley Oxnam (a principal figure in the ecumenical movement) was called before the McCarthy hearings, evangelical reservations about ecumenism seemed confirmed. (Oxnam, who had been chosen American Protestantism's man of the year in 1944, had been president of the Federal Council of Churches and replaced Fosdick during the post-war years as the symbol of what evangelicals deemed wrong with traditional Protestantism and ecumenical efforts.)[46]

Du Plessis, on the other hand, classified Pentecostalism as

a distinct stream of Christianity. "There are three main streams of Christianity," he noted. "They are Roman Catholicism, which emphasizes structure of the church; Protestantism, with its emphasis on doctrine; and Pentecostalism, which accents the Holy Spirit."[47] A similar observation made in 1958 by Du Plessis's friend Henry Pitney Van Dusen had received wide publicity. In an article in *Life* magazine entitled "The Third Force in Christendom," Van Dusen had focused on the contemporary vitality of several groups of religious "outsiders," especially Churches of Christ, Pentecostals, Adventists, and Jehovah's Witnesses. Citing impressive growth statistics, Van Dusen noted among mainstream Christians "a chastened readiness to investigate the secrets of [this] mighty sweep, especially to learn if it may not have important, neglected elements in a full and true Christian witness."[48]

Van Dusen listed several reasons for the third force's growing appeal:

> Its groups preach a direct biblical message readily understood. They commonly promise an immediate, life-transforming experience of the living-God-in-Christ which is far more significant to many individuals than the version of it normally found in conventional churches. They directly approach people—and do not wait for them to come to church. They have great spiritual ardor, which is sometimes but by no means always excessively emotional. They shepherd their converts in an intimate, sustaining group-fellowship: a feature of every vital Christian renewal since the Holy Spirit descended on the Disciples at the first Pentecost. They place a strong emphasis on the Holy Spirit—so neglected by many traditional Christians—as the immediate, potent presence of God both in each human soul and in the Christian fellowship. Above all, they expect their followers to practice an active, untiring, seven-day-a-week Christianity.[49]

The perception of Pentecostalism as a "third force" enabled ecumenical leaders to link the movement's focus on the Holy Spirit with their own ecumenical objectives. Du Plessis shared their views, which few evangelicals or Pentecostals attempted to understand. Van Dusen put it succinctly: "A correct understanding of the Holy Spirit is the crucial issue in the Doctrine of the Church. And it is a commonplace among students of the divisions of Christendom that the differences which divide Christians into separated Churches all center in their divergent Doctrines of the Church."[50] From this perspective, the Holy Spirit was the "point of contact" through whose presence and activity the fundamental oneness of all believers could be acknowledged.

A major source of tension over issues raised by this growing Protestant interest in ecumenism and the Holy Spirit had been nurtured in the Assemblies of God throughout its history by songs, sermons, literature, and testimonies. They celebrated the believer's passage from "dead," "cold" denominations into a movement that proclaimed the "full gospel." Recalling his youth in an Assemblies of God congregation, for example, Cecil Robeck of Fuller Theological Seminary has written:

> One would think by the way we Pentecostals assessed the spirituality of the "other Christians" that we used a thermometer. Triumphantly we lumped the "others" together in groups, ranging by degrees from "dead" (Catholics and "liberals"), to "cold" (mostly mainliners), to "lukewarm" (evangelicals and holiness folk), to "on-fire" (us). . . . Lots of these pastors had "D.D.s" after their names. That usually meant, I was told, that they couldn't be trusted. They were "false shepherds," "broken cisterns," "whited sepulchres," or, an early favorite, "Dumb Dogs," who had graduated from theological "cemeteries."[51]

More than a hint of triumphalism pervaded the literature and assured the persistence of such stereotypes. Pentecostals typically neither attended other churches nor read the people they fervently denounced. After 1941, they were deeply influenced by the leadership of the NAE, people who arguably influenced Assemblies of God attitudes far more extensively than the Assemblies of God influenced them. Du Plessis discovered the inadequacy of the stereotypes and rejected them with a winsomeness that won him wide acclaim, actions that helped mitigate stereotypes of Pentecostals as well. Just as Pentecostals had heard and believed stories about other segments of the church (and about church history), so mainline Protestants and Roman Catholics had preconceptions about Pentecostals. Many never bothered to discover whether their preconceptions were true. They simply passed them on, with the result that they often "[bore] 'false witness' against [their] neighbors."[52]

Protestants in general and Pentecostals in particular harbored deep suspicions about Roman Catholic intrigue, fed by a popular book, Paul Blanshard's *American Freedom and Catholic Power*.[53] When Du Plessis joined ecumenical leaders at Vatican II and then took every opportunity to proclaim his message to Catholic audiences, he defied longheld assumptions about the nature, design, and prophetic role of Roman Catholicism.

Shortly before, during the 1960 John Kennedy/Richard Nixon campaign for the presidency, Assemblies of God anti-Catholicism had become unusually focused.[54] Anti-Catholic rhetoric was preserved not only by the denomination's converts from Catholicism (worldwide), but by the official paper of the Assemblies of God as well: The *Pentecostal Evangel* carried an article by the denomination's general superintendent, Thomas F. Zimmerman, explaining why a Catholic should not be president. Political policies were not considered—the accent was on religion:

> So strong is the influence of the President of the United States that he could begin a major tide in the direction of a Roman Catholic-controlled and -directed America through his appointments if he so desired. The question is, Would he do so? The answer is a clear, simple, and short, "Yes."
> . . .
>
> Every Roman Catholic is completely under the control of his church: mind, soul and body. . . . A Roman Catholic cannot make a decision on any level which runs counter to the thinking and expressed policy of Papal authority. In other words, under threat of excommunication . . . every Catholic is bound by Rome.
>
> . . . We must not now let down the guard and lose our time-honored and sacred position by giving the highest position in the land to the Roman Catholic Church. But, to avoid doing so, we must take a positive stand both in

conversation with others and at the polls in November. It is not sufficient to hope and pray, for faith without works is dead.[55]

Such explicit political advice seldom found its way into the pages of the *Pentecostal Evangel* unless the politics in question raised issues that touched vital religious nerves. Culturally rooted distrust of Catholicism certainly marked most Pentecostals, as it did many other Protestants in the 1950s and early 1960s. The Assemblies of God General Presbytery endorsed Zimmerman's views and recommended their wide circulation. Though the presbyters' news release disclaimed "religious bias," it charged the Catholic church with "bigotry," citing its stance on papal infallibility.[56]

By 1960, generations of Pentecostals had passed along stories about other traditions that had become, in a real sense, Pentecostal "habits of the heart." Since, to some extent, the ecumenical and charismatic movements were at first perceived as related (especially given the influence of David du Plessis in each), opposition to ecumenism influenced reservations about charismatics. And suspicions about the nature and ultimate purpose of Catholicism assured distrust of Vatican II and the charismatic renewal that emerged in Roman Catholicism in the mid-1960s.

In spite of the reservations, some Assemblies of God congregations were deeply influenced by the charismatic movement. In an era of cultural and political unrest marked by challenges to institutions, charismatics reveled in religious experiences that seemed to infuse their traditions and liturgies with vitality. Their preference for spontaneity and informality ultimately influenced traditions that theoretically opposed charismatic teaching. The widespread use of Scripture choruses is but one of several examples of their enduring effect. Although the movement's impact on the Assemblies of God is difficult to measure, several generalizations can be made.

First, the charismatic movement, with its enthusiastic witness to the Spirit's activity in contemporary life, stimulated some Pentecostals to rediscover their heritage. Third and fourth generation birthright participants in the Assemblies of God were challenged to seek renewal and to abandon themselves to experiences in the Spirit. At the same time, contact with charismatic believers encouraged trends already evident toward more participation in this-worldly pursuits. Charismatics did not generally exhibit the radical behavioral changes that had routinely been urged on Pentecostals.[57] They danced, drank, smoked, attended theaters, bowled, swam at public pools and beaches, owned television sets, dressed fashionably, and generally failed to embrace the taboos that had long helped reinforce Pentecostal identity as "peculiar people." Yet they spoke in tongues and exercised spiritual gifts more frequently than did many Pentecostals. The shifting in recent years of the boundaries that once defined acceptable behavior for Pentecostals cannot be attributed to any single cause. Certainly, however, the charismatic movement played a role that should not be overlooked.

The charismatic movement not only brought new visibility to classical Pentecostalism, it also enhanced the membership of Pentecostal denominations: some charismatics leaving their historic denominations for the less formal worship settings of Pentecostal congregations. But deep cultural and theological differences typically distinguished these new members from long-standing adherents of Pentecostalism. The charismatic movement also spawned a wide variety of independent institutions and greatly enhanced the strength of independent Pentecostalism. It generated its own devotional literature and supported Bible schools and evangelistic efforts whose stress on charismatic phenomena and faith resembled (superficially at least) early Pentecostal efforts. They sometimes rediscovered early "prophets" like E. W. Kenyon, Smith Wigglesworth, and Maria Woodworth-Etter. And they facilitated the emergence of prosperity evangelism, which exhorts believers to claim their rights to health, wealth, and worldly success. And although Assemblies of God leaders have deplored the "humanistic" and "materialistic" orientation of prosperity evangelism, it has nonetheless infiltrated their ranks.[58]

For many reasons, then, Assemblies of God leaders were

cautious about endorsing the charismatic renewal. Finally, in 1972, they declared their desire to identify the Assemblies of God with "what God is doing in the world today":

> The winds of the Spirit are blowing freely outside the normally recognized Pentecostal body. . . .
>
> The Assemblies of God does not place approval on that which is manifestly not scriptural in doctrine or conduct. But neither do we categorically condemn everything that does not totally . . . conform to our standards.
>
> . . . It is important to find our way in a sound scriptural path, avoiding the extremes of an ecumenism that compromises scriptural principles and an exclusivism that excludes true Christians.[59]

Meanwhile, to meet the need for a forum where Pentecostals and charismatics of all persuasions could reflect on the movement's development and meaning, several scholars created the Society for Pentecostal Studies (SPS) in 1971. An independent scholarly society, the SPS has promoted annual conferences where scholars working in the Pentecostal and charismatic traditions bring their various perspectives to focus on issues of mutual concern. Faculty members from several Assemblies of God colleges as well as Assemblies of God scholars representing other institutions have occasionally given leadership to the SPS. Not surprisingly, until his death in 1987, David du Plessis was a regular participant.

Conclusion

Assemblies of God positions on ecumenism and charismatic renewal have been influenced by many factors. A denomination with many members who had been dissatisfied in other denominations naturally nurtured stereotypes that few bothered to verify. And with millions of members and hundreds of missionaries keenly aware of physical persecution at Catholic instigation in Latin America and elsewhere, the Assemblies of God could not easily endorse Catholic charismatic renewal.[60]

Prophetic speculation gave form and content to much of the anti-ecumenical diatribe as well. And it is significant that in the post-war years, as many evangelicals participated whole-heartedly in the "communist watch" of the McCarthy era, communism and ecumenism seemed inextricably linked. Participation in the NAE also reinforced Assemblies of God preconceptions about ecumenism and charismatic renewal.

By the post-World War II years, most, if not all, of the American white Pentecostal denominations had shed the movement's early restorationist stress on unity among the Spirit-baptized. Despite early enthusiasm about the spread of the charismatic movement in the historic churches, hesitations emerged about some aspects of the renewal. As a result, Assemblies of God leaders found it much simpler to continue identifying with evangelicals rather than charismatics. In an interview with *Christianity Today,* General Superintendent G. Raymond Carlson acknowledged a charismatic contribution to classical Pentecostalism, but called for balance in a statement that aptly summarizes the consensus of Assemblies of God leaders: "I'm grateful for what the charismatic movement has brought with regard to celebration. . . . We need more than celebration. We always need that balance of the Word and the Spirit. You need to anchor solidly in the Word."[61]

The remarkable growth and continued vitality of charismatic renewal movements helped reveal how thoroughly "denominationalized" classical Pentecostalism had become. Evangelical priorities seem solidly entrenched. But the sense of "third force" potential survives, as well, sustaining a tension that holds potential for future reflections on Pentecostal identity.

David du Plessis (1950s), Assemblies
of God pastor and international Pentecostal leader

Officers of the NAE for 1962–1963 (l-r): Cordas C. Burnett, Bob Cook,
Carl Gundersen, Jared F. Gerig, Rufus Jones

5. Education

Assemblies of God education programs began inauspiciously in the basements of frame churches, in storefront missions, in residences, at district campgrounds. Without accreditation or endorsement, they struggled to provide the movement's youth with the training necessary for implementing the Assemblies of God's evangelistic objectives. The present situation would surprise (and perhaps dismay) the founders. In effect, the schools became structured Bible institutes, then accredited colleges. As such they offered young people more training than their parents often had. They ultimately facilitated—or at least helped legitimate—college training among parts of a constituency that had previously resisted higher education.

Today the list of Assemblies of God endorsed colleges includes Bethany Bible College (Santa Cruz, California), Central Bible College (Springfield, Missouri), Evangel College (Springfield, Missouri), North Central Bible College (Minneapolis), Northwest College of the Assemblies of God (Kirkland, Washington), Southeastern College of the Assemblies of God (Lakeland, Florida), Southern California College (Costa Mesa), Southwestern Assemblies of God College (Waxahachie, Texas), Trinity Bible College (Ellendale, North Dakota), and Valley Forge Christian College (Phoenixville, Pennsylvania). Berean College of the Assemblies of God (Springfield, Missouri) is a nontraditional (correspondence) college. In addition, six endorsed institutions offer Bible institute level training: American Indian Bible College (Phoenix), Central Indian Bible College (Mobridge, South Dakota), Latin American Bible Institute of California (La Puente), Latin American Bible Institute (San Antonio), Southern Arizona Bible College (Hereford), Western Bible Institute (Phoenix).

Despite the proliferation of schools and the expansion of their programs, Assemblies of God institutions attract fewer than 4 percent of the denomination's college-age youth. At the same time, they train over half of its missionaries, some 80 percent of its chaplains, and a considerable (though undetermined) number of its ministers. Berean College offers a ministerial studies diploma, which satisfies most districts' requirements for ministerial preparation, enabling those who choose not to attend Assemblies of God residential schools to have basic courses.

The denomination's schools today resulted from a combination of shifting perceptions of denominational need in the 1940s and the leadership of several forceful men whose vision for the Assemblies of God included a strong commitment to education. The cultural pressures of the immediate postwar years permanently influenced the denomination's schools.

In 1940, Education Secretary Fred Vogler defined the purpose of Bible institute training:

> The question is often asked, "Why go to Bible School when the coming of the Lord is so near? Does not the King's business require haste?"
>
> When I was a lad of fifteen years I started to learn the carpenter trade. We had a number of houses to build and of course those for whom we were building were anxious to have the work finished. There was no time to be lost. Every man was doing his best to finish these homes. But I soon learned, as an apprentice, that the foreman expected every man to use sharp tools. If he saw a man using a dull saw, plane, chisel, or other tool, he would tell them to go and sharpen his tools, that "there is no time lost in whetting."
>
> The same principle is true with those who are called to preach. "Shall we take time off to go to Bible School?" Yes, indeed, for in a Bible School is where you get your tools sharpened.
>
> The first thing for a young man or woman to determine is, Am I called of God to preach the gospel? If you are, then

it is your duty to do all in your power to secure the training that you need.

Jesus called twelve disciples, or apostles; these He trained for three years and over before He said to them, "Ye shall be witnesses unto Me both in Jerusalem, and in all Judaea, and in Samaria, and unto the uttermost part of the earth." Time is never lost in preparing for service and studying the Word. Three years in any one of our Bible Schools will equip you with a knowledge of the Word that should make you an able minister of the Word. Prepare now to enter one of these Schools.[1]

By the next decade the need to convince eager young people to take time for training had been replaced by concern about the composition of the student population at Assemblies of God schools. In 1952, representatives of all eleven Assemblies of God Bible schools met in Chicago to discuss the denomination's educational program. Cultural expectations, combined with changing student needs, seemed to jeopardize the Bible institute's future. The men called for thorough reevaluation of Assemblies of God educational trends. At stake, some thought, was the role Bible institutes played in the movement. The larger issue was acculturation and the consequent collision of two opposing attitudes toward accommodation.

Two years earlier, the Assemblies of God Education Department had reminded the constituency of the purpose of the denomination's Bible institutes—to provide "training for the evangelization of the world in the shortest possible time at the lowest possible cost."[2] Yet already during the 1940s, fewer and fewer Bible institute students acknowledged a "call" to the ministry. Academic adjustments in Bible institute curricula accommodated those who did not anticipate ministry upon graduation but raised strong protests from others who feared the loss of the Bible institutes' practical emphasis. By 1952, the situation seemed desperate.

On the one hand, those who were deeply committed to Assemblies of God education programs had failed over the years to adequately cultivate and convince the constituency. On the other hand, those who urged educational programs did not necessarily agree among themselves about the nature and purpose of such programs. Debates over educational policies in the 1940s and 1950s are significant not so much for the institutions they shaped as for the attitudes toward culture they revealed. Although the discussions exposed deep differences of opinion, several areas of agreement soon became apparent.

The people who sought to influence the denomination's stance on education were usually associated either with one or another of its institutes or with the headquarters. Few of those with decision-making authority had any training outside of Bible institutes, yet they spoke for young people who lived in an increasingly technological society that placed high priorities on education. Arthur Graves, W. I. Evans, Charles W. H. Scott, Ralph Riggs, and Millard Collins were a few of those who felt deeply about education and argued passionately, though not always persuasively, that educational policies would influence the denomination's integrity and cultural force.

Not surprisingly, such men regarded an obligation to provide Pentecostal education as central to their Pentecostal heritage. After all, they said—with reference to Topeka, Kansas, in 1901—"notice where the Holy Spirit fell. Not in a church or even in an upper-room prayer meeting, but in a Bible school."[3] It therefore followed that Bible schools offered a setting uniquely conducive to spiritual renewal; "this is where diligent search of the Scriptures and earnest prayer combine to seek and find God in the best way possible."[4] Institutes provided an "ideal situation" for nurturing the movement's spiritual power; "Bible schools have not only been the womb of modern Pentecost, but its cradle as well."[5]

Some, however, rejected that reading of history, questioning the need for any formal training for ministry outside the local church (a position that had been revived forcefully by advocates of the Latter Rain, a movement that ironically had also emerged in a Bible school setting). Others doubted that Bible institutes in fact served the movement adequately. Even a casual glance at statistics reveals further that the debate over appropriate education for Pentecostal young people seldom addressed the obvious fact that the vast majority of Assemblies of God youth who sought education did so in non-Assemblies of God schools.

When this discrepancy was noted, it was usually used to support the creation of denominationally-sponsored liberal arts education.

At midcentury, Assemblies of God educators advocated at least four discrete approaches to denominational education. The first sought to conserve the Bible institutes as nonaccredited training schools with primarily practical and spiritual emphases. A variation on this was articulated by Ernest Sumrall at the 1949 General Council: "We are not against others having an education, but we want to keep it out of our organization. Don't mix up the Bible school with the intellectual trends of the world today. We want to keep our organization pure and holy and simple."[6] The second approach endorsed the expansion of the Bible institute concept to embrace accredited and nonaccredited programs, advocated establishing a seminary, and forcefully asserted the need for both an Assemblies of God liberal arts college and local church-sponsored day schools. The third, and by some estimates the most representative, constituted in effect a silent majority, which seemed only mildly perturbed (in spite of constant warnings to the contrary) by secular education. They probably agreed that Bible institutes were advisable for training missionaries and ministers but had no strong desire to send their children to Assemblies of God liberal arts programs—or, for that matter, to any post-high school institutions. The fourth approach opposed all Pentecostal schools on principle, maintaining that formal education "quenched the Spirit." As the debates between exponents of the first, second, and fourth views raged, the third group was often ignored. Assumptions and predictions about them fueled the debate over various approaches, but time would challenge those predictions.

More than most of the denomination's efforts, its contemporary program of education evidenced evolving perceptions within the movement about Pentecostalism's changing cultural role.

Institutes, Colleges, and the Liberal Arts

In October 1947 Arthur Graves, Nicholas Nikoloff, Millard

Collins, J. Roswell Flower, and Ralph Riggs traveled to Winona Lake, Indiana, where a popular fundamentalist summer conference grounds was the setting for a consultation among representatives of fifty Bible institutes, thirty-eight of which were non-Assemblies of God. Representing "all shades of fundamental faith" in the United States and Canada, the men discussed their common perception of the need for uniform standards for Bible institutes. Among the participants were representatives of several schools that had strongly opposed Pentecostals over the years, Moody Bible Institute and the Bible Institute of Los Angeles, for example. After a candid discussion of the advisability of allowing Pentecostal participation in their plan, the non-Pentecostal majority voted unanimously to include them. Not surprisingly, Assemblies of God delegates decided that this unanticipated welcome presented an opportunity "made of the Lord" for the Assemblies of God. Institute representatives agreed that cooperation would not limit doctrine or practice; it would simply enhance their ability to address common needs.

The number of Bible institutes across the nation had grown dramatically since A. B. Simpson and D. L. Moody had opened the first such schools in the 1880s. As colleges and seminaries had become hospitable to the new science, progressive education, and liberal theology, separatist fundamentalists had opted increasingly for Bible institutes; these they had made influential centers with key roles in perpetuating their movement. Many of these institutes were shaped by expectations of Christ's imminent return (making the rapid evangelization of the world a priority).

The Winona Lake meeting sought means for standardizing the work offered at participating schools. It gave shape to the Accrediting Association of Bible Institutes and Bible Colleges, which the Assemblies of God was a founding member of. This association reflected the inability of the National Association of Evangelicals to mobilize Bible institute administrators, many of whom inclined toward separatism. The NAE had tried in April 1947 to form its own accrediting association, the North American Association of Bible Institutes and Bible Colleges. Since many influential Bible institutes refused to cooperate through the NAE, the NAE association deferred its accrediting function but continued to offer a forum for discussion and advice. Its representatives attended the Winona Lake meeting and relinquished the accrediting function to the larger association organized there. Accreditation was a vital issue among Bible institute leaders in the 1940s. Assemblies of God educational trends were influenced by the same cultural factors that (in a quest for viability, influence, and respectability amid cultural transition) encouraged evangelical cooperation via associations. During the trying years of World War II, Bible institute leaders had encountered both opportunities and regulations that they were not prepared to address. Recognition of their graduates by the Veteran's Administration or by chaplaincy offices, for example, was uncertain. During the war years, pressing needs had allowed some to serve in capacities they did not formally qualify for; peacetime chaplaincy appointments, however, proved another matter. The continuing cold war kept the right of exemption from the draft timely. Government recognition of Bible institutes as legitimate theological schools would assure exemption of ministerial students.

Government approval of institute programs offered obvious benefits, but Bible institute educators also hoped that uniform academic standards would stimulate all cooperating schools. Such standards would also facilitate transfer from one school to another, assist students who wanted to continue their education in secular academic institutions, and enable foreign students to enroll in institute programs.[7]

On their return from Winona Lake, Assemblies of God representatives reported to the Executive Presbytery on the formation of the Accrediting Association of Bible Institutes and Bible Colleges. The executives summoned representatives of each of the Assemblies of God schools to Springfield for a discussion with the Executive Presbytery. By unanimous vote, those involved approved conforming Assemblies of God institutions to the standards of the accrediting association. The unanimity, Education Secretary Ralph Riggs reported, "bespoke the approval of the Lord."[8]

Assemblies of God schools applied for accreditation; visited by teams from the association, the schools were advised how to make their programs and facilities meet the association's standards. Several districts and individuals registered prompt protests about the process; the idea of review of Pentecostal institutions by non-Pentecostals, and potentially by some avowed anti-Pentecostals, repulsed some of them.[9] The Potomac and the Ohio districts sought specifically to forestall the accreditation of Central Bible Institute, a strategy welcomed by the institute's longtime dean, W. I. Evans.[10] The General Presbytery, however, overwhelmingly defeated motions that would have referred accreditation to the 1949 General Council, reserving for itself the prerogative to act.[11]

Because of the unique position of Central Bible Institute as a General Council (rather than a district) school, it became the focus of the denomination's discussions about education: All the districts had an interest in decisions about its curriculum, the executive presbyters constituted the school's board of directors, and the General Presbytery approved its faculty, administrators, and educational policy.

Concern that accreditation would interfere with the school's "Pentecostal character" reflected long-held assumptions about the role of formal education in shaping effective ministers. Although early Assemblies of God leaders had opted for Bible institutes that resembled fundamentalist institutions in important ways, they had not entirely rejected the earliest Pentecostal educational models: short-term, nontraditional settings in which charismatic leaders like Charles Parham or D. C. O. Opperman had substituted inspired utterances for textbooks and days of prayer for study hours. They tended to value nothing more than periods of intense spiritual fervor during which classes were set aside and charismatic worship filled the hours. In 1950, for example, President Bartlett Peterson's annual report on Central Bible Institute reported that on "many occasions" class periods became "times of prayer" and chapel "continued spontaneously as the Holy Spirit . . . moved" on them. During the spring semester, he continued, "a spontaneous Holy Ghost revival" had swept the campus; "[s]ome stated that it was the deepest revival they can recall. Though regular classes were forgotten, it was evident that we were in one large classroom with THE TEACHER and THE TEXTBOOK."[12]

In the end, many agreed with W. I. Evans' assessment: Accreditation—with its academic readjustments—was not worth the cost. "Divine things come by revelation," the veteran Bible school dean insisted. "Is our movement branching from experience to intellect? The trend is starting down a road that we may be sorry for in the future. This is the rock of stumbling which has brought about decline in every other denomination's ministry."[13]

In immediate terms, accreditation at Central Bible Institute meant longer classes, two additional weeks of work per semester, academically qualified faculty, and expansion of the curriculum to include basic work in English composition and literature. According to opponents of accreditation, the time that accreditation mandated for general education would be taken from the hours allotted for prayer and ministry. Accreditation also forced discrimination between students who had completed high school and those who had not. Although denominational leaders promised not to remove faculty members who lacked adequate formal training, they began to encourage them to further their educations during summer vacations.

In 1948 Central Bible Institute's board approved the addition of a fourth year, and the concept of a fifth year, for ministerial training. They hoped that the additional semesters would allow further study in four areas: theology, Christian education, missions, and music. The changes had been authorized by the 1947 General Council, which had also endorsed the provision of a "full theological seminary course" at Central Bible Institute at a future date.[14] (As an expression of intentions for expanding its curriculum, the name of Central Bible Institute was changed briefly to Central Bible Institute and Seminary.) Throughout the postwar years, the school continued to expand its facilities, purchasing war surplus materials to construct classroom and dormitory space.

Meanwhile, in addition to accepting accrediting association standards, the Executive Presbyters, functioning as the Educational Committee of the Assemblies of God, voted to set standards for the denomination's endorsement of all its Bible institutes. This involved pointing out deficiencies in existing programs and creating a workable timetable for changes to be implemented. All eleven Bible institutes were granted denominational endorsement, provided certain adjustments would be made. The same meeting approved membership for Assemblies of God Bible institutes in the NAE-related North American Association of Bible Institutes and Colleges.[15]

While the debate about accreditation focused primarily on Central Bible Institute (where it was nurtured by the strong, dominating personality of W. I. Evans), ten other Assemblies of God schools were moving in a similar direction. Three of them—Southern California Bible College (now Southern California College), Southwestern Bible Institute (now Southwestern College), and Northwest Bible Institute (now Northwest College)—added a fourth year of studies before Central Bible Institute (now Central Bible College) did. Southern California Bible College offered five years of work and both B.A. and B.Th. degrees.

Meanwhile, these schools, like Central Bible Institute, were seeing a dramatic increase in the percentage of students who did not anticipate full-time ministry. In 1946 Ralph Riggs noted that fully 43 percent of Assemblies of God Bible school students felt no call; 30 percent were under nineteen years old; and 36 percent had not completed high school.[16] Riggs interpreted the figures to mean that many Assemblies of God young people would attend an Assemblies of God liberal arts college if such a college were available. "They are afraid of the regular colleges and universities," he claimed, ". . . willing to spend three years of their lives attending some kind of school beyond high school even though there is no secular credit to be gained thereby."[17] Whether as part of a calculated strategy or from sincere conviction, Riggs connected the great percentage of high school dropouts attending Assemblies of God Bible schools to spiritual sensitivity, not social background or economic need: "The large number who have not even finished high school . . . indicates a fleeing from the modern high school with its sin and infidelity."[18]

Ernest Sumrall, pastor of the Stone Church in Chicago, spoke for a numerically significant faction when he responded, "If our young people can't go out into the world and uphold their testimony, they don't have a testimony."[19]

In fact, since 1919 district and regionally sponsored schools had adjusted curricula to meet the needs of nonministerial students, a high percentage of whom were not high school graduates.[20] When as much as two-thirds of their curriculum had become devoted to general education, some of the schools set up junior college programs. The first was in Waxahachie, Texas, where two years of college-level work was made available, leading to a teaching certificate or a transfer into third-year studies in state universities. Arkansas, which operated a small Bible institute between 1948 and 1952, followed suit in 1948, and Southern California organized a regionally-accredited, four-year liberal arts college along with its Bible college in 1950. In Oregon, Canyonville Bible Academy attracted between 125 and 150 Assemblies of God high school students yearly. In Waxahachie, Texas, a high school operated by Southwestern College also enrolled approximately 150.[21]

By the early 1950s, Assemblies of God educators used such statistics to serve two purposes: first, to urge the creation of an accredited, denominationally-sponsored liberal arts college and, second, to argue that the Bible institutes needed revamping. To some of these educators a new generation of Assemblies of God pastors seemed to be out of step with the hopes of early denominational leaders. Those who dreamed of a strong, accredited, denominationally-sponsored Bible institute and liberal arts education program rooted their hopes in at least two sources—their reading of Assemblies of God history and the presumed dissatisfaction of adherents with secular education. Both were open to interpretation.

The appeal to history stressed the alleged intentions of the conveners of the first General Council in 1914 to create a Council-operated school. In fact, the Council had recommended Neshoba Holiness School, a Mississippi-based literary school run by R. B. Chisolm. The school offered a wide variety of courses in addition to Bible: English and American literature, composition, grammar, history, Virgil, Cicero, Caesar, Latin, Greek, solid and plain geometry.[22] Conceived primarily as a school for children, it was recommended by the Council to parents who wanted their children to prepare for college under Christian auspices. In 1916, Chisolm moved to Eureka Springs, Arkansas, where he joined D. C. O. Opperman in a school that combined his literary emphases with Opperman's Bible school experience. Expectations that their cooperative effort would become a Council-sponsored institution offering both liberal arts and Bible training foundered when both Chisolm and Opperman embraced oneness Pentecostalism and left the Assemblies of God at the end of 1916.

Educators in the 1950s used the endorsement of Chisolm's work between 1914 and 1916 as evidence that Assemblies of God founders had planned "for the protection of Pentecostal youth."[23] Yet, when some of the same founders convened five years later as denominational executives to begin the long process of creating the first Council-sponsored educational institution, they did not opt for a "literary school" but rather for a Bible institute. The kind of education that was important to them was essentially task-oriented training. They fully shared fundamentalist assumptions about the encroachments of secular humanism on public education and substituted instead training that emphasized the knowledge and use of the English Bible. Pentecostalism grew rapidly before World War II among population sectors that did not generally anticipate a college education and for whom graduating from high school was not a foregone conclusion. The practical use of the Bible and the cultivation of Pentecostal spirituality, in either lay or clerical outreaches, was the primary objective.

Assemblies of God adherents often exhibited a fundamental ambivalence toward education. Uniformly devaluing secular training and castigating American higher education, they nonetheless took pride in those few of their own who excelled in academics. A few early leaders, E. N. Bell, S. A. Jamieson, and P. C. Nelson, for example, had seminary training and were exceptions to the rule that suggested successful pastors with teaching abilities (but usually without more than Bible institute training) should be the denomination's educators: Two longtime Central Bible Institute faculty members who deeply influenced Assemblies of God education, Frank Boyd and William Evans, had trained at the Christian and Missionary Alliance Bible Institute in Nyack, New York, for example. By the 1950s, however, a few from the next generation, like J. Robert Ashcroft and Klaude Kendrick, had ventured into secular programs and emerged satisfactorily unscathed to offer educational leadership to their denomination. And six years before the Assemblies of God opened its liberal arts college, the Executive Presbytery urged the denomination's youth to train to become "teachers in our public schools." Curiously, at the same time, the denomination encouraged its churches to sponsor Christian day schools.[24] So even as the Assemblies of God sought to flee public education, some of its leaders began to promote public school careers as ministry.

If the intentions of Assemblies of God pioneers supposedly buttressed the case for liberal arts schooling on one side, assumptions about the sentiments of adherents upheld it on the other. Alarmist views about public education regularly recurred among denominational leaders in the late 1940s and early 1950s. A casual glance at *United Evangelical Action,* the publication of the NAE, demonstrates that such sentiments had broad support—Assemblies of God leaders were expressing views shared by many contemporary fundamentalists and new evangelicals. They presumed, however, to speak authoritatively about trends that were open to question. In the end, they committed the denomination to educational programs that have continued to serve only a small percentage of Assemblies of God youth.

"There now exist in public schools not only the worldliness and wickedness from which our parents sought to escape in 1914 (and that intensified) but a systematic, thorough system of education taught mostly by non-Christian teachers from atheistic textbooks which orients the pupils entirely away from God and the Bible," Assemblies of God educators warned in

1951.[25] The dimensions of the problem, it followed, had forced Assemblies of God young people to apply to the denomination's Bible institutes, even though the institutes often lacked appropriate general education courses for nonministerial candidates. According to educators, "[T]here was a hostile, poisonous public educational system driving our young people to flee for their lives. No safe place but in our Bible schools!"[26]

Such reasoning supported tentative efforts to arouse support for the creation of a liberal arts college. In 1945 General Secretary J. Roswell Flower had noted a growing demand for Assemblies of God liberal arts education.[27] That year the General Council had confirmed the role of the Executive Presbytery as the Educational Committee responsible for the denomination's schools. Perceived as a "safeguard" for Assemblies of God institutions, this supervision by men who were subject to reelection every two years presumably assured both the doctrinal purity and the Pentecostal character of the schools. Given a broad mandate in 1945 to "provide for that academic education of the youth of our Fellowship for which there shall be need and demand," the Executive Presbyters had been limited by a resolution precluding their establishing a liberal arts college unless expressly authorized by a General Council in session.[28] Such authorization had failed to gain the necessary votes at the 1947 General Council. The situation was undoubtedly complicated by misunderstandings about accreditation (part of a broader questioning of the alleged trade-offs in Assemblies of God identification—through associations—with evangelicals) and upgrading Bible institute programs during the same period.[29]

Proponents of restructuring denominational education to include Bible institutes (three-year diploma courses), Bible colleges (four-year, degree-granting institutions), and a liberal arts college charged that their opponents both betrayed their heritage and reversed earlier (i.e., 1914–1929) General Council support for a broad education program. They noted several themes in the typical stance against change: "Schools had made other denominations backslide;" degrees for faculty and students alike signaled a lowering of "Pentecostal standards;" academic credentials would be substituted for spirituality; education would take the place of "the power of God."[30]

Observing that degrees were nothing more nor less than "the modern symbol for a specified amount of post-high school education," Riggs and others patiently answered each objection. "[T]he only way our schools can backslide," they asserted, "is for our constituency to backslide first and elect an Executive which will allow spiritual deterioration in our schools. If our constituency is backslidden the damage is already done."[31]

A deeply rooted concern that education would someday be a prerequisite for ministerial credentials surfaced again in the discussions. Twenty years earlier, the same argument had been introduced to oppose the proliferation of Bible institutes. In 1952, forty percent of Assemblies of God ministers and eighty-seven percent of Assemblies of God missionaries had attended, though not necessarily graduated from, one of the denomination's schools. Reflecting the fear that the growing trend toward Bible school attendance would become a requirement rather than a preference, the 1951 General Council passed a constitutional amendment that forbade districts to require formal education for ordination.

The concern was warranted, however. Denominational leaders naturally sought to assure the availability of qualified leadership, and the same people who recommended accreditation and liberal arts training encouraged districts to conduct ministers' seminars that offered work comparable to Bible school courses. In 1952, Michigan and Louisiana complied, and the Kansas and New Mexico districts announced plans for ministers' seminars for the next year.

In addition, a correspondence school under the direction of Central Bible Institute instructor Frank Boyd had taken over much of the correspondence course work done earlier at Central Bible Institute. Organized as a separate entity in 1948, the correspondence school offered ten courses and in four years had an enrollment of 1,952. The Home Missions Department cooperated with Boyd to make the courses available to prisoners in twenty-four penal institutions.

In 1951 the headquarters contacted each district, offering the correspondence courses for training of prospective ministers who chose not to attend Bible institutes. Ten districts immediately adopted the suggestion, and others indicated interest.

Denominational commitment to correspondence education grew steadily throughout the period. By the early 1980s, the Berean School of the Bible (as the program was named) enrolled over thirty-five thousand students, the majority of whom were lay people. Early in 1985, the Executive Presbytery authorized the incorporation of the correspondence program into Berean College of the Assemblies of God. Accredited by the National Home Study Council, Berean College offers three levels of correspondence training: college courses, ministerial credentialing courses, and personal enrichment programs.

Discussion about expanding traditional education programs after World War II was stimulated by the availability of a choice piece of property in Springfield. During World War II, the United States Government had operated a hospital on the northeast side of the city, ultimately constructing and equipping some two hundred buildings on 152 acres. As early as 1946, the Assemblies of God had considered uses they might find for the property, suggesting such programs as enlarged facilities for Gospel Publishing House, administrative offices, radio broadcasting facilities, housing for headquarters employees, an old age home, an orphanage, and a college.[32] After prolonged negotiations, the Assemblies of God obtained fifty-nine acres and sixty-eight buildings for a token payment of one dollar.

In 1953 the General Council approved the creation of a denominationally-sponsored liberal arts program. The Tennessee, West Central, Oregon, Alabama, and Michigan districts had formally requested the action. It was assumed that it would address the problem of young people who "were being lost to our cause forever because of the philosophies with which they become indoctrinated in colleges outside our Christian confession."[33] Ratification of the plan in 1953 was timely—The same General Council chose Ralph Riggs, one of the denomination's most forceful proponents of an expanded, accredited education program, as its new general superintendent.

Although much of the discussion about education programs emphasized negative, adversarial motives for providing an alternative to secular education, by the 1950s a growing group of younger leaders articulated a more positive approach. Prominent among them was Klaude Kendrick, first president of Evangel College and later president of Southwestern College in Waxahachie. Kendrick believed that in the aftermath of World War II an increasingly technological society mandated more support for education. "Pentecostal parents," he wrote, "now able to pay for their children's schooling, began to question their sect's traditional suspicion of education, and some began to support establishment of church-sponsored educational institutions."[34]

Kendrick noted with apparent approval the likelihood that, in partial response, Pentecostal colleges would expand general education course offerings. Still, the oppositional motive surfaced, for he observed that parents who distrusted higher education considered church-sponsored colleges "the best alternative."[35] He supported, as well, the creation of Pentecostal seminaries, arguing that future leaders needed training in "an environment that reflects Pentecostal traditions."[36]

In 1955 the long-debated liberal arts school, Evangel College, began classes on the newly acquired government property. Klaude Kendrick had been selected as president, and another longtime supporter of expanded denominational education, Assistant General Superintendent Charles W. H. Scott, served as chairman of the board of directors.

Evangel College's framers had decided that the college would qualify for regional accreditation, which required at least four years of full-time operation before consideration. On February 23, 1959, the Springfield city newspaper announced that the Education Commission of the State of Missouri had recognized Evangel College's teacher-training program; the school had also received accreditation by the Committee on Accredited Schools and Colleges of the University of Missouri.[37] In 1965, the North Central Accrediting Association granted Evangel College full accreditation.

Both Central Bible Institute and Evangel College had serious financial problems during the 1950s. Some recommended that Central Bible Institute be regionalized, so that its financial needs would be borne primarily by those districts that did not already support another institute.[38] It quickly became evident, however, that those who served on a special committee to discuss regionalization personally opposed it. Instead, they proposed as an alternative the creation of a theological seminary on the campus of Central Bible Institute. Meanwhile, in 1958 J. Robert Ashcroft, having served the denomination as national education secretary, accepted the presidency of both schools as part of an effort to foster efficiency and coordination by combining administrative offices.

The expansion of educational efforts necessitated some administrative restructuring at the headquarters too. In 1945 the Education Department had been separated from Home Missions. The 1955 General Council authorized the creation of an education committee (later known as the Board of Education) apart from the Executive Presbytery. Discussion of the need for a unified education plan continued through the period and formed the basis for proposals presented by an Educational Planning Commission for reordering the headquarters Education Department.[39] A thorough restructuring did not occur until 1971; discussion of further reorganization continues.

Assemblies of God Theological Seminary

As a result of the World War II chaplaincy service of several Assemblies of God ministers, the denomination had been requested to consider forming a theological seminary. Appointments as military chaplains ordinarily required college education and seminary graduation. Consequently, during the 1940s and 1950s, Assemblies of God men and women who sought such appointments enrolled in educational programs outside Assemblies of God auspices; typically having no course work in Pentecostal doctrine or Assemblies of God history and polity, they sometimes felt inadequately prepared to represent the denomination. In addition, of course, denominational executives noted an unspecified number whose Pentecostal commitments were successfully challenged in the presumed hostile environments of non-Pentecostal seminaries. Evangel College, and by 1959 some other Assemblies of God Bible colleges as well, made available the minimum 120 hours of undergraduate work required, but Bible institutes did not qualify as seminaries.

By the late 1950s a committee of the denomination's educators again recommended the creation of a seminary at Central Bible Institute. But since the seminary was envisioned as a General Council project, they also opposed the regionalization of the Bible institute.

During 1959 Charles Scott and Cordas C. Burnett, national education secretary, completed a thorough analysis of the need for a seminary. Noting that in 1957, over one hundred Assemblies of God men and women had been enrolled in (non-Pentecostal) seminaries and that "many more" anticipated such enrollment, they predicted potentially serious implications for future denominational leadership.[40] The Committee on Education hoped to persuade the 1959 General Council to authorize an Assemblies of God seminary.[41]

The men who envisioned the seminary hoped to do far more than educate chaplains and clergy. They had far-reaching plans, which included providing "spiritual leadership in Biblical exposition" through faculty scholarship. They hoped to gather an academically qualified faculty whose work would have integrity outside the Pentecostal movement.[42]

Both economic and doctrinal considerations seemed to make Springfield the most desirable location for the school. Central Bible Institute offered housing, classrooms, and a library that could form the nucleus of a seminary collection; direct denominational supervision would be most easily available in Springfield as well.[43] The proximity of Evangel College would enable prospective seminary students to make up academic deficiencies. Every provision should be made, educators urged, to "lend dignity" to the seminary, such as appointing a distinct seminary faculty and building a graduate library. They further suggested that entrance requirements include a bachelor's degree from a liberal arts college, maintaining that "consideration" should be given to Bible college graduates, who would be expected to take additional liberal arts courses to qualify.

Not surprisingly, when the General Presbytery considered the report, discussion revealed a division of opinion on the subject. Some remained hesitant about seminary education; others believed that the pressing financial needs of Evangel College should take precedence over creating a seminary. A consensus emerged that a seminary should be part of the denomination's long-range education plan, that the school should be located at Central Bible Institute, but that its inauguration should be deferred indefinitely.

Not until 1973 did the long-awaited seminary open its doors. Known as the Assemblies of God Graduate School (it was re-named Assemblies of God Theological Seminary in 1984), it was located in the headquarters complex rather than at nearby Central Bible College (its own name change had occurred in 1965). By 1973, establishing it independently of a Bible college seemed the best way to present it as a school operated by and for the entire constituency. In a bid to reassure Bible college personnel that the seminary was not intended to jeopardize their role, the seminary's entrance requirements were devised to favor graduates of Bible colleges. In effect, the seminary reversed the expectation of its early framers, creating programs that favored Bible college graduates and requiring most liberal arts graduates to make up a wide variety of deficiencies in Bible.

Conclusion

The debates over appropriate educational policies revealed uncertainties about the influence of culture on the denomination. Proponents of change as well as proponents of the status quo appealed to history to justify their schemes; and although both groups shared a view of "outsiders" (especially in the educational world), according to each of them it seemed to warrant a radically different response. Fear of the unknown and assumptions about secular education proved powerful incentives for both sides. As the denomination inched toward approval of liberal arts and seminary education, some warned of the radical implications such programs had for the denomination's self-image.

As the Assemblies of God inclined toward accredited institutions and additional programs, it participated in broader evangelical trends. Fellow participants in the NAE, for example, encouraged evangelicals to shoulder their obligation to be Christian intellectuals. Evangelical colleges and seminaries strove, with varying success, for academic excellence.

Sometimes the objections reminded the denomination's executives of the persistence of a mentality most members probably associated with an earlier era. In 1959, for example, the North Texas District forwarded to the General Presbytery a recommendation that Assemblies of God schools "refrain from maintaining ball teams for the purpose and intent of playing intervarsity contest games with teams of other schools and colleges, which we believe would have a far-reaching detrimental effect upon our entire fellowship." Claiming that such competition (as distinct from campus-wide recreational activities) was "contrary to the fundamental beliefs and doctrines of the Assemblies of God," the district urged the proscription of intercollegiate sports.[44] In the end, the matter was left to the discretion of individual schools, with the stipulation that General Council funds not be used to finance intercollegiate sports.[45]

Evangel College continued to struggle financially. In 1962, administrators were instructed to reduce costs by reducing "the breadth of instruction offered."[46] The situation revealed a continuing need for the cultivation of support for educational institutions in Assemblies of God churches. Throughout the period, enrollment in Assemblies of God colleges failed to keep pace with either population growth or student population increases. In some years, it declined. During the early 1950s, declining numbers were due in part to the expiration of G.I. educational benefits. Immediately following World War II, G.I. enrollment had contributed to the pressure for stronger academic programs.

As the educational expectations of American young people

have increased, Assemblies of God youth have enrolled in secular colleges and universities in ever higher numbers. A considerable number, too, proved responsive to the persuasions of Assemblies of God evangelist Jimmy Swaggart, who opened his independent Bible school in Baton Rouge in 1984. Some eighteen thousand applied for four hundred places in its first class. Jimmy Swaggart Bible College was adamantly opposed to accreditation and other trends in Assemblies of God education and advertised its programs as more authentically Pentecostal.[47] Even so, within two years, the school had sought and achieved applicant status with the American Association of Bible Colleges (AABC) and applied for regional accreditation with the Southern Association of Colleges and Schools even while maintaining that its program represented a more historically credible alternative to the denomination's institutions. After Swaggart's public disgrace in 1988, some students and faculty of his college opted for the less opulent, but also less controversial, settings of the denomination's schools, and the college itself withdrew its application from AABC.

The number of Assemblies of God church-related schools (prekindergarten through high school) has grown steadily, especially in the past decade. This growth is related to the larger cultural debate about the intrusion of secular humanism in the public schools and is consistent with a pattern of providing alternative educational models. In 1987, over 110,000 children were enrolled in schools sponsored by local Assemblies of God congregations.[48] Although some administrators refused to comply with legal requirements (as in Iowa in 1986[49]), most did not think that registration and teacher certification violated scruples.

Statistics indicate that in 1986 nearly two-thirds of Assemblies of God missionaries attended either Assemblies of God colleges or the Assemblies of God Theological Seminary.[50] Thus, fully one third obtained their education in nondenominational schools. Similar figures for the denomination's ministers are not compiled.

As 1987 ended, 8,369 students were enrolled in the denomination's senior colleges. Of these, 57.1 percent anticipated full-time ministry; 36.2 percent were preparing for other vocations; and 6.7 percent were undecided.[51] Over the past ten years, some colleges have grown dramatically: North Central Bible College enrollment increased 96.1 percent; Southern California College, up 46.5 percent; Evangel College, up 23.2 percent. Others have declined: Central Bible College, down 23.8 percent; Southeastern College of the Assemblies of God, down 20.3 percent; Northwest College of the Assemblies of God, down 15.9 percent.

Assemblies of God educational institutions today are very different from those the denomination sponsored in the 1940s. The constituency still embraces some who devalue education, some who blame it for much of what they perceive as wrong within the denomination, others who hail it as the hope for the future.

Over the years denominational debates and discussions about education have documented the movement of the Assemblies of God from its early restorationist character. Once, the fundamental impulse was toward recovery of primordial perfection, achievable by a leap over history to the pristine and harmonious beauty of God's intention for humankind. In its place has evolved a quest for the integration of faith and learning, an effort to understand and live within history. Some who opposed post-World War II trends did so because they sensed a shifting of the focus from a faith that "transcended life's difficulties" to a faith that explained them.

In educational trends perhaps more vividly than elsewhere, a powerful conviction that the exigencies of the times demand adaptation is evident. Putting aside rhetoric that affirms continuity with the past, general education and the liberal arts have not only enabled most Assemblies of God Bible colleges to survive, they have also fundamentally changed what the colleges are about. Although the schools remain committed to providing a Pentecostal educational alternative, they stand as a monument to a fundamental modification of the definition and character of Pentecostalism. In significant ways, a movement once "out of step with the times" has come increasingly into step. Students can hardly avoid what W. I. Evans once feared—the temptation to substitute trained abilities for what was once understood as "the power of God." The change has not been without cost.

W. I. Evans, dean of Central Bible Institute during the controversial issue of accreditation

J. Robert Ashcroft accepted the presidency of both Central Bible Institute and Evangel College in 1958 as part of an effort to improve efficiency and coordination of the schools.

Central Bible Institute campus, 1944

Cordas C. Burnett (right) with a professor of religious studies from Southwest Missouri State College (Springfield), Gerrit J. tenZythoff, at the opening of the graduate school

Frank Boyd and a secretary at Berean School of the Bible, ca. 1955

Reading newspaper articles about the purchase of O'Reilly Hospital for Evangel College in 1954 are (l–r) J. Roswell Flower, Bert Webb, J. Robert Ashcroft, Gayle Lewis, Thomas F. Zimmerman, and (seated) Ralph Riggs

J. R. Ashcroft, Ralph Riggs, and Thomas F. Zimmerman in prayer for the new school

6. Denominational Programs

Growth and institutionalization have resulted in the proliferation of programs for mobilizing varied Assemblies of God groups and resources. Such programs are generally coordinated through the denomination's headquarters in Springfield, Missouri, an operation that also mirrors the growth of the denomination. In January 1941, for example, 125 people were employed at the headquarters; in 1987, over 1,000 were on the payroll.[1]

A major restructuring of headquarters administration in the early 1970s makes efforts to trace the evolution of programs under specific divisions and departments unwieldy.[2] (The restructuring eliminated the five assistant general superintendents who had supervised the various departments, substituting one assistant general superintendent and appointed heads for reorganized programs. The new system allowed the executives to select people with special aptitudes for various roles.) What follows is not a detailed study of headquarters-administered programs; rather, it is a brief listing of the agencies and services that have emerged over the past forty-five years to sustain and extend the denomination's outreach.

Evangelism

Home Missions

By 1941 the Home Missions Department (now Division of Home Missions) had under its purview not only church extension, but also the oversight of the Assemblies of God presence in Alaska. Missions to American Jews, native Americans, and the service personnel stationed at domestic military bases com-

137

pleted the assignment. Since 1941 several more special ministries have been added to the responsibilities of the division. In the late 1980s, nearly four hundred home missionaries, under Division of Home Missions appointment, served in intercultural ministries among forty-one ethnic groups.[3]

Native Americans. Evangelism among native Americans was undertaken by individuals without official denominational appointment or support during the 1930s.[4] In 1943 the Home Missions Department organized the American Indian Division to coordinate these efforts.[5] Two hundred and eighty tribes scattered on three hundred reservations, many of them small and isolated, made this a difficult and challenging ministry.[6]

An important step in the Indian ministry was the opening of the American Indian Bible Institute in Phoenix, Arizona, in the fall of 1965.[7] Jointly sponsored by six western Assemblies of God districts and the national Home Missions office, the school trains indigenous leadership for Assemblies of God native American missions.[8] Over the years, three more schools have been organized to assist native Americans in receiving educational training, both ministerial and vocational. In 1987, the four Bible colleges had a record enrollment of 258.

Alaska. Assemblies of God evangelism in Alaska dates from 1917 when Charles C. Personeus and his bride, Florence, arrived in Juneau.[9] By 1941, they and others had developed a thriving outreach. In 1965, following Alaska's statehood, the Alaska District Council of the Assemblies of God was created, the denomination's Home Missions office retaining supervision of only remote stations and native evangelism.[10] Ninety missionaries were under appointment when the transition was made. In 1970 nearly forty native churches and outstations remained under the guidance of the Home Missions Department.[11] In 1987 the Division of Home Missions reported forty-five such congregations.

For many years, Home Missions personnel staffed a children's home in Juneau, which is now operated by the Alaska District. Since 1962, when Arvin Glandon of Fairbanks conducted a short-term mobile school to improve the skills of pastors and missionaries, others have conducted similar short-term leadership training around the state. Traveling by air to remote points, Far North Bible College personnel also seek to develop lay leadership for an indigenous Alaskan church.[12]

The Hearing Impaired. The Assemblies of God Deaf Fellowship was organized in the Home Missions Department in 1952, one year after the first Assemblies of God summer camp for the hearing impaired was conducted in California. Such camps as well as courses in signing at Assemblies of God schools have met with positive response.[13]

The denomination also sponsored a School for the Deaf, a department of Central Bible College begun in 1962. It offered a three-year Bible course for the deaf (since discontinued).[14] In 1964 the Home Missions Department placed the first chaplain ever appointed at Gallaudet College, the nation's oldest college for the deaf.[15] In the mid-1980s, The Deaf International Bible College was begun at North Central Bible College in Minneapolis to train deaf ministers.[16] The Division of Home Missions published a monthly newsletter, *Signs of Life,* for ministers and workers among the hearing impaired;[17] it has since been replaced by a quarterly, *Co-signer,* for a general readership, including the hearing impaired.

The Visually Impaired. In March 1961 Mrs. E. W. Whitney of Waukesha, Wisconsin, became the first appointee of the Home Missions Department to minister to the visually impaired.[18] Using a Braillewriter provided by the Home Missions Department, she had for several years been preparing literature; the main piece was *The Pentecostal Digest,* which circulated throughout the United States and in fifteen foreign countries.[19] In addition to Braille literature, a tape service has been offered since 1960 (reel-to-reel tapes and now cassettes). This tape library and a new Braille library are sponsored by the Division of Home Missions.[20]

Teen Challenge. A well-developed effort to address the needs of urban America is Teen Challenge. In 1987 over one hundred Teen Challenge Centers served inner city youth.[21] Each of the centers had its own constitution and bylaws, but all operated under the oversight of the executive director of the Division of Home Missions and the superintendent of the district the center was located in. The permanent staff of many of the centers have been augmented each summer by students from various Assemblies of God colleges.[22]

The New York Center is the original center. It resulted from the vision of a young Pennsylvania minister who felt impressed to reach out to youthful street-gang members he had read about in the news. David Wilkerson's dramatic story is recounted in a series of books, the best-known of which is *The Cross and the Switchblade*.[23]

In February 1958, on an impulse he believed to be from God, Wilkerson went to New York City to the trial of a young gang member. Wilkerson's eviction from the courtroom and the publicity that followed became the means for winning some of the gang members' confidence. In July he began a series of rallies in the St. Nicholas Arena, during which several gang leaders professed conversion. That October, Wilkerson opened an office on Staten Island as a local headquarters for his street-witnessing program. By then, he had resigned his Pennsylvania pastorate and moved his family to New York. In 1959, just a year after his first encounter with urban street gangs, through the backing of local ministers and churches, Wilkerson purchased a building in Brooklyn as an inpatient center for drug addicts on withdrawal therapy. In 1962 this fledgling Teen Challenge program expanded by turning a farm near Rehrersburg, Pennsylvania, into a Teen Challenge Training Center, a 200-acre rehabilitation school for addicts. The next year, the rapidly growing sphere of teen ministries included the purchase of an estate on the Hudson River at Rhinebeck, New York, for the training of workers. Former alcoholics, drug addicts, and prostitutes followed an intensive program that offered three years of Bible institute-level training in two calendar years of study.[24]

In 1964 three additional buildings were purchased on Clinton Street in Brooklyn near the original center. One of them served as a residence for workers; the others were "re-entry" residences for former addicts who were being reoriented to society. In 1965 a half-million-dollar "spiritual therapy clinic" was built to serve as the nerve center of the New York operation. Another acquisition was an estate at Garrison, New York; large enough for a summer camp, it was intended primarily for the rehabilitation of delinquent girls.[25] Meanwhile, similar centers were opening in other urban areas.

Teen Challenge attempts to prevent drug abuse as well as to treat it: Since 1965, Teen Challenge workers have presented a Bible-based drug education program in over four thousand schools and colleges. Teen Challenge is receiving national attention for its effective program.

Military/Institutional Chaplains

Military. An action of the 1941 General Council committed to Home Missions the responsibility of devising means for Pentecostal ministry to military personnel.[26] During the war years this ministry absorbed much of the department's energies. Its first project was the preparation of a small nondenominational devotional paper called *Reveille.* Edited by Myer Pearlman until his death in 1943, the paper apparently filled a need not met by any other agency. During the war years, fourteen million copies were supplied to thousands of chaplains of all faiths for distribution to servicemen, all costs being met by Assemblies of God contributors.[27]

In 1944 a Servicemen's Department was set up, with a staff of twenty-four full-time and twenty-eight part-time workers handling an enormous volume of private correspondence from, and printed mailings to, servicemen.[28] The department coordinated the efforts of eleven field representatives stationed at military bases, hospitals, and in communities adjacent to them. Forty-one Victory Service Centers were operated by the department—the Long Beach, California, center in one year alone having a quarter of a million visitors.[29] Contact was maintained with the thirty-four Assemblies of God chaplains serving the United States Army.

In June 1946 a Reveille Reunion in Springfield brought together for the last time many of the denomination's chaplains and military personnel who had seen active duty during the war. Soon after, the Servicemen's Department was disbanded, and curtailed services to military personnel were offered by the national Christ's Ambassadors (now Youth) Department. During the Korean conflict, and more recently during the Vietnam War, such work on behalf of servicemen again increased greatly. At the end of 1969, fifteen thousand men and women were on the mailing list of the Servicemen's section of the Christ's Ambassadors (CA) Department (an estimated thirty-four thousand Assemblies of God adherents were in uniform around the world). Forty-five chaplains, more than at the peak of World War II, were in military service. A total of more than seventeen million copies of *Reveille*, in thirty-three editions, had been distributed.[30] In 1987, with the department again under the jurisdiction of the Division of Home Missions, *Reveille's* replacement, *At Ease*, a publication designed to communicate with Assemblies of God armed forces personnel serving around the world, had a circulation of seventeen thousand. A quarterly publication, *The Assemblies of God Chaplain*, was produced for military and Veterans' Administration chaplains.

The number of Assemblies of God military chaplains has increased steadily as the denomination's growth has warranted more slots for its chaplains. The formal training of an increasing percentage of military chaplains is completed at the Assemblies of God Theological Seminary in Springfield, Missouri. Annual chaplains retreats provide inspiration and denominational contact for this far-flung constituency.

Institutional. The Division of Home Missions also supervises the denomination's ministries to prisoners. Before 1941, individual attempts were made at prison ministry. And only one Assemblies of God minister, Arvid Ohrnell of Walla Walla, Washington, actually served as a state-appointed prison chaplain.[31]

Later, Paul Markstrom, an Assemblies of God pastor in Newburgh, New York, was apprised of the need for denominational assistance in correctional institutions by Clifford Scrimshaw, a Methodist chaplain at the Elmira (New York) Reformatory. Markstrom visited Springfield, Missouri, in August 1950 to present the challenge of prison ministry to the executive officers of the Assemblies of God. As a result, Markstrom was invited to return the following month to discuss a proposal with the assembled General Presbytery. The Presbytery invited Arvid Ohrnell to move to Springfield to develop a denominational prison outreach.[32]

Ohrnell spent much of his time visiting prisons, working with both chaplains and inmates. Recognizing that the correspondence materials offered by the denomination through the Berean School of the Bible were not directed toward the special needs of prisoners, Ohrnell began in 1955 to prepare a series of courses of his own. By 1969 nearly two hundred thousand courses had been mailed to inmates across the country, located in 240 federal, state, and county prisons.[33]

The number of Assemblies of God men and women serving as prison chaplains has steadily increased. In 1963 there were only six full- and part-time chaplains; in 1969, thirty; in 1983, sixty.[34] In recent years, Assemblies of God chaplains have been placed in other industrial and institutional settings as well. In 1988 seventy-three men and four women were under appointment as industrial/institutional chaplains.[35]

Foreign Missions

World War II curtailed missionary activity around the world. Twenty-nine Assemblies of God missionaries were interned in the Far East, most of them expatriated during the war. Anna Ziese in North China never returned home and contact with her was lost for many years.[36] However, eight new countries were entered during the war in spite of severe restrictions.[37]

Missionary Secretary Noel Perkin refused to permit restrictions to curtail his vision. In April 1943 he called a conference to consider strategy for world outreach so that the Assemblies of God would be poised for a new missions emphasis when the war ended. More than sixty missionaries from eighteen countries gathered in Springfield to set new goals with Foreign Missions Department personnel.[38] The group stated five objectives: (1) appointing field secretaries for all major areas; (2) recruiting 500 new missionaries; (3) providing additional training for missionary candidates and missionaries on furlough; (4) conducting conventions in strategic centers to present various phases of the missionary enterprise to the constituency, and (5) raising a reserve fund of five million dollars for a calculated expansion in the immediate postwar years.[39] Much of this was implemented in the immediate postwar period, which saw considerable structural and methodological change.

Implementation began promptly. The first field secretary had been appointed a year earlier, when H. C. Ball, veteran Latin American missionary, accepted responsibility for coordinating all Latin American work.[40] By 1944 H. B. Garlock (Africa) and Gustav Kinderman (Europe) had been added.[41] Howard Osgood became the first Far East field secretary in 1945.[42] In 1944 Borneo missionary Kenneth Short launched the first major missionary department publication, the *Missionary Challenge*.[43] The title of this promotional monthly was changed to the *World Challenge* in 1956 and continued under that title until 1959, when the magazine was discontinued. In 1959 a new promotional magazine was launched, this time not as a subscription item, but for free distribution. *Global Conquest* became the symbol of vigorous missionary outreach, designed in part to compensate for the increasing competition from independent missions agencies originating in the salvation/healing movement.[44] The name of this periodical was changed in September 1967 to *Good News Crusades* to avoid the militaristic connotation of the previous title. In 1987 this magazine, now known as *Mountain Movers*, had a circulation that exceeded 170,000.

Another important structural change was the creation of a series of advisory bodies to enlarge the scope of counsel for the growing operation of world missions. In 1955 the Foreign Missions Board, consisting of representatives of the national office and missionaries, was created by the General Council to formulate policy.[45] In 1957 the General Council in session authorized the formation of a Foreign Missions Advisory Committee, to consist of "six consecrated, Spirit-filled men from among our fellowship, known for their spirituality, good judgment and faithfulness, as an advisory committee to work in cooperation with the Foreign Missions Board in the promotion of World Missions."[46]

One of the goals enunciated at the 1943 conference had been improved training for missionary personnel. A preliminary means to that end was a second missionary conference held in Springfield in June 1948, attended by more than a hundred missionaries.[47] The concept of such a gathering as an annual event resulted in the 1957 General Council approving a school of missionary orientation.[48] Each year since, all missionaries on furlough join with new candidates for intensive study and prayer in Springfield. Through the years the general level of formal training of the missionary staff increased so that by 1967 fully half of all furloughing missionaries were attending graduate schools of various kinds.[49] In the period from 1914 to 1949, 74 percent of the missionary force was trained in Bible schools; from 1949 to 1953 the figure climbed to 93 percent having some undergraduate preparation.[50] Figures for recent decades are not compiled.

Another of the goals envisioned in 1943 was the raising of funds for strategic postwar deployment. In the years that followed, several auxiliary agencies created within the headquarters structure provided large sums of money for special missionary projects, supplementing regular church support for missionary personnel. Perhaps most striking of such programs was Speed-the-Light, the special section of the youth department that raised funds to enable missionaries to purchase vehicles and radio and printing equipment.[51] By August 1948 Speed-the-Light funds had purchased a twin-engine C-46 transport plane to shuttle missionary personnel to and from various foreign fields. Christened the *Ambassador,* it attracted considerable attention for its novel employment of modern means in missionary endeavors. In 1950 the first plane was succeeded by a four-engine converted B-17, the *Ambassador II.*[52] Its frequent stops at exotic points helped extend awareness of Assemblies of God missions. However, such planes became economically impractical as commercial carriers improved their service, and within a few years missionaries were transported by the latter. Speed-the-Light funds, with amounts increasing annually, enabled missionaries to expand their resources. By the end of 1986 almost $53 million had been appropriated through Speed-the-Light to provide equipment and construct evangelistic centers.[53]

Another auxiliary agency that has been a significant financial source for missions is the Boys and Girls Missionary Crusade (BGMC), a project of the Sunday School Department designed to furnish Sunday school and training literature in missionary territories. Since 1985, over one million dollars has been raised annually by Assemblies of God children participating in BGMC.[54]

Since 1951, Women's Ministries has recorded aggregate giving exceeding $113 million, much of it related directly to the work of missions.[55] The Men's Ministries project, inaugurated in 1961 as Light-for-the-Lost, has been the supply of evangelistic literature for overseas crusades. In 1987, Light-for-the-Lost provided over $2.5 million for the Division of Foreign Missions.

Local church missions giving was refined by the adoption of the World Missions Plan, a means of distributing undesignated funds among priority categories.[56] Funds specified for individual missionary support are forwarded to the field in total, the costs of maintenance of the Foreign Missions Department coming from undesignated funds and other sources. A report by the auditing committee assigned to investigate the operations of the Foreign Missions Department in 1961 commended the department for its efficiency of operation, noting that it spent only 4.9 percent of the total income on administrative expense, apparently among the lowest of any church body in the country.[57] In addition to funds from auxiliaries, Assemblies of God congregations contributed eight million dollars to world missions in 1969, more than half of the total receipts of the General Council.[58] By 1986, annual World Ministries giving had reached a staggering $135 million, representing some 74 percent of the denomination's total expenditures and exceeding the per capita missions giving of every mainline denomination.

In 1957 a new missions strategy, known as Global Conquest, was introduced. This program, instituted in the final years of

Noel Perkin's farsighted administration, represented a shift in focus from rural and remote areas to rapidly growing urban centers.[59] To do this a three-pronged emphasis was detailed: (1) increasing the distribution of gospel literature, (2) emphasizing the evangelization of key metropolitan centers, and (3) increasing efforts to train a national leadership through Bible school programs.[60] Two years later *Global Conquest* magazine was introduced and became the chief instrument for informing the constituency of the advances on this new missions front. In keeping with this new thrust, goals were announced at the 1957 General Council that projected 818 missionaries, 10,000 national workers, and 600,000 members in foreign lands by 1960. (At that time there were 758 missionaries, 8,005 national workers, and 574,653 members of the Assemblies of God congregations overseas.[61]) By 1960 appointed missionaries were still below the 800 mark, but national workers exceeded 12,500, and membership abroad was approaching 750,000.[62] Since the institution of the Global Conquest strategy, the emphasis has not been on seeking new fields.[63] In general, fields entered since 1958 have been added in response to the appeal of nationals for assistance from the Assemblies of God.

In practice, the first thrusts of Global Conquest were in the areas of literature and the creation of urban "evangelistic centers." Gradually, the Boys and Girls Missionary Crusade and the Light-for-the-Lost programs became the instruments for implementing the literature feature of the new strategy. By 1965 the Light-for-the-Lost program formally became the literary agency of Global Conquest. In the meantime, urban evangelistic centers were being developed in several major cities: Seoul, Korea, becoming the pilot project. Seoul was not only the first, but also the most successful of the evangelistic centers, having 7,000 adherents by 1967. In 1983, it celebrated its twenty-fifth anniversary and had 615 full-time staff and 280,000 members.[64] Its continued dramatic growth is well-known and has helped make its pastor, Yonggi Cho, a familiar figure in church growth and charismatic conferences around the world.

By 1965 half a dozen other such centers had been launched. It was the hope that each would be a hub for urban evangelism, serving as "feeders" for multiplied small churches in the regions around them. However, this hope was not realized, and the evangelistic centers tended to become simply large metropolitan churches in places like Manila (Philippines), Dakar (Senegal), and Managua (Nicaragua).[65]

Between 1963 and 1965, Global Conquest made way for Good News Crusades, an emphasis on mass evangelistic crusades in which personnel and funds from the United States were to be employed in close cooperation with the missionaries and nationals in the field. The object was to stimulate existing congregations and, through intensive follow-up campaigns, to channel contacts into Assemblies of God churches.

The third prong of the original Global Conquest strategy, the training of nationals, contributed to the growth in the number of Bible schools abroad. They increased from 19 in 1941 to 91 by 1969 to 283 by 1987.[66]

Late in 1967 a supplement was inaugurated. Headed by Dr. George Flattery, the International Correspondence Institute (ICI) was to coordinate the various programs of correspondence work currently operating on many mission fields. At its inception about two hundred thousand were enrolled in the existing courses. In 1987, tons of ICI literature were sent to 164 countries. In ICI's twenty year history, over five million people have enrolled in one or more of its courses.[67]

In 1981 two other international ministries were added to the Division of Foreign Missions' administrative structure. The Center for Ministry to Muslims strives to make Christians aware of the hundreds of millions of unevangelized Muslims. International Media Ministries coordinates the Division of Foreign Missions' efforts to train missionaries and nationals to use the electronic media.[68]

Mobilization and Placement Service. The Mobilization and Placement Service (MAPS), which also supports foreign missionary outreach, is an outgrowth of the Memphis General Council of 1963. MAPS is a means of coordinating the efforts of lay personnel who wish to contribute their services in such activities as construction projects at mission stations. Vocational volunteers, laypersons who serve overseas and assist missionaries, are also supervised by MAPS. In 1985–1986, over 950 such volunteers filled one- and two-year special appointments in home and foreign missions. In 1986, over 560 college interns served up to eight weeks in the MAPS intern/summer program.[69] A similar outreach, coordinated by the Youth Department, is Ambassadors in Mission, a program organized in 1966 to facilitate the involvement of the denomination's youth in overseas evangelism. Over ten thousand have been involved.[70] A recently developed MAPS program is RV volunteers, through which retired people who own recreational vehicles volunteer for special home missions projects.

Campus Ministry

In February 1949 J. Robert Ashcroft, then a member of the national Christ's Ambassadors Department staff, introduced a resolution to the National Sunday School Convention meeting in Springfield, challenging the denomination to develop a program for ministering to Assemblies of God youth attending secular colleges. In the fall of 1948 the CA Department had begun publishing *The College Fellowship Bulletin,* issued free four times during the school year. By the 1951–1952 school year, 338 names were on the mailing list.[71]

In the fall of 1952 the paper was renamed *Campus Ambassador.* When Ashcroft assumed new duties as secretary of the Education Department in 1954, J. Calvin Holsinger became the editor of the paper and also developed a new phase of the program, the guidance of campus youth groups, called Chi Alpha chapters. William Menzies, instructor at Central Bible Institute, served as part-time director of the college program following Holsinger, from 1958 to 1962. The first full-time director was Lee Shultz, who spearheaded the first national Chi Alpha conference in 1963. Chi Alpha activity was reported at the beginning of 1970 on seventy campuses. The circulation of the *Campus Ambassador* magazine reached fourteen thousand as the 1970s began.[72] In 1987, with campus ministries coordinated through the Division of Home Missions, Chi Alpha Chapters, served by 175 campus pastors at 100 colleges and universities, represented the denomination's efforts among America's twelve million collegians.[73]

Bible Quiz and Teen Talent

In 1962 the Christ's Ambassadors Department introduced a Bible quiz program; it featured intensive study of one or more books of the New Testament each year. In the same year a talent search program was launched; its objective was to encourage young people to develop skills in church music. These programs led to a modified return to national youth conferences, where regional quiz and talent winners compete for national honors. Ten thousand young people participated in these ventures in 1969.[74] By 1987, Teen Talent had been expanded to include competitions in creative writing, painting, drama, preaching, photography, etc. Its name was changed to Fine Arts Festival. The denomination's first National Fine Arts Festival was held in 1987 in Oklahoma City.

Women's Ministries

A well-established department, Women's Ministries has consistently provided strong auxiliary support for the denomination's evangelistic programs. With aggregate giving now hovering near $113 million, Women's Ministries has played a vital role in mobilizing Assemblies of God women to assume supportive roles in district and national endeavors. Over 372,000 women, their activities coordinated by district Women's Ministries presidents/directors, participated in the U.S. in 1987. The national Women's Ministries office issues an inspirational magazine, *Woman's Touch,* with a circulation over twenty thousand.[75]

Rainbows, Missionettes, Royal Rangers

The Assemblies of God offers age-appropriate programs for children that roughly parallel Girl Scouts and Boy Scouts. Missionettes, the girls' auxiliary program, was launched in 1955.[76] In 1987, it registered over 131,000 members. Rainbows, the denomination's program for three- and four-year-old boys and girls, had nearly thirty-seven thousand participants. Royal Rangers, created in 1962, strives to "reach, teach, and keep boys for Christ."[77] In 1986 some 125,000 boys met weekly in over 5,000 churches. In the mid-1980s, the denomination developed a National Royal Rangers Training Center in Eagle Rock, Missouri.

Men's Ministries

The World War II years marked a change in the status of laymen in the Assemblies of God. A generation of young men came home from the war and took advantage of government-sponsored educational opportunities that opened the door to larger horizons. And, at home, many in the denomination had come into a new prosperity undreamed of in the days of the Great Depression, when so many of them had affiliated with the Assemblies of God. The Men's Fellowship Department was formed to provide service opportunities for this growing reservoir of abilities and energies that had largely been unharnessed and unrecognized.[78]

The prototype of Men's Fellowship began in 1947 at Calvary Assembly of God in Inglewood, California, under the leadership of Jack Epperson.[79] The immediate response to this program precipitated an appeal to the General Presbytery the next year for the creation of a national men's association to stimulate lay witnessing and encourage stewardship.[80] A committee was appointed to study the appeal, and its report at the 1949 General Presbyters' meeting revealed some reluctance to initiate a program at a national level without a prior significant grass-roots demand, such as the Women's Missionary Council (Women's Ministries Department) had had.[81] However, in spite of some reluctance of a few ministers who apparently feared the creation of a strong laymen's organization, the General Council in 1951 authorized a Men's Fellowship Department.[82] Assistant General Superintendent Ralph M. Riggs early in 1952 set up an advisory committee and selected Gospel Publishing House General Manager J. Otis Harrell to serve as the first national secretary of the new department.[83] Harrell had been the prime mover in the appeal for a national laymen's organization since 1948. Don Mallough and Burton Pierce followed Harrell in the office.

The various men's programs have not enjoyed the same consistent growth as the Women's Missionary Council.[84] Although the department was denominationally oriented, in its early years it competed with Full Gospel Businessmen's Fellowship International in some churches.[85]

Benevolences

In 1947 the General Council authorized setting up a Department of Benevolences to coordinate the denomination's growing welfare activities.[86] Now under the Division of the Treasury, care for aged ministers, child welfare, and disaster relief immediately meet such needs in the growing denomination.

Care for Aged Ministers. As early as 1933 the General Council recognized a growing need to provide for aging ministers, many of whom had no savings or insurance.[87] The 1935 General Council voted to create a fund for needy ministers, to be administered by the Executive Presbytery upon recommendation of the district councils: the Ministers' Benevolent Fund.[88] The fund was supplied through earnings from Gospel Publishing House and from donations. By the end of 1944 a balance of $146,224 had accumulated in the fund. At that time it was reconstituted as Aged Ministers Assistance.[89] Currently, Aged Ministers Assistance receives contributions from churches and individuals exceeding $1 million per biennium. During 1986, over 350 ministers received assistance.

In 1945 another important step was taken to make material provision for aging ministers. The General Council arranged for a retirement fund that ministers and churches could contribute to.[90] In the first seven months more than a thousand ministers joined the new retirement program, called the Ministers' Benefit Association.[91] Through the years several changes have been made in the program, the most important occurring in 1956 when it incorporated as an entity separate from all other General Council structures.[92] At the end of 1986, more than twelve thousand licensed and ordained ministers were participating in the retirement program.[93]

In 1946 a committee recommended to the General Presbytery that the Assemblies of God "proceed with the establishing of Homes for the Aged as soon as possible, thus meeting a real need in our fellowship, not only toward those ministers who have spent their strength and lives in the Gospel ministry and now face their declining years with no place to go or without anyone to care for them, but also for those of the laity who may be in the same position of need."[94] Two years later the Pinellas Park Hotel, an old facility near St. Petersburg, Florida, was purchased for this purpose. Since it housed only twenty-five residents, however, it eventually became too costly to maintain.[95] In 1959 construction began on the Bethany Retirement Center at Lakeland, Florida. This new facility, with a capacity of forty-two persons, was dedicated on May 15, 1960. Five years later an infirmary with a twenty-nine bed capacity was added.[96] A larger complex, Maranatha Village, was opened in the headquarters city in 1972 and presently has more than four hundred residents. It offers four levels of residential care: independent living, village apartments, semi-independent residential suites, and constant nursing care.

Child Welfare. In 1942 Gladys Hinson, a public schoolteacher, decided to open a home for deprived children in Hot Springs, Arkansas.[97] In 1944 Hinson began negotiating with the executive presbyters, securing their endorsement for her project. She opened the home on September 22, 1944, with three children. By year's end the home's capacity of seventeen had been reached.[98] Upon the creation of the Department of Benevolences, the National Children's Home, as it came to be called, came under denominational jurisdiction. Over the years, new buildings have been added to the property in Hot Springs, so that by 1967 the assets of the home amounted to over $367,000.[99] The purpose of the home (more recently renamed Hillcrest Children's Home) has been for long-term care for children who are abandoned, unwanted, or abused. Between eighty and eighty-five live in the home at any given time.

A second children's home (Highlands Child Placement Services) was opened in August 1966 in Kansas City, Missouri. A large mansion was donated to the Assemblies of God and extensively remodeled to provide an adoptive care center, primarily for short-term housing until placement arrangements were made. Within the first year of operation 16 children had been placed in either adoptive or foster homes.[100] The 92 adoptions in 1987 brought the total to 480. A program for unmarried mothers has served over 725 women.[101]

Disaster Relief. In 1962, as a result of a hurricane striking the Louisiana coast and causing considerable damage to Assemblies of God churches, steps were taken by the Benevolences Committee of the General Council to set up a disaster relief fund. By 1964 the Department of Benevolences had set up such a fund for the aid of churches, parsonages, and ministers in disaster-stricken areas. Churches suffering from flood damage in Northern California and Oregon in 1965 were the first beneficiaries.[102] During the biennium of 1985–1987, twenty churches received a total of $46,604 because of floods, fires, and/or hurricanes.[103]

Additional financial services through the headquarters include the Church Extension Loan Plan and the Church Builders Plan. A Deferred Giving and Trusts Department offers adherents assistance in estate planning, and a Stewardship Department urges responsible use of "life, treasures, time, talents, and testimony."[104]

Gospel Publishing House

Gospel Publishing House continues to offer a full line of Sunday school literature, developed by the Church School Literature Department, in English and Spanish. A new and growing effort is the production of curriculum for Christian schools and daycare centers. Publishing house earnings underwrite the activities of other headquarters departments. The denomination operates two bookstores, called Radiant Book & Music Centers.

Its presses churn out some ~~twenty-three tons of literature daily~~, using the most modern equipment.[105]

Among the most visible of Gospel Publishing House's publications in the constituency over the years has been the *Pentecostal Evangel.* Having a paid weekly circulation of over 280,000, the *Evangel* claims to be one of the world's most widely distributed Protestant weeklies. In addition to paid subscriptions, 7,500 copies are distributed weekly to prisons by the Chaplaincy Department of the Division of Home Missions and 1,000 are provided for employees at the denomination's headquarters.[106]

Another magazine, *Advance,* is printed monthly to provide pastors with promotional presentations from all headquarters divisions and departments. *Advance* also offers ministerial helps, articles, book reviews, and program ideas.

In addition to the literature it produces, Gospel Publishing House also supplies a wide variety of church supplies and evangelical literature. In some ways, the Gospel Publishing House *General Catalog* reveals more about the movement's ethos than do official denominational documents. It offers at least a limited glimpse of the broader sampling that denominational leaders feel is acceptable for the constituency, and it suggests what appeals to Assemblies of God adherents in Christian literature and music. Popular evangelicals and/or charismatics like Charles Swindoll, James Dobson, Josh McDowell, Beverly and Tim LaHaye, Hal Lindsey, Jack Hayford, and Walter Martin are well represented in the *General Catalog* alongside such prominent Assemblies of God writers as Kenneth Barney, Stanley Horton, and Ralph Harris. The sections of the catalog reflect the popular culture Assemblies of God adherents share with many other evangelicals. In addition to older sectional headings such as Bible, Bible study, evangelism, Christian education, and music are sections offering books and tapes on counseling, family life, marriage enrichment, and contemporary issues.

Conclusion

The expansion of headquarters activities symbolizes, in one

sense, the growth and stability of the Assemblies of God. Denominational polity, of course, allows individual churches to use denominational promotion selectively, and it is apparent that what happens in a local church may show little relationship to what occurs in Springfield. Clearly, the headquarters has developed beyond the denomination's founders' dreams or hopes. Those who seventy-five years ago confidently awaited Christ's return generally had little interest in the kinds of programs and services that have emerged to nurture the denomination's mission in the modern era. The programs now sustain the denomination's evangelistic outreaches, however. Yet the overwhelming sense of the end that marked the founding generation is less thoroughly compelling among a constituency poised to perpetuate itself.

The changes are not simply a chronicle of the transformation of sect to denomination; sociological categories are essential, but they do not tell the whole story. As American religious historian Grant Wacker observed recently in *Christianity Today,* many men and women whose convictions are shaped by the assumptions of the apostolic faith daily commit their time and tithe to evangelism. Further, in the first and second generation, Pentecostals forged a new vision of what Christianity was about. Faith enabled them to transcend life's difficulties and affirm with assurance the presence and power of the supernatural in history.[107] Their religion offered certainty and promised experience and truth untainted by the historical process. Wacker has further noted: "The ideas and sensibilities of the movement unfolded—and rather luxuriantly at that—within a set of premises untouched and for many years impervious to the governing assumptions of twentieth-century culture."[108] Since World War II, however, the governing assumptions of the culture have rapidly permeated American Pentecostalism. By 1976, historian Martin Marty noted that once Pentecostalism "was 'true' because it was small and pure, but now it is 'true' because so many are drawn to it."[109]

The Assemblies of God's recent past is a story of dramatic growth, increasing popular acceptance, and rapid cultural accommodation.

Chaplain Jim Cotton, 1962. Home Missions was given the responsibility of military chaplains for the Assemblies of God in 1941.

Arvid Ohrnell (left), 1955. (The "prisoner" in this photo may have been a man who worked with Ohrnell in giving talks on prison ministry.)

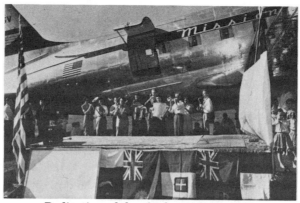

Dedication of the *Ambassador I*, 1948

Parade in front of the headquarters building in Springfield, Missouri, representing the vehicles purchased in one year with Speed-the-Light funds, 1967

Good News Crusades, like this one in Honduras, have been responsible for the salvation of millions of people.

The staff of Gospel Publishing House praying over the first shipment of BGMC materials. Front (l–r): Bartlett Peterson, J. Roswell Flower, Fred Vogler, Noel Perkin, Wesley Steelburg, Ralph Riggs, Bert Webb, J. Z. Kamerer, Paul Copeland

Packing barrels of literature for BGMC, 1958

Light-for-the-Lost layman Lance Warn, with Brother David of Kenya (Africa), preparing literature for distribution

MAPS workers in Guatemala

Edith Whipple and Martha McLean in the Women's Missionary Council office (later Women's Ministry Department), 1953

Women's Ministry Department staff (Sandra G. Clopine, national secretary, front, center)

Flag raising ceremony at the National Royal Ranger Training Center, 1,533 acres located in the heart of the Ozarks near Eagle Rock, Missouri

Robert Cunningham looks at a copy of the *Pentecostal Evangel,* ca. 1949. Over the years it has been the most visible publication in the denomination.

The headquarters, publishing plant, and distribution center of the General Council of the Assemblies of God, Springfield, Missouri. (The Assemblies of God Theological Seminary is on the fifth and sixth floors of the distribution center.)

7. The Recent Past

Sandwiched between articles on medical mysteries, Carl Sagan, and discipline in the U.S. Marines in a summer 1982 issue of *The Saturday Evening Post* was a brief popular profile of the Assemblies of God by evangelical journalist Edwin Plowman. Written in cooperation with a Youth Department fundraising project at a time when the denomination was winning attention among observers of American religion for its rapid growth, the article presented the Assemblies of God sympathetically in a medium that had often ignored it. In conversations with Assemblies of God members across the country, Plowman probed the Pentecostal ethos and discovered a disparity between popular perceptions of Pentecostals as fanatical "holy rollers" and the realities he encountered. "Tongues speaking," he commented, was not "a consuming issue." Rather, according to Plowman, Pentecostal core commitments differed little from those of other evangelicals: "Love for God" and "intense desire that others might come to know and love Him, too" coupled with "rock-ribbed belief in the authority of the Bible" were, he decided, the elements uniting the denomination's largely middle-class constituency.

Plowman also called attention to the considerable diversity the Assemblies of God encompassed, correctly observing that a typical U.S. Assemblies of God congregation did not exist. Such diversity, especially in worship style and affluence, has characterized the Assemblies of God throughout its history and has, perhaps, become most apparent in contemporary attitudes toward such musical expressions in worship as Christian rock, dancing, and Scripture choruses as alternatives to hymns.

Plowman meant as well the extreme variations in the size of congregations and church staffs, in church income, and in attitudes toward culture nurtured in the local congregation. Opulent suburban "plants," small unassuming buildings, inner-city missions, are all settings local congregations—the assembly of God—meet in. In recent decades the denomination's rapid growth, aided by interest in Pentecostalism generated in part by the charismatic movement and televangelism, has attracted attention that has helped give visibility to the widely different styles of worship and life that coexist under the Assemblies of God name.

Mission in the Modern Era

The denomination's rapid expansion in the 1970s and 1980s followed a period of slowed growth in the 1950s and 1960s. At the 1959 General Council in San Antonio, several prominent leaders with roots in the movement's earliest phases (Ralph Riggs, J. Roswell Flower, Noel Perkin) were replaced by younger executives. With the change in leadership came an opportunity to reassess denominational objectives and to define new concerns.

Assemblies of God leaders had typically stressed that renewal in local churches was essential to the denomination's momentum. Articulating the conviction that Spirit baptism, not attendance at a Pentecostal church, made people Pentecostals, Assemblies of God executives from 1959 concentrated on attempting to encourage renewal in local congregations. The 1963 General Council acted to make the general superintendent's office responsible for coordinating a Spiritual Life–Evangelism Commission; it was entrusted with devising ways to support local revival. This headquarters-based team set specific growth goals; meanwhile, the Executive Presbytery launched a denominational self-study.

The self-study focused on the need of a well-defined sense of mission and, in five years of study and planning, shaped an agenda that culminated in a Council on Evangelism in St. Louis in 1968. This council addressed concerns raised by committee reports over the past several years. Its operating assumption was that the Assemblies of God had been "brought into being and built as an instrument of divine purpose" in the end times. A scrutiny of the denomination's past resulted in an articulation of a threefold denominational purpose: evangelism, worship, nurture. The Council on Evangelism approved a Five-Year Plan of Advance, which set specific goals for the immediate future.

The newly focused sense of mission after 1968 derived largely from the work of the Committee on Advance appointed by the Executive Presbytery to diagnose needs, evaluate programs, and project goals. Serving with the general superintendent on the committee were fourteen men selected to represent various geographic areas and ministry skills. At the 1967 General Council, the Committee on Advance had been given the charge "to rearticulate our purpose";[1] the denomination's leaders were convinced that the best analysis of their movement's needs could be provided from within, by men who had a participant's familiarity with the denomination's wide-ranging programs.

In its quest to articulate the denomination's reason for being, the Committee on Advance had examined documents from the 1914 Hot Springs (Arkansas) General Council that had launched the Assemblies of God. A subcommittee attempted to discover how contemporary members viewed the denomination's purpose. Their analysis of the documents and reports revealed a sense of ambiguity about purpose within the denomination, an ambiguity contributed to by an action of the 1963 General Council that identified evangelism as "the whole work of the whole church."[2] Not surprisingly, preliminary surveys indicated confusion in the constituency about the meaning of the word "evangelism." The St. Louis Council on Evangelism was an attempt to examine the practical dimensions of evangelism; the examination was shaped by the report of the Committee on Advance, stressing what it called the "traditional" meaning of evangelism. The Assemblies of God existed primarily as "an agency of God for evangelizing the world," the committee maintained. Listed second and third were its purpose to be "a corporate body in which man may worship God" and its resolve to be "a channel of God's purpose to build a body of saints being perfected in the image of His Son."[3]

The document also affirmed the continuity of the Assemblies of God with "the New Testament apostolic pattern" as expressed in the denomination's teaching on Spirit baptism, observed to have three primary purposes: evangelism ("with accompanying supernatural signs"), worship (which it was said to add a "necessary" dimension to), expression of spiritual fruit, gifts, and ministries ("as in New Testament times").[4]

The Council on Evangelism met the denomination's expectations in many ways. It was an enthusiastic gathering of thousands of the faithful who joyously approved the committee's work.[5] It attempted to mobilize the constituency to a new sense of purpose at a time when denominational leaders believed that traditional values and certainties were being assailed everywhere. The decade of the sixties was critical for the denomination.

During the 1960s, it disavowed ecumenism and distanced itself officially from the first phase of the charismatic renewal, stances symbolized by the dismissal of David du Plessis; it expanded its Statement of Fundamental Truths to conform more closely to the NAE's, thus symbolizing the completion of a significant phase in the formal identification of the Assemblies of God with the new evangelicalism; it ignored much of the social disarray in the nation as well as the burgeoning charismatic renewal and defined evangelism as its primary task. In a sense, this was an attempt to recommit the denomination to its historical position of cultural alienation. Yet at the same time, tension between that cultural alienation and a growing interest in cultural custodianship became apparent. As "the salt of the earth," a few Pentecostals began direct attempts to penetrate the culture with Christian values. Eventually this yielded results as diverse as the controversial efforts of Jim and Tammy Bakker to preside over a Christian amusement park, dinner theater, and fashion trends; the appointment of James Watt, an Assemblies of God layman, as secretary of the interior; and the election of John Ashcroft, another Assemblies of God layman, as Missouri governor. At the same time, the impact of American culture on American Pentecostals became increasingly apparent in their embracing new technologies as well as in their growing accommodation to the values of middle America.

During the 1960s, the Assemblies of God, like all American denominations, operated amid bewildering social change marked by an apparent liberal Christian crisis and the public emergence of evangelicalism. Part of the trauma of the time for some was the emerging sense of moral pluralism (which differed from the denominational pluralism Americans were accustomed to). Out of the perceived breakdown of core values emerged a more aggressive evangelicalism and a more strident fundamentalism. Assemblies of God mobilization for the task of evangelism can be accurately evaluated only from the perspective of the larger context of the 1960s.

Denominational leaders addressed organizational as well as religious needs during the 1960s under Thomas Zimmerman's executive leadership. After many hours of committee discussion, in 1972 the headquarters structure was reorganized in an effort to offer more efficient and specialized services to the constituency. The proliferation of programs administered through the denomination's headquarters and the rapid expansion of home and foreign missions following World War II is chronicled in chapter 6, "Denominational Programs."

Although institutional and organizational changes are easy to summarize, the movement's character and diversity are not. Even as ongoing efforts at the denomination's headquarters sought to cultivate certain emphases and attitudes, the constituency's popular ethos was more closely tied to the perceptions and activities of local pastors, evangelists, and lay leaders. And, more than the official record may suggest, women played important roles in the life of local congregations.

Among the significant issues the denomination addressed was that of its relationship to ethnic minorities.

Ethnic Ministries

Early in its history, the Assemblies of God had focused attention on major European population groups by organizing districts (German, Hungarian, Polish, Ukrainian, etc.) composed of foreign-language-speaking congregations. As European groups were assimilated, without being replenished by significant new immigration, churches once affiliated with foreign-language districts were absorbed by the geographic districts they were located in.

Although acculturation meant the decline of older European districts, new oriental immigration challenged the denomination to consider forming Asian-directed outreaches. This would represent an important reorientation, from a European to a Pacific Rim hegemony.

Recognizing the growing Korean presence across America, in 1981 Assemblies of God leaders looked favorably on the creation of a Korean district. At the time, approximately 47 ministers served 60 organized Korean Assemblies of God churches totaling some 7,000 members. They became the nucleus of the fifty-seventh district council of the Assemblies of God. The rapid influx of Korean immigrants in the 1980s shaped this district's special challenge, which it has met with determination. In 1988 this newest district was coordinating the efforts of over 260 ministers in some 100 churches of over 14,000 members.

Spanish-Speaking

Assemblies of God ministries to Spanish-speaking Americans are as old as the General Council and have been the most successful ethnic-directed efforts of the denomination. In motion as the denomination organized, they saw sustained growth: Without them the denomination could not have claimed the growth rate that made it, at times, America's fastest-growing denomination. By 1987, Assemblies of God membership was approximately 15 percent Hispanic.[6]

Mexican Americans had participated in the Pentecostal movement at least since its Azusa Street days, and some who affiliated with the newly formed Assemblies of God in 1914 were already actively engaged in ministries targeting Mexican communities from Texas to southern California. Organized Assemblies of God efforts among Spanish-speaking Americans began after Henry C. Ball, a young Methodist, embraced Pentecostalism and was ordained by the Assemblies of God in 1915. The next year, he organized a congregation in Kingsville, Texas; it became a center from which he launched a broader outreach. Converts became lay workers and spread the message among cotton pickers and other migrant workers. Ball selected the most promising participants in his fledgling congregation and assigned them to evangelize in farflung Texas communities.[7]

Constant calls for more workers resulted in the introduction of programs and literature to train Hispanic converts for leadership. Ball and Alice Luce, a former British missionary to India who devoted the second half of her life to ministry among Spanish-speaking Americans, organized and led Bible institutes in Texas and California; prepared Spanish correspondence courses; published a Spanish gospel hymnal; and provided the periodicals, tracts, and other literature that typically gave Pentecostals an inexpensive forum for presenting the testimonies to religious experience that formed the core of their message.[8]

In January 1918 Ball's successful efforts among Hispanics were acknowledged by the Texas-New Mexico District of the Assemblies of God when the district commissioned him to organize Assemblies of God congregations among Spanish-speaking people wherever he found them. Undaunted by the magnitude of the commission, Ball simply continued the activities he had begun. He devoted virtually all his time to personal evangelism. His marriage in June 1918 to Sunshine Marshall united him with one who felt a similar calling. The Hispanic ministers, the Balls, and Alice Luce worked with electing Ball the first superintendent of the Latin American District when the Hispanic outreach became independent of the auspices of the Foreign Missions Department in 1929.[9]

The Latin American District grew rapidly. At first concentrating especially in the Southwest, from Texas to California, efforts among Spanish-speaking Americans soon spread to the East Coast as well. By the post-World War II era, Hispanics formed a growing percentage of the Assemblies of God constituency, and the Latin American districts of the Assemblies of God together constituted the largest Protestant presence among Hispanics in the United States. By the late 1980s, the Latin American District had been divided into four districts: Pacific Latin American, Gulf Latin American, Central Latin American, and Midwest Latin American. The Spanish Eastern and Southeastern Spanish districts coordinated efforts among Spanish-speaking Americans on the East Coast. The present Puerto Rican District, the seventh Spanish district, was organized in 1975. These districts were served by three denominationally endorsed schools: Latin American Bible Institute (San Antonio), Latin American Bible Institute of California (La Puente), and Southern Arizona Bible College (Hereford).[10] In 1988, the seventieth anniversary of the formalizing of Assemblies of God efforts among Hispanics, statistics helped describe the appeal the Assemblies of God has had among Spanish-speaking North Americans: From 7 ministers, 6 churches, and 100 members in 1918, the Spanish and Latin American districts together had grown to embrace 164,105 adherents in 1,217 churches. The constituency was served by 2,517 ordained and licensed ministers.

In 1987 well over 200,000 of the members of Hispanic Pentecostal denominations traced their Pentecostal commitments to efforts coordinated by Ball and his coworkers from 1915. The influence on Puerto Rican Pentecostals was indirect, having been mediated through the efforts of Juan L. Lugo, who was supported first by Bethel Church, a prominent Anglo Assemblies of God congregation in Los Angeles, and Francisco Olazabal, men influenced in the formative stages of their ministries by Ball. Olazabal, who was converted to evangelical faith through the efforts of George and Carrie Judd Montgomery at the turn of the century, became a Methodist evangelist until the Montgomery's influence encouraged him to pursue the Pentecostal experience. In 1917 he received Assemblies of God credentials. Before long he was acknowledged as a dominant figure among Hispanic Pentecostals. Although he left the Assemblies of God in 1923 to head a newly created Hispanic association, the Latin American Council of Christian Churches, Olazabal's efforts to spread Pentecostal teaching among Mexican and Puerto Rican Americans contributed substantially to Assemblies of God growth.

Thus by midcentury the Assemblies of God had several clusterings of Hispanic workers and congregations: The largest concentrations were in Texas, California, and the Northeast. Separated by both distance and culture from Mexican Americans, Puerto Rican members urged that a district independent of the Latin American District be organized: In 1956 the Spanish Eastern District was formed. Until 1973, both the Latin American District and the Spanish Eastern District were supervised by the Home Missions Department. In 1973, the Latin American District was further subdivided, and all the Hispanic districts were given status equal to the denomination's geographic Anglo districts.

Efforts to provide Hispanic Pentecostals with support for their evangelism have continued to expand. Gospel Publishing House and the denomination's LIFE Publishers in Miami provide Sunday school curriculum and other literature in Spanish. Berean College, the denomination's accredited nontraditional college, has begun issuing Spanish courses. For several generations, then, Hispanic Assemblies of God leadership has been in the hands of talented Hispanic men who, at first by virtue of office and then in recognition of their abilities as well, have been integrated into the denomination's General Presbytery and leadership structure.

Blacks

Although Hispanic and Korean minorities posed no special problems for the Assemblies of God and carved out their niche with relative ease in the overwhelmingly white denomination, the story of Assemblies of God attitudes toward American blacks was complicated from the start.

Presuppositions of white American Pentecostals about black Americans came from many sources. It is evident that Assemblies of God adherents differed little in their racial attitudes from other white Americans of similar social class and educational background. With the exception of its efforts among

Latin Americans (which until 1929 were considered foreign missions work), the denomination had historically been predominantly white. The constituencies that united to create it were, too. Though they claimed to revere black Pentecostals like Charles Mason, Thoro Harris, and G. T. Haywood, most white Pentecostals did so at a distance. Predominantly southern and often nationally led by men of decidedly southern views, the Assemblies of God failed to attract a sizable black membership. No workers dedicated to evangelizing black Americans—as the Balls, Alice Luce, Mack Pinson, and others had dedicated themselves to Hispanics—were on the denomination's early rosters. During the denomination's early years, the name of only one black minister appears: that of E. S. Thomas, a pastor from Binghamton, New York, whose name was followed by the designation "colored." I. S. and Mattie Neeley, black missionaries to Liberia before 1914, affiliated briefly with the General Council for further service in Liberia.

Before World War II, scattered evidence indicates the presence of a few licensed black ministers, especially in the Eastern District (where General Presbyter and prominent pastor Robert Brown encouraged them). In general, a few black men (and, from 1922 to 1935, at least one talented black woman, Cornelia Jones Robertson) acquired district licenses; a few (mostly in New York and on the West Coast, including Robertson) were ordained. Most districts, however, hesitated to ordain them, citing the difficulties inherent in the potential national visibility that would allegedly follow. For ordination, it was recommended that they look to the Assemblies of God "sister organization," the predominantly black Church of God in Christ.[11]

During the 1940s, a suggestion that the Assemblies of God create a "Colored Branch" was introduced several times, but met with little enthusiasm. In his report to the General Presbytery in 1949, J. R. Flower commented: "If anything is to be done for the colored people, it would seem that someone must get a burden for some type of evangelistic or philanthropic work and devote themselves to it."[12] Discussions about evangelizing American blacks became more frequent during the 1950s. A committee on race relations, appointed by the 1956 General

Presbytery, prepared a report entitled "Segregation vs. Integration." The appointment of a committee was intended to counter allegations that the denomination was ignoring the problem even as mounting civil rights activism raised the national consciousness. At the General Presbytery meeting in Oklahoma City, after discussing issues raised by the civil rights movement, the presbytery expunged all of its actions from the minutes. "We could not afford to go on record as favoring integration," Ralph Riggs explained; "neither did we want it to be known that we were in favor of segregation."[13] (In correspondence with "the black Billy Graham," Nicholas Bhengu, Riggs agreed with him that integration could be "disastrous";[14] J. R. Flower cautioned that integration might well result in the loss of white members.[15]) The solution seemed obvious: "[A] convenient and deliberate approach" would be to appoint a study commission. "Our answer to those who challenged us," Riggs maintained, "would simply be that we have a commission appointed to study the problem."[16]

Interest in the subject was stimulated by the aggressive civil rights stance of the Truman administration, the emerging civil rights movement, and the 1954 unanimous Supreme Court ruling against "separate but equal" public schools. This state of affairs had elicited responses from northern mainline Protestant bureaucracies—though not necessarily equally from their constituencies. In February 1956, the *Reader's Digest* published an article entitled "The Churches Repent"; it chronicled the mainline churches' response to moral questions raised by the predicament of American blacks. Some Assemblies of God adherents who read the article were challenged to discover their denomination's official stance on civil rights.[17] General Superintendent Ralph Riggs's response to one such inquiry indicated again the leadership's dilemma. Riggs, a native of Tennessee who had spent his childhood in Mississippi and begun his ministry as a missionary to South Africa, noted that the General Presbytery had discussed both creating a colored branch and attempting to integrate the constituency.[18] The subject had purposely been considered in the Presbytery and excluded from the floor of the General Council. Riggs reported:

> We did not feel free to create a Colored Branch for this
> would be condoning segregation and even creating seg-
> regation when this is not felt the right thing to do at the
> present time. On the other hand, the intense social conflict,
> particularly in the deep South, makes it unwise to intro-
> duce integration at the present time. For these reasons we
> felt that it would be best for us to mark time at the moment
> until the matter had developed further in the public con-
> sciousness and practice.[19]

This willingness to wait for cultural accommodation to the
concept of integration and then to bring the Assemblies of God
into line characterized the denomination's leaders in the Eisenhower years. Although Riggs assured others that "we are
thoroughly alert as to the trend of the times and also what our
Christian duty in this regard is," he and his colleagues sensed
no compulsion publicly to define that Christian duty until they
had been satisfied that other factors had inclined the constituency to acquiesce.[20]

Also in the Eisenhower years, by forging stronger ties to the
Church of God in Christ, Assemblies of God leaders attempted
to counter charges that they had "excluded blacks from the
great commission." Such contact was facilitated by acquain-
tances made at the World Pentecostal Conference, one of the
few associations black and white Pentecostals mingled in.
Charles Mason (whom Ralph Riggs, thirty years his junior,
routinely addressed in correspondence as "Venerable Father")
and others welcomed Riggs and Flower to the Church of God
in Christ's National Convocation in Memphis in 1955; for several years the two denominations discussed a potential business relationship (that never materialized) through which the
Church of God in Christ would purchase its Sunday school
literature from the Assemblies of God. The aging Mason sent
a representative to the 1957 General Council; Ralph Riggs and
Thomas Zimmerman represented the Assemblies of God at the
fiftieth anniversary convocation of the Church of God in Christ,
also in 1957. But such contacts failed to issue in long-term
cooperation.

Meanwhile, in the Northwest and in New York, a few black
men were quietly ordained by Assemblies of God districts.[21] In

1958, a request from the Northern California-Nevada District about receiving a black church into membership and ordaining its pastor opened the question for renewed discussion in the General Presbytery.[22] A committee once again considered a "colored fellowship," this time recommending that it be supervised by the national Home Missions Department.[23] Concern about possible involvement "in the present agitation regarding racial problems prevalent in society at large" resulted in the tabling of the committee's report.[24] Meanwhile, denominational leaders chose to ignore approaches like those from the National Association for the Advancement of Colored People, calling on the religious community to support financially their quest for civil rights.[25]

During the 1960s, as various African colonies became independent nations, some missionaries became anxious about their welcome abroad. In a letter to *Christianity Today,* an Assemblies of God missionary, after commenting on Americans who refused to integrate their own churches but willingly evangelized in Africa, noted the likelihood that nationalist African leaders would "look into the parent body of missions in that country and see if in the home churches segregation is practiced."[26] Bringing this sentiment to the attention of Thomas Zimmerman, missionary John Garlock noted a condition that apparently some assumed to be true in the American Assemblies of God: "If it is true that Negro students are not welcome at CBI (unless they come from overseas); if it is true that most of our districts are reluctant to ordain Negro ministers; if it is true that in many districts local congregations would be unwilling to accept Negroes into membership, our missionary work overseas may become a great deal more difficult than it is now."[27]

In June 1963 Zimmerman and Bartlett Peterson, Assemblies of God general secretary, participated in a White House conference on civil rights at which President John Kennedy and Attorney General Robert Kennedy encouraged religious leaders to cultivate a climate of understanding. President Kennedy's excusing himself and announcing that discussion would continue under the auspices of National Council of Churches leadership prompted the departure of about a third of the two hundred discussants. Among those who left were Zimmerman and Peterson.

But the tide was slowly beginning to turn. Ending years of hesitation and responding to the accelerating civil rights movement, the 1965 General Council adopted a resolution affirming civil rights. (The resolution, like many General Council actions, had first been approved by the General Presbytery):

> RESOLVED, That we reaffirm our belief in the teachings of Christ including His emphasis upon the inherent worth and intrinsic value of every man, regardless of race, class, creed, or color and we urge all our constituency to discourage unfair and discriminatory practices wherever they exist; and, be it further RESOLVED, That we believe those in authority in political, social and particularly in evangelical groups, have a moral responsibility toward the creation of those situations which will provide equal rights and opportunities for every individual.[28]

The above resolution was prefaced with the statement that "the teachings of Christ are violated by discriminatory practices against racial minorities" and the insistence that Christian conversion "breaks down prejudice and causes justice to prevail."[29] By the 1970s the sentiments of the resolution were beginning to be implemented in some places as renewed denominational attention to inner city evangelism resulted in several thriving racially integrated urban efforts, which have continued to expand in the 1980s.[30] This refocusing was prompted in part by the tendency of Assemblies of God congregations in some places to move to the suburbs, as well as by the emergence in the denomination of a handful of talented young blacks with a vision for inner city outreaches.

Other Cultural Issues

As the Vietnam War accelerated and contributed to increased social upheaval in the late 1960s, the Assemblies of God General Presbytery adopted a "social statement" in August 1968.[31] The socially conservative document repudiated "devised confrontations between those alienated" as well as the view (which seemed popular on college campuses among the Students for a Democratic Society) that "revolution is the key to social progress."[32] "Community-betterment projects and legislative actions on social improvement" could alleviate merely the symptoms of the fundamental human problem: sin. The church's most significant social contribution would always be preaching "the Biblical gospel of the Lord Jesus Christ."[33] This document and the actions of the St. Louis Council on Evangelism in the same year are revealing. In a period of intense cultural disarray, the denomination mobilized for evangelism. It rejected the agenda of the era's social activists, but—in spite of the best efforts of some—it was ultimately influenced by the cultural climate it tried to ignore. Its accommodation to the values of middle America became more apparent; relaxed standards for social behavior became easier to rationalize.

Assemblies of God leaders and constituents have tended to opt for conservative stances (because they justify them as biblical stances) on major social questions as well as on domestic and foreign policy issues (Vietnam, the Grenada invasion, Oliver North, etc.). Several of a series of position papers released by the General Presbytery during recent decades have reiterated the denomination's longstanding opposition to abortion, homosexuality, alcohol, and gambling. Although the Assemblies of God has no official statement on the women's movement, it is easy to document both diversity and anxiety in responses to issues raised by secular and evangelical feminists. In 1978, an instructor at one Assemblies of God college, Evangel, reported to Thomas Zimmerman her concern about trends revealed by women students' comments: "More and more we are hearing of young ministers' wives who do not have a complete dedication to God and to their husband's calling," she lamented.[34] Such women tended to opt for "independent careers in the secular world." Liberation movements, especially those promoting biblical feminism, she noted, presented a growing challenge.[35]

Awareness of the emerging evangelical feminist movement was, of course, inevitable. Several wives of Assemblies of God executives attended an Evangelical Women's Conference at

Fuller Theological Seminary in Pasadena; it seemed to justify their fears that evangelical feminism jeopardized life as they knew it. In an address on "Women and the Evangelical Movement," Faith Sand, a Protestant missionary to Brazil, called on her audience to acknowledge how thoroughly cultural biases influenced their "communication of God's message." She noted various inconsistencies in evangelical uses of Scripture, several of which were highlighted for Zimmerman's attention by the Assemblies of God women (having obtained a copy of the address). The following items seemed the most threatening: an indictment of "our worship of capitalism," a call to boycott religious institutions that gave only lip service to women's rights, and an insistence that "women's liberation portends the end of evangelical chauvinism."[36]

It is evident that Zimmerman and other leaders tended to sense in the women's movement a serious threat to traditional social institutions; it is equally evident that a small but growing number of younger women, especially at the denomination's colleges, objected to the denomination's failure to address (or even acknowledge) both the ambivalence in its own stance on women and the issues raised by evangelical feminists.[37] Declining numbers of active ordained women (i.e., those who have responsibilities independent of their husband's) have marked the recent past.[38]

Feminism seemed integrally related to a larger discussion about the family that emerged in evangelical ranks in the 1970s. Assemblies of God leaders and lay people looked askance at rising divorce rates and at a widening array of marital problems affecting expectations in local churches. From their perspective, the women's movement seemed inextricably linked to the breakdown of core values inherent in moral pluralism. In response, like other evangelical constituencies, the denomination reiterated in numerous ways its commitment to the traditional family. Assemblies of God adherents avidly read James Dobson, Chuck Swindoll, and other evangelical authors whose books emphasized traditional family roles and values. Pentecostals also discovered the newly visible popular evangelical counseling and self-help literature that filled Christian bookstores. Before long, the general catalog of Gospel Publishing House carried it too.

Another dilemma of the post-1960s was divorce and remarriage. In spite of frequent, lively discussions about alternatives, the denomination had consistently opposed the remarriage of a divorced person whose spouse was living. Assemblies of God ministers were forbidden to perform such marriages; in 1973, the General Council acted to make it permissable. Such permission was not intended to approve divorce but rather to help ministers handle difficult situations, especially those resulting from marital entanglements prior to conversion. As divorce became more common in the culture, divorced people formed an increasing segment of Assemblies of God adherents. Their appropriate roles in local churches among a constituency that had long disapproved divorce generated discussion as well.

The Assemblies of God has consistently refused to ordain to the ministry any married person with a living former spouse. Those who believe that their situation merits review and/or special consideration may request it: If the district credentials committee agrees that fraud occurred (at least eighteen guidelines amplify the meaning of fraud), annulment may be granted, and the divorced and remarried candidate may receive credentials. Although it is more difficult to trace, the pattern and frequency of annulments is probably more revealing than the course of debates over divorce for the clergy. The 1973 General Council, meeting in Miami, Florida, not only redefined the Assemblies of God stance on divorce and remarriage for members, it also implemented a rehabilitation program that had been developed over the past decade. Until 1973, the denomination had no formal rehabilitation program: Disciplined ministers, depending on the nature of their offense, were excluded from all ministry for a minimum time; afterwards they could apply for reinstatement.

In 1963 R. J. Carlson, district superintendent from Washington, suggested to the General Presbytery that it consider "preventative" and "redemptive" phases of rehabilitation. Noting that "the greatest endowment we have in our Movement are men whom God has filled with the Holy Spirit" and that "everyone we lose is an irreparable loss," Carlson moved the appointment of a committee of "mature men" to address the subject.[39] In response the Executive Presbytery appointed a committee, chaired by former General Superintendent Gayle F. Lewis.

The report of this Rehabilitation and Morals Study Committee summarized the problem and recommended solutions. Presumably addressing its task to discover preventive measures, the committee recommended "great care" in the examination of ministerial candidates—not only in testing biblical knowledge, but also in probing character and self-discipline.[40] The report recommended a distinction between one having "a moral weakness," evidenced by "repeated acts which have gone unconfessed," and one "who may have been subjected to unusual temptation, resulting in a fall."[41] It was the latter group the committee recommended for rehabilitation.

The report recommended as well that homosexuality be grounds for permanent dismissal: "Psychotherapy," the committee noted, "indicates that for a homosexual to be cured, he must get a new image of himself and undergo a personality reconstruction."[42] According to the report, this coincided with the biblical perspective on conversion; the report therefore maintained that ministers whose conduct required discipline for homosexual offenses should not be reinstated because they had presumably "not . . . allowed [Christ] to effect the necessary transformation of personality."[43]

Rehabilitation, the report advised, should begin with integration into a local congregation and continue in active involvement in lay ministries; no acts reserved distinctly for the ordained ministry should be performed.[44] The presbyters accepted the report but requested further study. In 1965 they again discussed how to help ministers prevent moral failure.[45] The denomination issued a policy manual for district credentials committees entitled *Moral Delinquencies and Rehabilitation Policies.* These preliminary efforts were displaced in 1973 by the institution of a full rehabilitation program. Administered by local districts, the multi-faceted program and its relationship to discipline are outlined fully in the denomination's Constitution and Bylaws.

Theological Trends

In recent years, Assemblies of God leaders have frequently expressed concerns about various teachings having an obvious appeal in the Pentecostal milieu. In partial response, the General Presbytery has authorized the release of position papers reaffirming the denomination's historic commitment to healing, the rapture of the Church, eternal punishment, and tongues speech as the uniform initial evidence of Spirit baptism. Other such papers have attempted to provide guidance on controversial issues raised largely by the charismatic movement: positive confession, discipleship and submission, and demon possession.

By the late 1970s, the General Presbytery chose to respond to the widely shared conviction that faculty members at some Assemblies of God colleges did not personally subscribe fully to the denomination's eschatological position. J. Philip Hogan agreed that his interviews with missionary candidates revealed that some failed to commit themselves on the rapture of the Church and other elements within the basic dispensational, premillenarian framework long approved by the denomination.[46] The 1979 General Presbytery authorized the appointment of a Committee on Loopholes to analyze language in the Constitution and Bylaws that might allow theological deviation.[47] In response to the consensus that Assemblies of God college personnel should fully endorse the denomination's theological stance, it was recommended that the committee seek ways "to assure doctrinal purity in all of our schools."[48]

When the committee reported to the 1980 General Presbytery, it immediately became apparent that the presbyters' concerns were far broader than had originally been indicated. Not only did the denomination's stance on the pretribulation rapture seem impaired, so also did its views on the initial evidence of Spirit baptism and the inerrancy of Scripture. The latter issue had been raised in the larger evangelical community, and

Harold Lindsell's *Battle for the Bible* (1976) and *Bible in the Balance* (1979), containing indictments of the alleged shifting attitudes of many evangelical institutions on the subject, seemed to support the worst fears of the denomination's leaders. The General Presbytery appointed a larger committee and solicited a new report.[49]

In 1981 the committee report called on district officials to examine credentials candidates thoroughly and carefully. It also suggested revisions for the annual credentials renewal forms that would require ministers to indicate annually any differences with the General Council on the core of issues that seemed most critical to the denomination's identity. The list is instructive: initial evidence of Spirit baptism (tongues); baptism by immersion (yes); premillennialism (futurist pretribulationist); divine healing (yes); eternal security (no); sanctification (progressive).[50]

Continued efforts to assure that Assemblies of God colleges promoted these views took the form in 1984 of urging faculty to use books published by Gospel Publishing House. This followed an Executive Presbytery action in November 1983, suggesting that presidents and academic deans encourage the use of such books as texts and required supplementary reading.[51] The denomination's Board of Education, chaired by Hardy Steinberg, pursued the matter by instituting "a careful, ongoing review of curricular offerings of our Bible colleges and institutions, with particular attention to . . . detecting textbooks that would include unscriptural philosophies leading to humanism, or other faith-destroying teaching that would undermine the acceptance of the supernatural."[52] The Board of Education recommended that each Assemblies of God educational institution set up a textbook review process "to assure compatibility with our Movement's commitment to the supernatural moving of God's Spirit."[53] For endorsed schools, reports on textbooks became part of the required annual questionnaire and statistical report. In addition, tenured Assemblies of God college faculty members were required to be Assemblies of God members and to conform to the moral standards for Assemblies of God ministers. Such efforts to assure "doctrinal purity" both indicated the extent of perceived unacceptable diversity and reflected the concerns of the elected leadership for conserving the Assemblies of God during a period of rapid social and theological change. The social complexion of the denomination changed rapidly too: The percentage of college graduates in the constituency, for example, nearly tripled between 1960 and 1970. Balancing a heritage that valued individual autonomy and a measure of diversity with the growing need to demand consensus has provided a continuing challenge.

Popular Pentecostalism

Like many other forms of evangelicalism, Pentecostalism is decidedly a popular movement. As an audience-conscious, popular expression of Christianity, it has adapted itself to the themes and styles running through American popular culture. Historian Peter Williams has outlined three basic characteristics of popular religions that help illumine Pentecostalism's character: Popular religions are, he observes, distinct in their social structure; their sociology of knowledge; and their symbolism, expression, and behavior.[54] They celebrate and expect the activity of the divine in daily life in such events as healing, Spirit possession, and revelations. Once they devise organizational structures, they cease, in some ways, to fit the description of popular movements. Assemblies of God polity, however, permits a measure of coexistence of organizational structure and elements of popular religion. Although the denominational records document concerns and triumphs, the picture they present often bears little resemblance to the Pentecostalism the rank and file identify with.

The General Council is by legal definition a ministers' fellowship. Most of the vital history of the Assemblies of God, however, is the story of hundreds of thousands of unnamed men and women who never spoke at General Councils or voted on denominational questions. But their commitments kept local churches thriving and their giving kept missions efforts flourishing.

Although organizational development has modified some

traits of popular Pentecostalism, the tradition continues to attract those who hope that faith will enable them to transcend life's difficulties and that the Spirit's indwelling will illumine and empower them. The Assemblies of God was cited several times late in the 1970s and early in the 1980s for rapid growth. However, unprecedented national visibility came late in the 1980s when the moral irregularities of Jim and Tammy Bakker and Jimmy Swaggart (both men held Assemblies of God credentials) became the subject of countless news stories, many of them exploring the history and character of the Assemblies of God. Bakker and Swaggart were part of a much larger group of televangelists and broadcasters whose efforts gave cohesion to the hopes and dreams of hundreds of thousands of Pentecostals and charismatics. The content of their programs captured the essence of important dimensions of popular Pentecostalism in ways that denominational procedures could not.

Significant elements in the denomination had for years identified with the rhetoric of televangelists who called the nation to repent and work for a Christian America. The relationship between televangelism and the new Christian political right is a fascinating one that has become the subject of scholarly inquiry.[55] As noted, in recent years the Assemblies of God clearly included people who were moving from cultural alienation to cultural custodianship, a trend accelerated by prominent televangelists.

A long-simmering feud between Bakker and Swaggart erupted early in 1987 when Bakker was accused of various improprieties and Swaggart called him "a cancer that should be excised from the body of Christ." The two understood better than most how to appeal to the popular culture that had been an integral part of the Pentecostal ethos since the movement's inception. Each represented an approach to ministry that had a long history within the movement. Several basic assumptions help explain the appeal of media ministries for Pentecostals. Some are ideological, others social.

First, Pentecostals respond readily to rhetoric promoting support of evangelistic outreach. Given their premillennialism and their priority on evangelism, it has been easy to convince them that televangelism is the most effective way to carry out the worldwide proclamation of their message, which they believe will prepare the world for Christ's return. It is obviously easier to give financial support to one who claims to be doing the job than to subscribe to the older Pentecostal emphasis on "each one win one."[56] And Swaggart claimed precisely that. Televangelism, he declared, was the one way to proclaim the gospel around the world. Pentecostals have virtually sanctified modern media technology, regarding it as providentially provided for their ends.

Second, many Pentecostals enjoyed seeing their own become stars. Having gone unnoticed for many years, they took pride in and lavished funds on those who gave them visibility. Like Bakker and Swaggart, many of them recalled years of deprivation. Some seemed inclined to revel in possessions (which, they rationalized, indicated God's blessing) and to accept the emphases of health and wealth for believers being so reasonably presented by independent Pentecostal centers. Swaggart's opulence did not disturb most of them, and when Jim and Tammy Bakker decided to open a lavish Christian amusement park and offer their devoted supporters the opportunity of participating in a setting that featured the stars of Christian pop culture, the faithful responded enthusiastically. The setting, after all, brought them about as close to the country club milieu as they were likely to get.

Third, the Pentecostal fascination for modern technology should not be overlooked. Although the movement has historically used antimodern rhetoric, its members have been among the first to embrace modern technology and to adapt it for their ends. Television, once a suspect medium (and in certain districts formally condemned), became a means to an end, and thus found its place in Pentecostal homes. Whereas the first generation of Pentecostals resisted the attractions of secular society to preach a culture-challenging gospel, recent generations have tended to accommodate readily to the technology and values of middle America.

Certainly the Pentecostalism modeled by these popular televangelists was demonstrably different in significant ways from that of earlier years, but it had continuities as well. Bakker's amiable religion, with its stress on Christianizing popular amusements, fashions, and communications, appealed to many who had at one level made their peace with this world. Bakker modeled what many Pentecostals had come to suspect: One could speak in tongues and exercise spiritual gifts while embracing much more of this world than had previously been supposed. The line between religion and entertainment had often been blurred: Bakker, Swaggart, and other televangelists were popular in part because they were consummate entertainers. PTL (originally "Praise the Lord," later "People That Love") became a forum in which the Bakkers and others presented their case for the "liberation" of the movement from the vestiges of "separation" thinking. While they repudiated "legalism," they did not directly embrace the secular. Instead, by featuring the stars of Christian pop culture, they set out to assist the "Christianization" of the arts and other pastimes. In so doing, they greatly accelerated the permeation of the Assemblies of God with the view that the Christian life allowed more self-expression than had previously been acknowledged. PTL's quest to permeate American culture with Christian values also had an affinity for the agenda of the Christian right, dominated in the 1980 election by Jerry Falwell's Moral Majority. Although support for individual candidates was absent, support for conservative political causes—like reviving and preserving moral values, prayer and creationism in the public schools, and support for Israel and military spending—was strong.[57]

In accordance with established denominational procedures, the Assemblies of God dismissed Jim Bakker in 1987 for conduct unbecoming a minister, including allegations of sexual misconduct. They could not as readily expunge his influence, however, for he represented an emerging redefinition both of how Pentecostal experience should influence one's relationship to culture and of how that experience should be understood. The earlier eschatological context for understanding Pentecostalism having been significantly modified in the mindset of increasing numbers of Pentecostals, Bakker's emphasis on a celebration of the Spirit often seemed more inviting than a stress on the imminence of the end.

In contrast to Bakker, Jimmy Swaggart called for a renewed focus on the place of themes like holiness, separation, and evangelism in Pentecostal self-understanding: He thereby struck a responsive chord in thousands of Pentecostals who felt bewildered by the growing acculturation of their movement. His warm style and honky-tonk sound attracted handclapping crowds who regarded him as the ablest exponent of the true Pentecostal message.

Yet, however much he thundered against contemporary Christian rock music, pastoral counseling, the charismatic movement, Catholics, and those fellow Pentecostals he thought compromised with modernity, Swaggart did not fully embrace the heritage he spoke for. Ironically, his opulent life-style helped make his stern message palatable and even popular. Whereas once Pentecostals who preached against popular culture consciously tried to conspicuously distance themselves from that culture (perhaps inconsistently, but nonetheless sincerely), by the 1980s even those who claimed to be true to the movement's version of the "old-time religion" often found that being outwardly different was unattractive. As in some other evangelical settings, the life of faith tended to become an alternative to the life of holiness, two elements that had once been generally acknowledged as complementary.

Despite pressure to treat Swaggart's indiscretions differently from those of other offending ministers, the Assemblies of God Executive Presbytery, supported by the General Presbytery, voted to demand Swaggart's compliance with a typical rehabilitation program. The pressures for special consideration came from inside as well as outside the constituency. Prominent charismatic personalities like James Robison and E. V. Hill urged that a restoration to ministry should quickly follow the confession of wrongdoing. Some thought Swaggart's substantial financial contributions to the denomination's Division of Foreign Missions assured him rapid reinstatement. Others thought his various ministries too vital to jeopardize by silencing him. But the Executive Presbytery (acting as the denomination's credentials committee) stood its ground, rejected the Louisiana District's plea for lenience, and emerged with its authority in credentials decisions enhanced.

The public disgrace of two of popular Pentecostalism's heroes has challenged Assemblies of God adherents to evaluate their personal motives and priorities. "God is calling us back to the trenches," Executive Presbyter Robert Schmidgall told a crowded congregation in his Naperville, Illinois, church in February 1988. Trenches hardly have the appeal of luxury cars and executive estates. But they are, Schmidgall insisted, where the movement began, with each member committed to personal evangelism. Movements, he reasoned, cannot shirk individual responsibility by paying one to perform a task assigned equally to all. Similar calls to repentance, holiness, and witness have issued from many Assemblies of God pulpits, often born in the hope that the denomination can emerge from the moral failures of its best-known exponents stronger and more united.

Conclusion

As the Assemblies of God moves into the last decade of the twentieth century—a decade that, at its end, will mark the centennial of the American Pentecostal movement—the denomination is mobilizing for a Decade of Harvest. Adherents are being challenged to involvement in a mammoth evangelistic thrust.

As Assemblies of God adherents pray and plan for a dramatic surge of growth and empowerment, their denomination's history offers instructive insights about both early Pentecostalism's dynamic and its stance toward culture. History shows that the denomination's first generation preached a sharp distinction between the holy and the unholy and, further, that the unholy was not limited by the proscriptions of white, conservative middle America. It reveals that despite a contemporary celebration of tongues speech, Pentecostal identity once came not through Spirit baptism but through life-style. As W. I. Evans put it, "Receiving the baptism of the Holy Spirit doesn't make you Pentecostal. It's what you do after you receive the baptism that makes you Pentecostal."[58]

The past suggests that the Assemblies of God, like American Pentecostalism more generally, grew at first not in spite of its culture-challenging message but because of it.[59] At least partly because it was out of step with modernity, it attracted people who were convinced that its message would bring them into step with God's end-times purpose.

Latin American Bible Institute graduating class in the early 1930s. (H. C. Ball founded this school in 1926.)

H. C. Ball was elected first superintendent of the Latin American District in 1929 and was active through the years in such educational efforts as the Latin American Bible Institute (pictured above).

Luncheon for black church leaders and students from Evangel College and Central Bible College, 1970. Seated (l–r): unidentified, Bob Harrison, C. W. H. Scott, Martin B. Netzel, Kermit Reneau, T. E. Gannon, unidentified, G. Raymond Carlson, unidentified, Phillip Crouch (CBC president). Standing: J. Robert Ashcroft (Evangel College president), Frank Davis, Thomas F. Zimmerman, unidentified, J. Philip Hogan, Bartlett Peterson, unidentified, Thurman Faison, unidentified

Executive Presbyters at the General Council in Long Beach, California, 1967 (l–r): Edgar W. Bethany, G. Raymond Carlson, N. D. Davidson, Joseph R. Flower, Howard Bush, T. E. Gannon, M. B. Netzel, Bartlett Peterson, C. W. H. Scott, Bert Webb, W. T. H. Richards (chairman of the Assemblies of God in Great Britain and Ireland), J. Philip Hogan, and Thomas F. Zimmerman

Under the leadership of Thomas F. Zimmerman the headquarters structure was reorganized in 1972.

A selection of position papers published in recent years by the Assemblies of God

ADMINISTRATIVE /

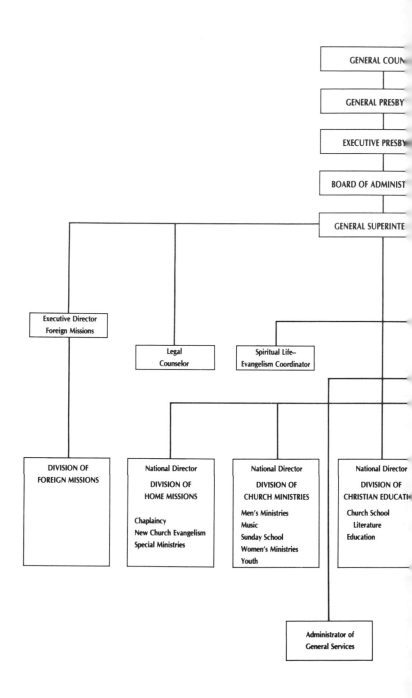

GENERAL COUN—

GENERAL PRESBY

EXECUTIVE PRESBY

BOARD OF ADMINIST

GENERAL SUPERINTE

Executive Director
Foreign Missions

Legal
Counselor

Spiritual Life–
Evangelism Coordinator

DIVISION OF
FOREIGN MISSIONS

National Director
DIVISION OF
HOME MISSIONS

Chaplaincy
New Church Evangelism
Special Ministries

National Director
DIVISION OF
CHURCH MINISTRIES

Men's Ministries
Music
Sunday School
Women's Ministries
Youth

National Director
DIVISION OF
CHRISTIAN EDUCATI◀

Church School
Literature
Education

Administrator of
General Services

OPERATIONAL FLOW CHART

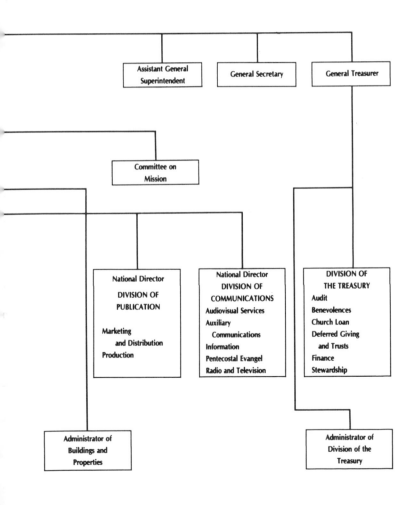

| Assistant General Superintendent | General Secretary | General Treasurer |

Committee on Mission

National Director
DIVISION OF PUBLICATION

Marketing and Distribution
Production

National Director
DIVISION OF COMMUNICATIONS
Audiovisual Services
Auxiliary Communications
Information
Pentecostal Evangel
Radio and Television

DIVISION OF THE TREASURY
Audit
Benevolences
Church Loan
Deferred Giving and Trusts
Finance
Stewardship

Administrator of Buildings and Properties

Administrator of Division of the Treasury

Officers of the General Council: 1914–1987

1. Hot Springs, Arkansas—April 2–12, 1914
Chairman: Eudorus N. Bell
Secretary: J. Roswell Flower

2. Chicago, Illinois—November 15–29, 1914
Chairman: Arch P. Collins
Assistant Chairman: Daniel C. O. Opperman
Secretary: J. Roswell Flower
Assistant Secretary: Bennett F. Lawrence

3. St. Louis, Missouri—October 1–10, 1915
Chairman: John W. Welch
Secretary: J. Roswell Flower

4. St. Louis, Missouri—October 1–7, 1916
Chairman: John W. Welch
Secretary: Stanley H. Frodsham

5. St. Louis, Missouri—September 9–14, 1917
(All officers reelected)

6. Springfield, Missouri—September 4–11, 1918
(All officers reelected)

7. Chicago, Illinois—September 25–30, 1919
Chairman: John W. Welch
Secretary and Editor: Eudorus N. Bell
Foreign Missions Secretary: J. Roswell Flower

8. Springfield, Missouri—September 21–27, 1920
Chairman: Eudorus N. Bell
Secretary: John W. Welch
Foreign Missions Secretary: J. Roswell Flower
Editor: J. T. Boddy

9. St. Louis, Missouri—September 21–28, 1921
Chairman: Eudorus N. Bell

Secretary: John W. Welch
Foreign Missions Secretary: J. Roswell Flower
Editor: Stanley H. Frodsham

10. St. Louis, Missouri—September 13–18, 1923
Chairman: John W. Welch
Assistant Chairman: David H. McDowell
Secretary: J. R. Evans
Foreign Missions Secretary: William Faux
Foreign Missions Treasurer: J. Roswell Flower
Editor: Stanley H. Frodsham

11. Eureka Springs, Arkansas—September 17–24, 1925
Chairman: W. T. Gaston
Assistant Chairman: David H. McDowell
Secretary: J. R. Evans
Foreign Missions Secretary–Treasurer: William Faux
Editor: Stanley H. Frodsham

12. Springfield, Missouri—September 16–22, 1927
General Superintendent: W. T. Gaston
Assistant General Superintendent: David H. McDowell
General Secretary: J. R. Evans
Foreign Missions Secretary: Noel Perkin
Editor: Stanley H. Frodsham

13. Wichita, Kansas—September 20–26, 1929
General Superintendent: Ernest S. Williams
Assistant General Superintendent: (vacant)
General Secretary: J. R. Evans
Foreign Missions Secretary: Noel Perkin
Editor: Stanley H. Frodsham

14. San Francisco, California—September 8–13, 1931
General Superintendent: Ernest S. Williams
Assistant General Superintendent: J. Roswell Flower
General Secretary: J. R. Evans
Foreign Missions Secretary: Noel Perkin
Editor: Stanley H. Frodsham

15. Philadelphia, Pennsylvania—September 14–20, 1933
(All officers reelected)

16. Dallas, Texas—September 12–19, 1935
General Superintendent: Ernest S. Williams
Assistant General Superintendent: J. Roswell Flower
General Secretary: J. Roswell Flower
Foreign Missions Secretary: Noel Perkin
Editor: Stanley H. Frodsham

17. Memphis, Tennessee—September 2–9, 1937
General Superintendent: Ernest S. Williams
Assistant General Superintendent: Fred Vogler
General Secretary: J. Roswell Flower
Foreign Missions Secretary: Noel Perkin
Editor: Stanley H. Frodsham

18. Springfield, Missouri—September 2–12, 1939
(All officers reelected)

19. Minneapolis, Minnesota—September 5–11, 1941
(All officers reelected)

20. Springfield, Missouri—September 1–9, 1943
General Superintendent: Ernest S. Williams
Assistant General Superintendent: Ralph M. Riggs
General Secretary: J. Roswell Flower
Foreign Missions Secretary: Noel Perkin
Editor: Stanley H. Frodsham

21. Springfield, Missouri—September 13–18, 1945
General Superintendent: Ernest S. Williams
Assistant General Superintendents: Ralph M. Riggs, Gayle F. Lewis,
  Fred Vogler, and Wesley R. Steelberg
General Secretary: J. Roswell Flower
Foreign Missions Secretary: Noel Perkin
Editor: Stanley H. Frodsham

22. Grand Rapids, Michigan—September 4–11, 1947
General Superintendent: Ernest S. Williams
Assistant General Superintendents: Ralph M. Riggs, Gayle F. Lewis,
  Fred Vogler, and Wesley R. Steelberg
General Secretary: J. Roswell Flower
General Treasurer: Wilfred A. Brown
Foreign Missions Secretary: Noel Perkin
Editor: Stanley H. Frodsham

23. Seattle, Washington—September 8–14, 1949
General Superintendent: Wesley R. Steelberg
Assistant General Superintendents: Ralph M. Riggs, Gayle F. Lewis,
  Fred Vogler, and Bert Webb
General Secretary: J. Roswell Flower
General Treasurer: Wilfred A. Brown
Foreign Missions Secretary: Noel Perkin
Editor: Robert C. Cunningham

24. Atlanta, Georgia—August 16–23, 1951
(All officers reelected)
(Wesley R. Steelberg died in Cardiff, Wales, July 8, 1952. Gayle F.

Lewis was chosen to fill the unexpired term of general superintendent by the General Presbytery on September 2, 1952. James O. Savell was selected as an assistant general superintendent to fill the vacancy created by Lewis's election.)

25. Milwaukee, Wisconsin—August 26–September 2, 1953
General Superintendent: Ralph M. Riggs
Assistant General Superintendents: Gayle F. Lewis, Bert Webb, J. O. Savell, and T. F. Zimmerman
General Secretary: J. Roswell Flower
General Treasurer: Wilfred A. Brown
Foreign Missions Secretary: Noel Perkin

26. Oklamhoma City, Oklahoma—September 1–6, 1955
(All officers reelected)
(Wilfred A. Brown died on September 19, 1955, in Springfield, Missouri. Atwood Foster was appointed by the General Presbytery to fulfill the unexpired term.)

27. Cleveland, Ohio—August 28–September 3, 1957
General Superintendent: Ralph M. Riggs
Assistant General Superintendents: Gayle F. Lewis, Bert Webb, C. W. H. Scott, and T. F. Zimmerman
General Secretary: J. Roswell Flower
General Treasurer: Martin B. Netzel
Foreign Missions Secretary: Noel Perkin

28. San Antonio, Texas—August 26–September 1, 1959
General Superintendent: Thomas F. Zimmerman
Assistant General Superintendents: Gayle F. Lewis, C. W. H. Scott, Bert Webb, and Howard S. Bush
General Secretary: Bartlett Peterson
General Treasurer: Martin B. Netzel

29. Portland, Oregon—August 23–29, 1961
(All officers reelected)

30. Memphis, Tennessee—August 21–26, 1963
(All officers reelected)

31. Des Moines, Iowa—August 25–30, 1965
General Superintendent: Thomas F. Zimmerman
Assistant General Superintendents: Howard S. Bush, Theodore E. Gannon, C. W. H. Scott, Bert Webb, and J. Philip Hogan
General Secretary: Bartlett Peterson
General Treasurer: Martin B. Netzel

32. Long Beach, California—August 24–29, 1967
(All officers reelected)

33. Dallas, Texas—August 21–26, 1969

General Superintendent: Thomas F. Zimmerman
Assistant General Superintendents: G. Raymond Carlson, T. E. Gannon, Kermit Reneau, C. W. H. Scott, and J. Philip Hogan
General Secretary: Bartlett Peterson
General Treasurer: Martin B. Netzell

34. Kansas City, Missouri—August 19–24, 1971

General Superintendent: Thomas F. Zimmerman
Assistant General Superintendent: G. Raymond Carlson
General Secretary: Bartlett Peterson
General Treasurer: Martin B. Netzel

35. Miami Beach, Florida—August 16–21, 1973

General Superintendent: Thomas F. Zimmerman
Assistant General Superintendent: G. Raymond Carlson
General Secretary: Bartlett Peterson
General Treasurer: Raymond H. Hudson

36. Denver, Colorado—August 14–19, 1975

General Superintendent: Thomas F. Zimmerman
Assistant General Superintendent: G. Raymond Carlson
General Secretary: Joseph R. Flower
General Treasurer: Raymond H. Hudson

37. Oklahoma City, Oklahoma—August 18–23, 1977

(All officers reelected)

38. Baltimore, Maryland—August 16–21, 1979

(All officers reelected)

39. St. Louis, Missouri—August 20–25, 1981

(All officers reelected)

40. Anaheim, California—August 11–16, 1983

(All officers reelected)

41. San Antonio, Texas—August 8–13, 1985

General Superintendent: G. Raymond Carlson
Assistant General Superintendent: Everett R. Stenhouse
General Secretary: Joseph R. Flower
General Treasurer: Raymond H. Hudson

42. Oklahoma City, Oklahoma—August 6–11, 1987

(All officers reelected)

Endnotes

Introduction

[1]Grant Wacker, "The Functions of Faith in Primitive Pentecostalism," *Harvard Theological Review* 77 (July/October 1984): 353–75.

[2]*1985–1987 Biennial Report,* by Biennial Report Committee, Lee Shultz, Chairman (Springfield, MO: Gospel Publishing House, 1987), 7, 8.

[3]In the biennium, 313 churches were removed from the list: 45 withdrew; 39 merged; 14 were removed; 215 closed. *1985–1987 Biennial Report,* 7.

[4]On religion since World War II, see Mark Silk, *Spiritual Politics: Religion and America Since World War II* (New York: Simon and Schuster, 1988); Robert Wuthnow, *Restructuring of American Religion: Society and Faith since World War II* (Princeton: Princeton University Press, 1988).

Chapter 1: From Isolation to Cooperation: The Assemblies of God and the New Evangelicals

[1]J. R. Flower to Ralph T. Davis, 3 December 1941, National Association of Evangelicals Collection, Assemblies of God Archives, Springfield, MO.

[2]In *Religious Outsiders and the Making of America* (New York: Oxford University Press, 1986), R. Laurence Moore notes the pervasive sense of persecution and conflict among Pentecostals, which they, like other "outsiders," seemed to cultivate. Luther Gerlach and Virginia Hine named persecution as one of five factors explaining Pentecostal growth. See their "Five Factors Crucial to the Growth and Spread of a Modern Religious Movement," *Journal for the Scientific Study of Religion,* 7 (1968): 36–37.

[3]For more information on the Assemblies of God and Oneness, see Edith L. Blumhofer, *The Assemblies of God: A Chapter in the Story of American Pentecostalism (Volume 1—To 1941)* (Springfield, MO: Gospel Publishing House, 1989), chapter 10.

[4]John Lake to Charles Parham, 24 March 1927, Assemblies of God Archives.

[5]Historian William McLoughlin has argued that the story of American evangelicalism was "the story of America itself" in the nineteenth century. See his *American Evangelicals, 1800-1900* (New York: Harper & Row, 1968), 1.

[6]For studies of fundamentalism, recent evangelicalism, and modernism, see Ernest R. Sandeen, *The Roots of Fundamentalism: British and American Millenarianism, 1800-1930* (Chicago: University of Chicago Press, 1970); George M. Marsden, *Fundamentalism and American Culture: The Shaping of Twentieth Century Evangelicalism, 1870-1925* (New York: Oxford University Press, 1980); George M. Marsden, *Reforming Fundamentalism: Fuller Seminary and the New Evangelicalism* (Grand Rapids: William B. Eerdmans Publishing Co., 1987); William R. Hutchison, *The Modernist Impulse in American Protestantism* (Cambridge, MA: Harvard University Press, 1976).

[7]Sandeen, *Roots of Fundamentalism.*

[8]Marsden, *Fundamentalism and American Culture.*

[9]Joel Carpenter, "The Fundamentalist Leaven and the Rise of an Evangelical United Front," in *Evangelical Tradition in America*, ed. Leonard I. Sweet (Macon, GA: Mercer University Press, 1984), 259.

[10]For a sense of how this fascination manifested itself, especially with regard to Israel, see Dwight Wilson, *Armageddon Now: The Premillenarian Response to Russia and Israel Since 1917* (Grand Rapids, MI: Baker Book House, 1977).

[11]Norman F. Furniss, *The Fundamentalist Controversy: 1918-1931* (Hamden, CT: Archon Books, 1963), 51-56.

[12]Stanley Frodsham, "Disfellowshipped!" *Pentecostal Evangel,* 18 August 1928, 7.

[13]Ibid.

[14]R. Bryant Mitchell, *Heritage and Horizons* (Des Moines, IA: Open Bible, 1982) gives an account of her meetings in Eugene, Oregon. Straton's pamphlet in defense of Utley is reprinted in Janette Hassey, *No Time for Silence* (Grand Rapids: Zondervan, 1986), 189-210. For Utley's life, see Uldine Utley, *Why I Am a Preacher: A Plain Answer to an Oft-Repeated Question* (New York: Fleming H. Revell, 1931).

[15]There were ties in the 1920s and 1930s between some Pentecostals and right wing politicians like Gerald Winrod and Gerald L. K. Smith. See Parham papers, Apostolic Faith Bible College, Baxter Springs, KS.

[16]Carl Henry, "Has Fundamentalism Lost Its Social Conscience?" *United Evangelical Action,* 1 June 1947, 3,5. Henry argued that fundamentalists—including those active in such ecumenical efforts as the NAE or the ACCC—desperately needed to couple their rejection

of liberal Protestant agencies (devoted to "attacking social ills") with a "forceful assault on social evils in a distinctly supernaturalistic framework."

[17]Marsden, *Reforming Fundamentalism,* 6.

[18]Ibid.; see also George M. Marsden, *The Evangelical Mind and the New School Presbyterian Experience* (New Haven: Yale University Press, 1970).

[19]Marsden, *Reforming Fundamentalism,* 6.

[20]Marsden, *Fundamentalism and American Culture,* 6–7. Moore discusses this at length in his *Religious Outsiders.*

[21]Carpenter, "Fundamentalist Leaven," 267.

[22]Ralph Davis letter, 11 December 1940, Herbert J. Taylor Papers, Box 14, File 27, Billy Graham Center Archives, Wheaton, IL.

[23]Minutes of the Committee for United Action Among Evangelicals, 27 October 1941, Herbert J. Taylor Papers, Box 14, File 27, Billy Graham Center Archives.

[24]Assemblies of God leaders noted the similarities of the two plans in their early stages and responded to an invitation from Davis and Wright to participate in their association with the information that the American Council seemed to be doing the same thing. Flower intimated that McIntire's associate H. McAllister Griffiths had led Assemblies of God leaders to believe that no objections would be raised on doctrinal grounds to Assemblies of God participation in the American Council. See Flower to Ralph T. Davis, 3 December 1941; Flower to R. L. Decker, 27 October 1949, National Association of Evangelicals Collection, Assemblies of God Archives.

[25]This attitude later figured in McIntire's attack on the Assemblies of God. He repudiated Pentecostal doctrine and accused the Assemblies of God of deceptive cooperation with the Federal Council of Churches.

[26]Minutes, Committee for United Action Among Evangelicals, 27 October 1941, 3; Herbert J. Taylor papers, Billy Graham Center Archives.

[27]Thomas R. Birch, the editor of *The Presbyterian Guardian,* listed these three areas of disagreement as reasons for the "stormy session" at Chicago and for continued charges that United Evangelical Action sponsors were "compromisers." *The Presbyterian Guardian,* 25 March 1942. It seems apparent that the ACCC was ready to accept Pentecostals. If McIntire could have consolidated the others in support of his program, he would by all indications have been as tolerant as the new evangelicals toward Pentecostalism and holiness people. However, having failed in Chicago, within a year he began criticizing the others for accepting Pentecostals.

[28]*The Lutheran Witness,* 25 November 1941, 395; *The Christian Century,* 1 October 1941, 19.

[29]Ibid.

[30]*The Church Times,* 27 September 1941, 19.

[31]Ralph Davis, letter of invitation to St. Louis, Herbert J. Taylor papers, Billy Graham Center Archives.

[32]Carpenter, "Fundamentalist Leaven," 261.

[33]J. Elwin Wright, "Reports to The Temporary Committee for United Action," Herbert J. Taylor Papers, Billy Graham Center Archives.

[34]Manuscript copy of Wright's opening remarks, 5, Herbert J. Taylor papers, Billy Graham Center Archives.

[35]Ben Hardin's comment is in his letter in "United We Stand: NAE Constitutional Convention Report," 8. Herbert J. Taylor Papers, Billy Graham Center Archives.

[36]Prolonged bickering discouraged some (like InterVarsity or independent Bible institutes) from maintaining early ties to the NAE (Decker to Herbert J. Taylor, 29 February 1948, Herbert J. Taylor Papers Collection 20, Box 66, File 14, Billy Graham Center Archives). Conservative voluntary associations needed support from the broadest possible constituencies. Aligning with one side or the other could have dire financial consequences.

[37]William Bell Riley, "The Fatal Weakness of Fundamentalism," *World-Wide Temple Evangelist,* 19 June 1942, 1, 6. See also William Bell Riley, "National Association of Evangelicals for United Action," *The Pilot,* November 1942, 53–54.

[38]See especially the editorial: Philip E. Howard, "St. Louis Convention," *The Sunday School Times* 84 (20 June 1942): 493–94, 498–99. See also "Four Significant Organizations," *The Sunday School Times* 85 (17 July 1943): 573, 574, 578, 587, 588.

[39]Ernest Gordon, "Survey of Religious Life and Thought," reprinted in Carl McIntire, *America Needs Christ,* 13. Another Baptist, Robert Ketcham, edited *The Baptist Bulletin,* the organ of the General Association of Regular Baptist Churches, in which he denounced the NAE. See, for example, "Facing the Facts," in the November 1942 issue. Some of his editorials—like "Shadow of the Federal Council"— were reprinted in pamphlet form. See also "Why the General Association of Regular Baptists Declared Itself in Fellowship with the American Council of Christian Churches (Rather than the widely-publicized National Association of Evangelicals for United Action)," undated article clipped from *The Baptist Bulletin,* National Association of Evangelicals Collection, Assemblies of God Archives.

[40]Samuel McCrea Cavert to Bishop Leslie R. Marston, 20 April 1945, Federal Council of Churches, Assemblies of God Archives.

[41]This series began in the 1 September 1948 issue of *United Evangelical Action*.

[42]A random selection of titles from *United Evangelical Action* evidences these views: on communism, "Enemy of Religion," (15 November 1947, 8); Daniel A. Reed, "Facts About Communism and Communists," 1 June 1948, 5–6; on Catholicism (much of this pertained to church and state questions), Glenwood Blackmore, "How Rome Seized an Ohio Public School System," (1 June 1947, 4ff); James Murch, "Threat to Liberty," (1 March 1947, 12–13); Glenwood Blackmore, "Is Roman Catholicism Broad and Tolerant?" (1 June 1948, 7ff); William Ward Ayer, "Romanism's Pied Piper: A Gospel-eye View of the Roman Catholic Church's Top Propagandist—Msgr. Fulton J. Sheen," (15 August 1948, 3ff); on patriotism, Samuel E. Boyle, "Jesus Christ and the American Tradition," (15 September 1947, 3ff); S. Richey Kamm, "The Christian and His Civic Responsibility," (15 May 1947, 3ff); V. Raymond Edman, "New Lamps for Old?" (1 October 1947, 3ff). The last article strongly implies that the desirable "old lamps" can be equated with traditional American values. Of the many derogatory comments about the designs of Federal Council leaders, Glenwood Blackmore, "It Can Happen Here!" (15 March 1947, 7–8) is typical. A sampling of liberal views on these subjects can be gained by an overview of *Christian Century* or the *Federal Council Bulletin*.

[43]Minutes, Board of Administration, 21 September 1943, 7; Herbert J. Taylor papers, Billy Graham Center Archives.

[44]There was considerable discussion in the NAE executive committee over admitting the International Church of the Foursquare Gospel, not primarily because the denomination was Pentecostal, but because of controversy surrounding its founder, Aimee Semple McPherson. The denomination ultimately was accepted. It is important to note, however, that the vast majority of American Pentecostal groups (numbering well over 250) neither sought nor were offered NAE membership. That was confined to longer-established, larger, white denominations. Of the many Pentecostal groups in existence in 1942, only the Assemblies of God and the Church of God (Cleveland) gained immediate prominence within the new organization.

[45]"Ockenga Disavows Barnhouse's Speech at N.A.E. Convention," *Christian Beacon*, 27 April 1944, 1. Apparently Barnhouse found his audience somewhat sympathetic: He found it necessary to "rebuke" those who shouted amen. Carl McIntire reported much "waving of hands around in the air" during prayer and claimed that during the NAE meeting a holiness advocate sought to convince him of sinless perfection and a Pentecostal tried to "sell him" on tongues. He charged that holiness and Pentecostal delegates had "well organized ground plans" and hoped to "Pentecostalize" the NAE. See W. O. H. Garman, "Analysis of National Association Convention and Constituency," *Christian Beacon*, 27 April 1944, 2. Both Barnhouse and McIntire

accurately gauged the potential situation. Before long, the Assemblies of God became (and it has remained) by far the largest affiliate of the NAE.

[46]Ibid.

[47]In fact, Okenga and Wright went so far as to offer positions of leadership despite Flower's frequently repeated deference to non-Pentecostal leadership. "We wish to assure you that the Assemblies of God desire no great prominence in this movement, although we are interested in its success.... We recognize that this association has done a new thing in the earth by the recognition of groups formerly excluded from 'Fundamentalist' associations.... If the publicizing of these groups will hinder other good evangelicals from uniting with the movement, then our advice would be that no prominence be given to them, but that they be kept in the background." Flower to Harold J. Ockenga, May 1943, National Association of Evangelicals Collection, Assemblies of God Archives. (It is widely rumored that J. Elwin Wright was reared in a Pentecostal home.)

[48]Garman, "Analysis of National Association Convention and Constituency," 2.

[49]Ibid.

[50]Robert Brown, "Hindrances to the Work of God," *Glad Tidings Herald,* May 1944, 2.

[51]News release, 3 May 1944, Herbert J. Taylor papers, Billy Graham Center Archives.

[52]Ibid.

[53]"United We Stand," 10.

[54]Ibid.

[55]Evangelicals were not the only Protestants to voice such sentiments. Both *The Christian Century* and the *Federal Council Bulletin* also published misgivings about Roman Catholic intentions and dreamed of a righteous America.

[56]Ibid.

[57]"United We Stand," 58.

[58]General Council Minutes, 1943, 8.

[59]Minutes, Board of Administration of the National Association of Evangelicals for United Action, 21 September 1943, 3, Herbert J. Taylor Papers, Billy Graham Center Archives.

Chapter 2: Fronts for United Action: Cooperation with Evangelicals and Pentecostals

[1]Samuel Cavert to Leslie R. Marston, 20 April 1945, National Association of Evangelicals Collection, Assemblies of God Archives.

²Fosdick's autobiography, *The Living of These Days* (London: SCM Press Ltd, 1957), remains an eloquent account of his aspirations and accomplishments. For a thorough assessment, see Robert Moats Miller, *Harry Emerson Fosdick: Preacher, Pastor, Prophet* (New York: Oxford University Press, 1985).

³See, for example, Ernest Gordon, "Ecclesiastical Octopus: Evangelism Without an Evangel," *United Evangelical Action,* 1 November 1948, 5–8, which includes a long segment entitled "The Radio and the FCC." Gordon alleges that Fosdick's ideas coincided with Nazi theology. That *United Evangelical Action* would publish Gordon's allegations indicates how close the National Association of Evangelicals and the American Council of Christian Churches actually were in these years.

⁴In a statement "Why I Joined the National Association of Evangelicals," Michigan Baptist Pastor H. H. Savage included these quotes from Wright's pamphlet, *Death in the Pot.* See Herbert J. Taylor Papers, Billy Graham Center Archives. In spite of such protestations about the Federal Council, it is striking to note similarities in the concerns of NAE and FCC proponents. In addition to shared anti-Catholicism, anticommunism, and strong patriotism, both groups urged prayer and preparation for revival, encouraged evangelism, urged morality in government and in public affairs.

⁵Though much popular fundamentalist thought anticipated a world church and world government, these fundamentalists chose not to acquiesce in the "inevitable" but rather to challenge it.

⁶Riley, "Fatal Weakness," 1.

⁷J. Elwin Wright to National Association of Evangelicals Board of Administration, 8 January 1944, Herbert J. Taylor Papers, Collection 20, Box 65, File 20, Billy Graham Center Archives.

⁸Ibid.

⁹See sample letter to pastors of churches whose denominations are affiliated, Herbert J. Taylor papers, Billy Graham Center Archives.

¹⁰Minutes of the Executive Committee of the National Association of Evangelicals, 7 December 1942, 11, Herbert J. Taylor Papers, Billy Graham Center Archives.

¹¹See Memo to Sponsors of Religious Radio Broadcasts, 16 April 1942, Herbert J. Taylor Papers, Billy Graham Center Archives.

¹²Under the farsighted leadership of R. J. Craig, Glad Tidings in San Francisco organized its own radio station in 1925. See Craig file, Assemblies of God Archives.

¹³Over the years, Zimmerman has played an important role on the executive committee of the National Religious Broadcasters. He has served both the National Religious Broadcasters and the National Association of Evangelicals as president. As of 1988, he had not missed

one of the forty-five annual National Religious Broadcasters conventions.

[14] See, for example, *United Evangelical Action,* 1 May 1948, 5; 15 September 1948, 5.

[15] Minutes, Executive Committee of the National Association of Evangelicals for United Action, 14 June 1944, 2; Herbert J. Taylor Papers, Billy Graham Center Archives.

[16] William Ward Ayer, *United Evangelical Action,* 1 June 1943, 17.

[17] Pentecostal participants in the NAE remained keenly conscious of the reservations of many fundamentalists—organized and independent—about them. Flower believed that independent fundamentalist organizations like Moody Bible Institute or such papers as *The Sunday School Times* in the end failed to support the NAE because of Pentecostal participation. He noted, for example, that the *Moody Monthly* and *The Sunday School Times* had refused to carry paid advertising for Assemblies of God uniform Sunday school lessons. Other independent leaders who at first identified with the NAE, then separated, were John R. Rice and Bob Jones, Sr. Through Flower's contact with the NAE, he won the friendship of Bob Jones. Bob Jones University (later vigorously anti-Pentecostal) conferred an honorary Doctor of Laws degree on Flower in 1946. See J. R. Flower to H. H. Foley, 12 September 1952; and Flower to J. Elwin Wright, 3 July 1947, Flower papers, Assemblies of God Archives.

[18] General Presbytery Minutes, 1949, 6; see also Flower to R. L. Decker, 29 September 1949, Flower papers, Assemblies of God Archives.

[19] R. D. Shaw to J. R. Flower, 13 June 1944, Assemblies of God Archives.

[20] *Christian Beacon,* 27 April 1944, 2.

[21] Alexander Clattenburg to J. Roswell Flower, 2 October 1942, Assemblies of God Archives.

[22] James DeForest Murch, "The Proposed National Council of Churches," *United Evangelical Action,* 1 October 1946, 6.

[23] Ibid., 7.

[24] See, for example, J. Alvin Orr in *United Evangelical Action,* 1 June 1943, 1. *United Evangelical Action* is the best source for a sense of the cultural issues that perturbed these evangelicals.

[25] *United Evangelical Action,* January [In 1944, wartime economy and financial setbacks forced the publication to go on a monthly schedule.] 1944, 3; Wilbur Smith, "The Urgent Need for a New Evangelical," National Association of Evangelicals Report, 1946, 42–48; Herbert J. Taylor Papers, Billy Graham Center Archives.

[26] *United Evangelical Action,* 10 September 1943, 2.

[27] Joel Carpenter, "Revive Us Again: Alienation, Hope, and the Resurgence of Fundamentalism, 1930–1950," unpublished mss., 19–20.

[28]"Report of Committee on Pentecostal Fellowship of North America," General Presbytery Minutes, 1949. Tapes of General Council sessions in the oral history collection of the Assemblies of God Archives further document reservations.

Chapter 3: Dissonance Among Pentecostals: The Assemblies of God Responds

[1]Unsigned letter addressed to the Guardians of Our Heritage, 28 February 1949, New Order of the Latter Rain Collection, Assemblies of God Archives.

[2]Ibid.

[3]Moorhead, a former missionary to India, accepted Pentecostal views in 1906 and became an itinerant, independent preacher, teacher, and author. After spending some time in England during World War I (where his objections to the war fervor of England patriots resulted in his imprisonment as a German spy) he taught at Beulah Heights and other schools before identifying with Ivan Spencer's efforts. See his obituary, *Elim Pentecostal Herald,* May 1937, 7.

[4]Mattsson-Boze, "Too Big to Bag," *Herald of Faith* (June 1944).

[5]Ibid.

[6]George Hawtin, *Church Government* (Los Angeles: Fox Printing Company, 1949), 8.

[7]Ibid. (see especially chapters 3 and 5).

[8]R. E. McAlister, "Apostles—True or False," *Truth Advocate,* 1, no. 1 (May 1949), 20.

[9]Unsigned letter to Guardians of Our Heritage, 28 February 1949, New Order of the Latter Rain Collection, Assemblies of God Archives. The Assemblies of God Archives has transcriptions of various prophecies by the Hawtins and Myrtle Beall, instructing the recipients about their gifts and callings.

[10]R. E. McAlister, "Prophets—True or False," *Truth Advocate,* 1, no. 1 (May 1949), 6.

[11]Assemblies of God Ministers' Letter, 20 April 1949, 4.

[12]R. E. McAlister to Ernest Williams, 23 April 1949, New Order of the Latter Rain Collection, Assemblies of God Archives.

[13]Ibid.

[14]R. E. McAlister, "The Restitution of All Things," *Truth Advocate,* 1, no. 1, (May 1949), 20.

[15]R. E. McAlister, "What Is Meant by the Manifestation of the Sons of God?" *Truth Advocate,* 1 (August, 1949), 11.

[16]Ivan Spencer, "In Memoriam," *Elim Pentecostal Herald* (May 1937), 6.

[17]Quoted in Marion Meloon, *Ivan Spencer: Willow in the Wind* (Plainfield, NJ: Logos International, 1974), 224.

[18]C. B. Smith (general superintendent of the Pentecostal Assemblies of Canada) to F. J. Lindquist, 7 December 1948, New Order of the Latter Rain Collection, Assemblies of God Archives.

[19]Ibid.

[20]Myrtle Beall file, Assemblies of God Secretariat.

[21]Ralph E. Northrup, "Belief of the Latter Rain People," New Order of the Latter Rain Collection, Assemblies of God Archives.

[22]General Presbytery Minutes (1949), 11, 18.

[23]*The Herald of Faith* 15 (July 1950), 3. As time passed, the dominant male leaders had serious reservations about women's participation in apostolic roles. It seems evident that Beall exercised more authority in discerning and bestowing gifts than her male counterparts thought appropriate.

[24]Unsigned letter to Guardians of our Heritage, 1 March 1949, New Order of the Latter Rain Collection, Assemblies of God Archives.

[25]"A Statement Pertaining to the New Order Latter Rain Movement," Assemblies of God Archives. The statement was prepared as a response to the many letters arriving in Springfield requesting information on the movement.

[26]These links are elucidated by Richard Riss in a summary of his thesis published as "The New Order of the Latter Rain: A Look at the Revival Movement on its 40th Anniversary," *Assemblies of God Heritage* (Fall 1987), 15–19.

[27]Ministers' Letter, 4.

[28]"Report of the Committee on the New Order of the Latter Rain," General Presbytery Minutes, 1949.

[29]Theodore Hofmeister to J. R. Flower, 9 July 1949, New Order of the Latter Rain Collection, Assemblies of God Archives. The Hawtins had apparently linked themselves with a former Assemblies of God employee who had turned in bitterness from the denomination years before, Jonathan E. Perkins.

[30]Ibid.

[31]H. F. Gambill to J. R. Flower, 7 May 1949, New Order of the Latter Rain Collection, Assemblies of God Archives.

[32]See, for example, "Great Swedish Revival," *The Voice of Faith* (May 1950), 1, 3, which links Freeman with the Latter Rain and also claims that Lewi Pethrus, veteran European Pentecostal leader, had "entered into Latter-rain revival, embracing its glorious truths" in the fall of 1949 (p. 3).

[33]One link between the New Order and the charismatic movement

is James Beall, popular advocate of that movement and son of Myrtle Beall. He is the current pastor of the church his mother founded.

[34]"A Last Minute Word from A. A. Allen," *Voice of Healing* special edition (1955), 2.

[35]Gordon Lindsay, "A Billion Souls for Christ," *Voice of Healing* (1955) 10.

[36]Ibid.

[37]For the story of the revival, see David Edwin Harrell, *All Things Are Possible* (Bloomington: Indiana University Press, 1975); David Edwin Harrell, *Oral Roberts: An American Life* (Bloomington: Indiana University Press, 1985).

[38]Eve Simson, *The Faith Healer* (St. Louis: Concordia Publishing House, 1977) analyzes their social backgrounds.

[39]"The Miracle of the Outpoured Oil," *Miracle Magazine* (January 1956), 2.

[40]Ibid., 3.

[41]Ibid., 4.

[42]Harrell, *All Things are Possible,* 55.

[43]Ibid., 56.

[44]*Jack Coe's International Healing Magazine* (May 1956), 22, 23; Harrell, *All Things Are Possible,* 62.

[45]A. A. Allen, "My Final Answer to the General Council of the Assemblies of God," *Miracle Magazine* (May 1956), 4; R. W. Schambach, "Has A. A. Allen Been Persecuted?" *Miracle Magazine* (May 1956), 5.

[46]Severe internal criticism came in the 1960s from a balanced, respected Pentecostal leader, Granville H. Montgomery. Montgomery had edited the *Pentecostal Holiness Advocate,* the official publication of the Pentecostal Holiness Church, for many years. He joined Oral Roberts' team, then left Roberts in 1961 and identified with Jack Coe's efforts, led by his widow, Juanita. In 1962, Montgomery published a series of articles he entitled "Enemies of the Cross," in which he castigated both major revivalists and the Pentecostal denominations which, he claimed, had forced the revivalists to extremes. Harrell rightly summarizes the force of Montgomery's critique: It was at once "the protest of a sympathetic insider" and that of a "true believer." *All Things Are Possible,* 141.

[47]William W. Menzies, *Anointed to Serve* (Springfield, MO: Gospel Publishing House, 1971), p. 334.

[48]General Presbytery Minutes, 1952, 14.

[49]Ibid., 15.

[50]Harrell, *All Things Are Possible,* 79.

[51]G. H. Montgomery, "Their Glory is Their Shame," *International Healing Magazine* (March 1962), 3.

[52]G. H. Montgomery, "Making Merchandise of You," *International Healing Magazine* (May 1962), 15.

[53]Harrell discusses this at length in *All Things Are Possible*, 140–144.

[54]For the story of recent related themes, see Bruce Barron, *The Health and Wealth Gospel* (Downers Grove, IL: InterVarsity Press, 1987).

[55]Harrell, *Roberts*, 460–462.

Chapter 4: Ecumenism, Renewal, and Pentecostal Identity

[1]"Rector and a Rumpus," *Newsweek*, 4 July 1960, 77. See also "Speaking in Tongues," *Time*, 15 August 1960, 53, 55. Bennett at one point was an electronics wholesaler, then a congregationalist minister, and finally an Anglo-Catholic Episcopalian.

[2]"Rector and a Rumpus," 77.

[3]Bennett did not permit charismatic intrusions in formal worship services, but added prayer and fellowship meetings to the schedule. In this, he duplicated Anglican Vicar Alexander Boddy's stance early in Pentecostalism's European history. Boddy's Anglican parish was the early focus of English Pentecostalism, but it remained thoroughly Anglican in its stated schedule. See announcements and accounts Boddy published in *Confidence*, 1909–1914.

[4]Dennis Bennett, *Nine O'Clock in the Morning* (Plainfield, NJ: Logos International, 1970).

[5]George Hawtin to Wayne Warner, 15 December 1987, 2–3, Assemblies of God Archives.

[6]"Miracles Today is on the Air," *Miracle Magazine,* December 1955, 2; "World Wide Revival," *The Voice of Healing*, January 1951, 5.

[7]Jack Coe, *Apostoles and Prophets . . . In the Church Today?* (Dallas: Herald of Healing, Inc., 1954), 3.

[8]Ibid., 4.

[9]Ibid., 12.

[10]Ibid., 30.

[11]Donald Gee, "Possible Pentecostal Unity," *The Voice of Healing* (January, 1951), 3.

[12]Ibid.

[13]Ibid., 7.

[14]For his biography, see David du Plessis as told to Bob Slosser, *A Man Called Mr. Pentecost* (Plainfield, NJ: Logos International, 1977).

[15]David du Plessis, *The Spirit Bade Me Go* (Plainfield, NJ: Logos International, 1970), 13.

[16]Ibid., 14.

[17]Charles W. Forman, "The Church Under the Cross," *The Christian Century,* 13 August 1952, 923–924.

[18]Du Plessis, *The Spirit,* 15.

[19]Ibid.

[20]They reconsidered their understanding of early World Council activities after the Council's third assembly in New Delhi in December 1961. Noting that before New Delhi, the World Council gave a stronger evangelical testimony than did the National Council of Churches. From 1961, their opposition to early World Council efforts was mitigated by their sense that 1961 was a watershed that had somehow allowed radical political, social, and religious agendas to take control. See, for example, G. Aiken Taylor, "New Delhi—Afterwards," *United Evangelical Action,* February 1962, 7–9; George Ford, "Ecumenicity: A Threat to Christian Unity," *United Evangelical Action,* May 1962, 8–11.

[21]Charles Clayton Morrison, "Protestants in the World Council of Churches," *The Christian Century,* 23 June 1954, 760.

[22]Du Plessis, *The Spirit,* 16.

[23]See, for example, Stanley Frodsham, "The Tarrying Meeting," *Pentecostal Evangel,* May 19, 1945, 4–5, which mourned the "discarding" of tarrying meetings and urged their revival; "The Early Days of Pentecost," *Pentecostal Evangel,* August 11, 1945, 2–3, reprinted a lengthy article from *The Upper Room* (1909) with the comment: "It is a very easy thing to drift away from the simplicity that characterized the Pentecostal Movement in its early days"; "Utter Dependence on the Holy Spirit," *Pentecostal Evangel,* October 20, 1945, 1, 5, noted: "It is not a flattering commentary on our spiritual state that so few members of our assemblies gather for prolonged seasons of prayer. Nor is it complimentary to have such small quarters for the places of prayer"; P. C. Nelson, "Shall We Surrender the Fort?" *Pentecostal Evangel,* November 3, 1945, 1, 12, noted declining emphasis on divine healing.

[24]Du Plessis, *The Spirit,* 67.

[25]Ibid., 64.

[26]"A World Council of Churches," *Pentecostal Evangel,* 20 November 1948, 15.

[27]"Church Union," *Pentecostal Evangel,* 27 November 1948, 15.

[28]"To Create a Superchurch?" *Pentecostal Evangel,* 10 December 1949, 9.

[29]Ibid., 8.

[30]Ibid.

[31]Quoted in "The 'World Church' Movement," *Pentecostal Evangel,* 26 March 1949, 10.

[32]"The World Council of Churches," *Pentecostal Evangel,* 4 February 1950, 9.

[33]"Unity—False and True," *Pentecostal Evangel,* 17 December 1950, 2.

[34]See, for example, "Pentecostal Leader Sees 'Awakening,' " *Seattle Post-Intelligencer,* 1 February 1969, 33.

[35]Carl McIntire, *Christian Beacon,* 15 June 1961, 8.

[36]Ibid.

[37]General Presbytery Minutes, 31 August 1962, 39.

[38]Ibid., 39–40.

[39]Du Plessis refused to withdraw: he received a letter from the denomination's general secretary, informing him that he was no longer a minister. Bartlett Peterson to David du Plessis, 14 September 1962, Du Plessis file, Assemblies of God Secretariat.

[40]General Presbytery Minutes, 31 August 1962, 40.

[41]John MacKay to David du Plessis, 17 April 1959, Archives of the David J. du Plessis Center for Christian Spirituality, Fuller Theological Seminary, Pasadena, CA.

[42]Henry P. Van Dusen, *Spirit, Son and Father: Christian Faith in the Light of the Holy Spirit* (New York: Charles Scribner's Sons, 1958), 84–85.

[43]Du Plessis to John MacKay, 28 May 1963, Du Plessis Center for Christian Spirituality. Although leaders of the turn-of-the-century revival emphasized Christ, most of them didn't overtly claim that that emphasis helped eliminate "excesses."

[44]Ibid.

[45]Ibid.

[46]See "No Pentecost," *Time,* 13 September 1948, 51–53.

[47]Quoted in newspaper clipping, "Visiting Cleric Sees Move to Christian Unity," from a Seattle paper, 1 February 1969, in Du Plessis file, Assemblies of God Archives.

[48]"The Third Force in Christendom," *Life,* 9 June 1958, 124.

[49]Ibid., 122.

[50]Van Dusen, *Spirit, Son and Father,* 84.

[51]Cecil M. Robeck, Jr., "Growing Up Pentecostal," *Theology News and Notes,* March 1988, 5.

[52]Ibid., 6.

⁵³Paul Blanshard, *American Freedom and Catholic Power* (Boston: The Beacon Press, 1951).

⁵⁴Zimmerman's article expressed sentiments that had been published in the NAE's *United Evangelical Action,* since the likelihood of a Kennedy nomination became apparent in 1958. See, for example, Don Hillis, "If We Elect a Roman Catholic as President," *United Evangelical Action,* 15 March 1958, 3–4; Don Hillis, "Will Rome Rule the World," *United Evangelical Action,* April 1959, 3, 6–7; George L. Ford, "A Catholic President: How Free From Church Control?" *United Evangelical Action,* May 1960, 5–7, 13. After Kennedy won, the NAE urged a strategy to assure continued religious freedom in Clyde Taylor and George Ford, "A Protestant Strategy for the Sixties," *United Evangelical Action,* December 1960, 5–7, 16.

⁵⁵Thomas F. Zimmerman, "A Protest Against Electing a Roman Catholic President," General Presbytery Minutes, 1960, Exhibit P, 3–4. This was published in the *Evangel* on 18 September 1960, 32.

⁵⁶News release, 2 September 1960, included in General Presbytery Minutes, 1960.

⁵⁷The Pentecostals' incredulity at this phenomenon are reflected in the titling of one work by an Assemblies of God author, J. Douglas Wead. In 1972 Wisdom House Publishers brought out his book, calling it *Father McCarthy Smokes a Pipe and Speaks in Tongues,* and the next year Creation House published it as *Catholic Charismatics: Are They For Real?*

⁵⁸Harold B. Smith, "America's Pentecostals: Where They Are Going," *Christianity Today,* 16 October 1987, 28.

⁵⁹Executive Presbytery, "Charismatic Study Report," *Advance,* November 1972, 3.

⁶⁰Catholic persecution left a wide variety of Protestants outraged. See, for example, *The Christian Century,* 16 June 1954, on Catholic persecution of Protestants in Colombia, South America.

⁶¹Smith, "America's Pentecostals," 28.

Chapter 5: Education

¹Fred Vogler, "Why Go to Bible School?" *Pentecostal Evangel,* 31 August 1940, 8.

²"Report of the Educational Department to the General Presbytery," 30 August 1950, 2.

³"Our Bible School Men Speak Concerning Education in the Assemblies of God," General Presbytery Minutes, 14–20 August 1951, 1.

⁴Ibid.

⁵Ibid.

[6]1949 General Council Debates, cassette, Oral History Collection, Assemblies of God Archives.

[7]By 1950, nineteen foreign students had been permitted by the Justice Department to enroll at Assemblies of God schools. (Some twenty-six thousand foreign students were in the United States.) The government required that schools be accredited and issue transferable credits for course work. Permission to enroll foreign students became increasingly attractive to Assemblies of God institutions as the denomination established overseas Bible institutes that produced graduates who sought further training in the United States.

[8]"Report of the Educational Department to the General Presbytery," 10 September 1948, 2.

[9]Of course this worked both ways. Assemblies of God men served on accrediting teams that evaluated cooperating non-Pentecostal schools.

[10]General Presbytery Minutes, 1948, 3. It is curious but revealing to note that these men deplored the raising of academic standards in the Bible institutes, a situation necessitated, according to them, by the lack of a denominational liberal arts college. Candidates for the ministry were being forced to meet higher standards, and "[t]he old-fashioned Bible school program" was no longer "free from academic intrusion" or fully "effective in the purely theological realm."("Our Bible School Men Speak", 4.) What passed for theology could be done better, contrary to most expectations elsewhere, with fewer academic constraints and without a broad academic context.

[11]Ibid.

[12]"Central Bible Institute Annual Report," 1950, General Presbytery Minutes.

[13]W. I. Evans, 1949 General Council Debates, cassette, Oral History Collection, Assemblies of God Archives.

[14]Ernest S. Williams, "A Report to the General Presbytery," 1948, 3.

[15]"Report of the General Secretary to the General Presbytery," 1948, 3.

[16]"Report of the Educational Department to the General Presbytery," 1946, 2.

[17]Ibid.

[18]Ibid.

[19]1949 General Council Debates, cassette, Oral History Collection, Assemblies of God Archives.

[20]Northern California in 1919; Southern California in 1920 and 1923; Oklahoma in 1927; North Central in 1930, Texas in 1931; Northwest and Illinois in 1934; Alabama and Kentucky in 1935; Eastern in 1938;

and Arkansas and New England in 1948 had established programs with as much as one-third of the curriculum devoted to academic studies. "Our Bible School Men Speak," 2.

[21]"Report of Educational Department to the General Presbytery," 1952.

[22]See Grade Card for Neshoba Holiness School, Chisolm Papers, Assemblies of God Archives.

[23]"Our Bible School Men Speak," 2.

[24]"Report of the Educational Committee to the Twenty-third General Council of the Assemblies of God," September 9–14, 1949.

[25]"Our Bible School Men Speak," 2.

[26]Ibid.

[27]J. Roswell Flower to General Presbyters, 3 August 1945, General Presbytery Minutes, 1945.

[28]"Our Bible School Men Speak," 3.

[29]In 1949, for example, W. I. Evans attempted to end Central Bible Institute's accreditation and to forestall the issuing of degrees on the grounds that the 1947 General Council had not specifically authorized granting degrees and that "questionable procedure" had been used to influence General Presbyters to vote for the school's accreditation.

[30]"Our Bible School Men Speak," 3, 4.

[31]Ibid., 3. An observation that the student body of an Assemblies of God school was only a reflection of the general constituency—as well as, perhaps, an expression of confidence in a system of electing spiritual leaders. This confidence in the correspondence between electability and spirituality is not surprising but nonetheless intriguing. One could argue with equal persuasion that the system tends to favor a particular personality type rather than necessarily to assure spiritual accountability.

[32]"Report of the Committee on the Purchase of the O'Reilly General Hospital Property," General Presbytery Minutes, 1946.

[33]"Education Committee Report," General Presbytery Minutes, 1953.

[34]Klaude Kendrick, "The Pentecostal Movement: Hopes and Hazards," *Christian Century,* 8 May 1963, 608.

[35]Ibid., 609.

[36]Ibid. By the 1980s, Assemblies of God colleges had progressed significantly in articulating their goal of integrating faith and learning. The bulletin of Southern California College includes the following statement that conveys the objectives that have emerged from recent positive statements on the potential of Christian college education:

> Southern California College, a liberal arts college, assumes that it is essential to offer educational opportunity

within a context of free inquiry and academic integrity. Such opportunity includes the examining of the Christian heritage, the claims of Christ, the charismatic involvement of the church, and the revelation of God. . . . The College therefore seeks—

Spiritually—To promote the values emerging from Biblical Christianity;

to encourage commitment to the Lord Jesus Christ and to the development of Christian character;

to serve the church by providing a trained membership with a missionary vision;

Intellectually—To provide a climate conducive to learning;

to encourage the acquisition of those skills required for meaningful participation in society;

to develop competency in the communication of ideas, in the use of research skills, and in the making of sound judgments;

Socially—To encourage informed, effective, and responsible service in contemporary society;

to enable students to discover the nature and implications of freedom in a democratic society;

to foster the development of integrated and purposeful human beings.

(*Southern California College 1988–90 Catalog*, 8–9.)

Notably absent is the sense of fear of secular training; instead, a positive alternative is offered.

[37]General Presbytery Minutes, 24 February 1959, 3.

[38]The districts not committed to the support of an Assemblies of God school were Kansas, Nebraska, Rocky Mountain, Tennessee, West Central, Michigan, Ohio, Illinois, Kentucky, Indiana, Southern Missouri, Wyoming, South Dakota, Oregon, Arizona, New York, Potomac, Southern New England, Northern New England. See "Central Bible Institute Regionalization Committee Meeting," General Presbytery Minutes, 1959, 1.

[39]See, for example, "Report of the Educational Planning Commission," General Presbytery Minutes, 1954.

[40]"Special Report to the General Presbytery from the Committee on Education," General Presbytery Minutes, 1959, 1.

[41]Ibid., 2.

[42]Ibid., 3.

[43]Ibid., 4.

[44]General Presbytery Minutes, 1960, 41–42.

[45]General Presbytery Minutes, 1961, 80. A survey of twenty-five Assemblies of God district superintendents and forty-eight Assemblies of God pastors on the subject revealed more support for, than opposition to, intercollegiate sports. See General Presbytery Minutes, 1961, 80a–80e.

[46]General Presbytery Minutes, 1962, 51.

[47]Grant Wacker, "America's Pentecostals," *Christianity Today,* 16 October 1987, 16.

[48]"Report of the Assemblies of God Education Department Secretary to the Assemblies of God Board of Education," 9 November 1987, 4.

[49]The Iowa case involved T. N. Taylor, pastor of First Assembly of God in Mount Pleasant, who was jailed in February 1987 for violating parole in reopening the congregation's Christian academy, which had been closed by state order. Alleging that the state wanted control of curriculum content, the Taylors were accused of violating a state teacher certification law. The case revealed that Assemblies of God adherents had strong affinities with vocal fundamentalists who also felt threatened by public school curriculum content. Lisa Getzler, "The State or Teachers: Who Says Who Teaches Children?" *Pentecostal Evangel,* 12 April 1987, 24–27.

[50]Report of the Assemblies of God Education Department Secretary to the Assemblies of God Board of Education, 9 November 1987, 2.

[51]"1987 Endorsed College Statistical Report," Education Department, 3.

Chapter 6: Denominational Programs

[1]*Pentecostal Evangel,* 11 January 1941, 14; *1985–1987 Biennial Report,* 3. For institutionalization in the Assemblies of God, see Margaret Poloma, *Charisma and Institutional Dilemmas Within the Assemblies of God: A Sociological Account* (Knoxville, TN: University of Tennessee Press, 1989).

[2]The flow chart in the appendix indicates headquarters administrative structure as of 1987.

[3]*1985–1987 Biennial Report,* 27.

[4]J. Irvine Harrison, "A History of the Assemblies of God," Th.D. diss., Berkeley Baptist Divinity School, 1954, 218.

[5]William Menzies, interview with Curtis W. Ringness, 10 October 1967.

[6]*Reaching our American Indians,* Home Missions Department pamphlet.

[7]General Council Reports, 1966, 119.

[8]*Presenting the American Indian Bible Institute,* Home Missions Department pamphlet.

[9]*Alaska Evangelism,* Home Missions Department pamphlet.

[10]*Branch Out,* Home Missions Department pamphlet.

[11]Home Missions Department statistics as cited in Menzies, *Anointed,* 236.

[12]News Release, Public Relations Office, 19 September 1967. Far North Bible College is now in Anchorage. It completed its own building in the spring of 1988 in conjunction with the Anchorage Native Assembly.

[13]Home Missions Department statistics. Seven states conducted such camps in 1969, with total attendance approximating 900; *Pentecostal Evangel,* 18 May 1952, 7.

[14]*Slant,* October 1966, 26; *Pentecostal Evangel,* 4 December 1955, 7. Central Bible College continues to offer course work to train ministers to work among the hearing impaired.

[15]*Branch Out,* Home Missions Department pamphlet.

[16]*1985–1987 Biennial Report,* 27.

[17]General Council Reports (1967), 117.

[18]General Council Reports (1961), 94.

[19]General Council Reports (1967), 118.

[20]"Blind Evangelism: Filling the Dark Emptiness," *Advance,* March 1968, 12.

[21]*1985–1987 Biennial Report,* 27.

[22]Menzies, *Anointed,* 238.

[23]David Wilkerson, *The Cross and the Switchblade* (New York: Bernard Geis, 1963).

[24]William Menzies, interview with David Wilkerson, 9 January 1968.

[25]Ibid.

[26]General Council Minutes, 1941, 64.

[27]Harrison, "History," 242–43.

[28]Ibid., 243–44.

[29]General Council Minutes, 1945, 84.

[30]National Christ's Ambassadors Department statistics cited by Menzies, *Anointed,* 276.

[31]William Menzies, interview with Paul Markstrom, 25 September 1967.

[32]Ibid.

[33]Ibid., Division of Home Missions statistics.

[34]Division of Home Missions statistics.

[35]Ibid.

[36]*Pentecostal Evangel,* 19 September 1965, 11.

[37]Ibid.

[38]Ibid., 12.

[39]Ibid.

[40]Harrison, "History," 210.

[41]*Pentecostal Evangel,* 1 July 1944, 11.

[42]General Council Minutes, 1945.

[43]*Pentecostal Evangel,* 1 July 1944, 11.

[44]See Menzies, *Anointed,* 330–335 for a discussion of the problems engendered by the salvation/healing movement.

[45]General Council Minutes, 1955, 23. Pastors were added to the Board by action of the 1957 General Council.

[46]General Council Minutes, 1957, 51.

[47]*Pentecostal Evangel,* 24 October 1965, 22.

[48]*Pentecostal Evangel,* 19 December 1965, 20.

[49]William Menzies, interview with J. Philip Hogan, 30 September 1967.

[50]General Council Reports, 1953, 34.

[51]The *1985–1987 Biennial Report* (p. 19) reported nearly $52.8 million in aggregate Speed-the-Light giving, with $3.3 million raised in 1986 alone.

[52]*Pentecostal Evangel,* 21 November 1965, 19.

[53]News Release, Public Relations Department, 16 January 1970; *1985–1987 Biennial Report,* 19.

[54]*1985–1987 Biennial Report,* 18.

[55]Ibid.

[56]*Pentecostal Evangel,* 19 December 1965, 19.

[57]General Council Minutes, 1961, 80.

[58]"Key," 1969 Annual Report of the Foreign Missions Department, 5.

[59]William Menzies, interview with David Womack, 11 January 1968.

[60]*Pentecostal Evangel,* 19 December 1965, 20.

[61]Ibid.

[62]Ibid.

[63]William Menzies, interview with Robert McGlasson, 9 October 1967.

[64]*Pentecostal Evangel,* 23 October 1983, 25.

[65]Menzies, interview with David Womack.

[66]"Key," 1969 Annual Report of the Foreign Missions Department, 3; *1985–1987 Biennial Report*, 25.

[67]*Our Campus Is the World*, Foreign Missions Department pamphlet, 1968.

[68]*1985–1987 Biennial Report*, 23.

[69]Ibid., 13.

[70]Ibid., 19.

[71]Rick Howard, *Chi Alpha Manual* (Springfield, MO: Gospel Publishing House, 1966), 6.

[72]National Christ's Ambassador's Department statistics as cited in Menzies, *Anointed*, 276–277.

[73]*1985–1987 Biennial Report*, 26–27. A high school ministry called Youth Alive is coordinated by the Youth Department.

[74]National Christ's Ambassador's Department statistics as cited in Menzies, *Anointed*, 277.

[75]*1985–1987 Biennial Report*, 18.

[76]William Menzies, interview with Mildred Smuland, 30 September 1967.

[77]*1985–1987 Biennial Report*, 17.

[78]William Menzies, interview with J. O. Harrell, 24 October 1967.

[79]William Menzies, interview with Wildon Colbaugh, 27 September 1967.

[80]General Presbytery Minutes, 1948, 4, 9.

[81]General Presbytery Minutes, 1949, 1.

[82]General Council Minutes, 1951, 24.

[83]Ralph M. Riggs, "The Men's Fellowship of the Assemblies of God," November 1952, unpublished report.

[84]Men's Fellowship Department statistics as cited in Menzies, *Anointed*, 282.

[85]Full Gospel Business Men's Fellowship, International, file, Assemblies of God Archives; Menzies, *Anointed*, 338.

[86]General Council Minutes, 1947, 37.

[87]General Council Minutes, 1933, 104.

[88]General Council Minutes, 1937, 66–68.

[89]William Menzies, interview with Evelyn Dunham, 15 December 1967.

[90]General Council Minutes, 1945, 49.

[91]Ibid.

[92]Menzies, interview with Evelyn Dunham.

[93]Statistics from Ministers Benefit Association office, 1987.

[94]General Presbytery Minutes, 1946, 7–8.

[95]William Menzies, interview with Stanley Michael, 22 September 1967.

[96]General Council Reports, 1967, 78.

[97]*Pentecostal Evangel,* 9 June 1945, 5.

[98]Ibid.

[99]Menzies, interview with Stanley Michael.

[100]Ibid.

[101]*1985–1987 Biennial Report,* 12.

[102]Menzies, *Anointed,* 286.

[103]*1985–1987 Biennial Report,* 11.

[104]Ibid., 12.

[105]Executive, Divisional, and Departmental Reports Presented to the 1988 General Presbytery, 40.

[106]*1985–1987 Biennial Report,* 22.

[107]Wacker, "Faith in Primitive Pentecostalism," 353–75; "America's Pentecostals: Who They Are," *Christianity Today,* 16 October 1987, 21.

[108]Wacker, "Faith in Primitive Pentecostalism," 353–75.

[109]Wacker, "America's Pentecostals," 21.

Chapter 7: The Recent Past

[1]"Why the Plan of Advance," in *Our Mission in Today's World,* Richard Champion, Edward Caldwell, Gary Leggett, eds. (Springfield, MO: Gospel Publishing House, 1968), 11.

[2]Ibid., 13.

[3]Ibid., 14.

[4]Ibid. This was a significant shift from early perceptions of what the "New Testament apostolic pattern" had called for. In 1968, the doctrine of tongues speech as uniform, initial evidence of Spirit baptism constituted proof that the denomination conformed to the apostolic pattern. Fifty-five years earlier, that doctrine had been a relatively minor component in a thoroughgoing restorationist worldview. The stress on evangelism, too, was different: it tended to de-emphasize an early stress on being as well as doing, on spirituality as well as on proclamation.

[5]"Declaration at St. Louis," *Our Mission in Today's World,* 212–213.

[6]Everett A. Wilson, "Hispanic Pentecostalism," in *Dictionary of Pen-*

tecostal and Charismatic Movements, ed. Stanley Burgess et. al. (Grand Rapids: Zondervan, 1988).

[7]Victor DeLeon, *The Silent Pentecostals* (Taylors, SC: Faith Printing Co., 1979), 43-44.

[8]Luce file, Assemblies of God Secretariat, contains letters that document the growth of these Spanish-language ministries.

[9]DeLeon, *Silent Pentecostals,* 45-48.

[10]The story of Hispanic Pentecostalism is told in DeLeon, *The Silent Pentecostals,* 43-44.

[11]In the mid-1920s, Mason apparently launched efforts to create a white branch of the Church of God in Christ. Assemblies of God minister August Feick resigned his credentials to direct Mason's white branch. Nothing is known about the immediate fate of these efforts. It is evident, however, that a viable white branch did not take shape.

[12]"Report of the General Secretary for Presentation to the General Presbytery" (1949), 5.

[13]Ralph Riggs to Frank Lindquist, 12 September 1956, Race Relations file, Assemblies of God Archives, 1.

[14]Ralph Riggs to Nicholas Bhengu, 12 October 1955, Race Relations file, Assemblies of God Archives.

[15]Ralph Riggs to Leonard Palmer, 11 February 1958, Race Relations file, Assemblies of God Archives.

[16]Riggs to Lindquist, 12 September 1956.

[17]Kenneth Roper (pastor, Assembly of God, Covelo, CA) to Ralph Riggs, 16 January 1956, Race Relations file, Assemblies of God Archives.

[18]Ralph Riggs to Kenneth Roper, 24 January 1956, Race Relations file, Assemblies of God Archives.

[19]Ibid.

[20]Ibid.

[21]"The 'Colored' Question," Race Relations file, Assemblies of God Archives, 2.

[22]General Presbytery Minutes, 1958, 36.

[23]"Report of the Committee to Consider a Colored Fellowship," General Presbytery Minutes, 1959.

[24]General Presbytery Minutes, 1959.

[25]"An Appeal to the Conscience, Concern, and Commitment of the Organized Religious Community," (October 1957), Race Relations file, Assemblies of God Archives; James Varner (Congress of African Peoples) to Assemblies of God Executives, 12 August 1970, Race Relations file, Assemblies of God Archives.

[26]Ernest G. Jones to the editor, *Christianity Today*, 10 April 1964, 17–18.

[27]John Garlock to Thomas Zimmerman, 18 May 1964, Race Relations file, Assemblies of God Archives.

[28]General Presbytery Minutes, 1965, 32–33; General Council Minutes, 1965, 60–61.

[29]General Presbytery Minutes, 1965, 32.

[30]An early effort in the recent attempt to focus attention on American blacks was a conference on Ministry to the Blacks in America held in October 1980. See list of participants and schedule in Race Relations file, Assemblies of God Archives.

[31]General Presbytery Minutes, 1968, 24–25.

[32]General Presbytery Minutes, 1968, 25.

[33]Ibid.

[34]Virginia Hogan to Thomas Zimmerman, 31 July 1978, Women's Movement file, Assemblies of God Archives.

[35]Ibid.

[36]These quotations are taken from a draft of Sand's address, Women's Movement file, Assemblies of God Archives, 4–5.

[37]Zimmerman made his opposition to the ERA clear in a letter to Mr. and Mrs. R. T. Highfill, 10 February 1977, Women's Movement file, Assemblies of God Archives.

[38]Robert Cunningham, "Let George Do It," *Advance*, February 1987, 4–6, noted the decline with concern.

[39]General Presbytery Minutes, 1963, 14–15.

[40]"Report of the Rehabilitation and Morals Study Committee," General Presbytery Minutes, 1964, 66.

[41]Ibid., 67.

[42]Ibid., 68.

[43]Ibid., 69.

[44]Ibid.

[45]General Presbytery Minutes, 1965, 17.

[46]General Presbytery Minutes 14 August 1979, 36.

[47]Ibid., 37.

[48]Ibid.

[49]General Presbytery Minutes, 19 August 1980, 13.

[50]General Presbytery Minutes, 17 August 1981, 10.

[51]General Presbytery Minutes, 24 August 1984, 27. Appended to the minutes was a list of titles, courses, and schools showing in which courses specific books were used.

[52]General Presbytery Minutes, 6 August 1985, 27.

[53]Ibid.

[54]Peter Williams, *Popular Religion in America: Symbolic Change and the Modernization Process in Historical Perspective* (Englewood Cliffs, NJ: Prentice-Hall, Inc., 1980).

[55]For example, Robert C. Liebman and Robert Wuthnow, eds., *The New Christian Right* (Hawthorne, NY: Aldine Publishing Company, 1983).

[56]Some of this material was previously published in two articles for *The Christian Century,* "Divided Pentecostals: Bakker vs. Swaggart," 6 May 1987, 430 431; "Swaggart and the Pentecostal Ethos," 6 April 1988, 333–335.

[57]See the brief essay, "Radical Right: Electronic Fundamentalism" based on David Edwin Harrell's work in *A Documentary History of Religion in America Since 1865,* ed. Edwin S. Gaustad (Grand Rapids: William B. Eerdmans, 1983), 539–544; Jeffrey Hadden and Anson Shupe, *Televangelism: Power and Politics on God's Frontier* (Henry Holt and Co., 1988); Grace Halsell, *Prophecy and Politics* (Westport, CT: Lawrence Hill & Co., 1986).

[58]Quoted in Kenneth D. Barney, "The Aftermath of Pentecost," *Paraclete* 21 (Summer 1987), 14.

[59]Grant Wacker, "America's Pentecostals: Who They Are," *Christianity Today,* 16 October 1987, 21.

Bibliographic Comments

In recent years, numerous significant resources for the study of American Pentecostalism have become available. The most comprehensive guide to sources is Charles Edwin Jones, *A Guide to the Study of the Pentecostal Movement*, 2 vols. (Metuchen, NJ: Scarecrow Press, 1983). See also, Grant Wacker, "Bibliography and Historiography of Pentecostalism (U.S.)," *Dictionary of Pentecostal and Charismatic Movements*, ed. Stanley M. Burgess, et. al (Grand Rapids: Zondervan, 1988). (This dictionary is a valuable compendium of entries covering a wide range of people and institutions as well as bibliography. It also provides a valuable overview of the literature.)

Several prior histories of the Assemblies of God trace the denomination's institutional development, the intricacies of which are largely beyond the scope of my present work. See Carl Brumback, *Suddenly... From Heaven* (Springfield, MO: Gospel Publishing House, 1961); William Menzies, *Anointed to Serve* (Springfield, MO: Gospel Publishing House, 1970). The two-volume set by Gary B. McGee, *This Gospel Shall be Preached*, documents the story of Assemblies of God foreign missions. Margaret Poloma, *The Assemblies of God at the Crossroads: Charisma and Institutional Dilemmas* (Knoxville: University of Tennessee Press, 1989) is an important sociological assessment of the recent period.

Index

Accreditation of schools, 114–115, 130, 222n.7
Accrediting Association of Bible Institutes and Bible Colleges, 114, 115
Adams, J. Davis, 21
Advance, 155
Allen, A. A., 67, 69, 72–73, 76, 81pl., 87
Ambassador I, 145, 158pl.
Ambassador II,, 145
Ambassadors in Mission, 149
American Council of Christian Churches, 22, 23, 26, 37, 41, 209n.27
Apostolic Faith Movement, 57
Apostolic Faith Movement (South Africa), 90
Ashcroft, John, 168
Ashcroft, J. Robert, 121, 126, 133pl., 135pl., 149, 193pl.
Assemblies of God, 24
  accreditation of Bible schools, 116, 118, 222n.10
  beginnings, 5
  Bible colleges, 109–110
  black relations, 173–178, 193pl., 231n.30
  charismatic renewal, views of, 53, 87, 103, 105
  church-related schools, 130, 225n.49
  divorce and remarriage, 181
  doctrine, 18
  ecumenical movement, views of, 91, 97, 99, 105
  education, 109, 113, 120–121
  as fundamentalists, 15
  growth, 5, 10, 12
  headquarters, 137, 163pl.
  missions, 43
  NAE involvement, 31, 32, 106, 168
  New Order, response to, 64–67
  PFNA involvement with, 47
  position papers, 183, 196pl.
  radio broadcasting, 39–40
  salvation/healing revival, response to, 73–74
  statistics, 10, 137, 207n.3
  Sunday schools, 41
  war, views on, 30
  women, views on, 179–180
  youth ministries, 42–43
Assemblies of God Chaplain, 142
Assemblies of God Theological Seminary, 142, 126–128, 162pl.
At Ease, 142
Ayer, William Ward, 38–39, 40

Bakker, Jim and Tammy, 168, 186, 187, 188
Ball, H. C., 144, 171, 192pl.
Baptism in the Holy Spirit (*see also* Holy Spirit), 166, 190, 229n.4
Baptists, 17
Barnhouse, Donald Grey, 27, 28, 40
Beall, James, 216–217n.33
Beall, Myrtle, 55, 63, 80pl.

Benevolences, Department of, 152–154
Bennett, Dennis, 85–86, 95, 218n.1, 218n.3
Berean College, 110, 124
Berean School of the Bible (*see also* Berean College), 123–124, 134pl.
Bethany, Edgar W., 194pl.
Bethany Retirement Center, 153
Bethel Temple, 42
Bethesda Missionary Temple, 53, 55, 60, 62–63, 80pl.
Betzer, Dan, 40, 50pl.
Bible institutes, 109, 111–112, 114, 131, 222n.7
Bible Quiz, 150
Billion Souls Crusade, 67, 68, 81pl.
Blomberg, Elvar, 64
Blue network, 37–38, 40
Boddy, Alexander, 218n.3
Bosworth, F. F., 70
Boyd, Frank, 121, 123, 134pl.
Boys and Girls Missionary Crusade, 146, 147, 159pl.
Branham, William, 66, 68, 70, 81pl.
Britton, C. E., 51pl.
Broadcasting (*see* radio)
Brown, Robert, 28, 39
Bruzelius, D., 64
Burnett, Cordas C., 107pl., 127, 134pl.
Bush, Howard, 194pl.

Campus Ambassador, 149
Carlson, G. Raymond, 193pl., 194pl.
Carlson, R. J., 181–182
Catholic Hour, 29
Catholicism, 11, 29, 100, 102
  charismatic renewal within, 86, 96
  views toward, 29–30, 31, 45, 103–104
Cavert, Samuel, 35
Center for Ministry to Muslims, 148
Central Bible Institute, 118, 133pl.
  accreditation of, 116, 117, 223n.29
  enrollment, 131
  financial situation, 125–126
  School for the Deaf, 139

Chafer, Lewis Sperry, 22
Chaplains, 11, 29, 139
  institutional, 142–143
  military, 141–142, 157pl.
  wartime, 142
Charismatic renewal, 53, 78, 86, 103–105, 216n.33
Chesser, W. L., 151pl.
Chi Alpha, 149
Chisolm, R. B., 119–120
Cho, Yonggi, 147
Christ for the Nations, 75
Christian America, 46
Christ's Ambassadors, 42, 142, 149, 150
Christ's Ambassadors Herald, 42
Church of God (Cleveland), 24, 26, 31, 47
Church School Literature, 154
Coe, Jack, 71–73, 81pl., 87
Coe, Juanita, 76
College Fellowship Bulletin, 149
Collins, Millard, 112, 113–114
Communications Act, 40
Congo Protestant Council, 23
Congregationalists, 17
Cook, Bob, 107pl.
Cooperation, 15, 44, 47, 49
Copeland, Paul, 159pl.
Coronodo Hotel, 13
Co-signer, 139
Cotton, Jim, 157pl.
Council on Evangelism (St. Louis, 1968), 166–168, 179
Credentialing of ministers, 14
Crouch, Phillip, 193pl.
Cultural influences, 9, 10, 11, 14, 29, 45, 156
Cunningham, Robert, 162pl.

Davidson, N. D., 194pl.
Davis, Frank, 193pl.
Davis, Ralph, 21, 22, 23
Dean, Horace F., 46
Decade of Harvest, 10
Dispensationalism, 15, 16, 17 18, 19, 20
Du Plessis, Anna, 90
Du Plessis, David, 12, 51pl., 86, 95, 96, 99–100, 107pl.
   dismissal from A/G, 168, 220n.39
   ecumenical movement, involvement with, 90–93, 102
   Spirit baptism, views of, 98–99
Durham, William, 56–57, 58, 59

Early rain, 55
Ecumenism, 11, 12, 90, 93–97, 100–101
Edman, V. Raymond, 21
Education Department, 111, 126, 149
Elim, 56, 63
Elim Pentecostal Herald, 63
End times, 19, 37, 54, 87, 93, 95, 191
Epperson, Jack, 151
Erickson, Clifton, 71
Evangel College, 133pl.
   enrollment, 131
   financial situation, 125–126, 129
   purchase of land, 124–125, 135pl.
   teacher-training program, 125
Evangelical Foreign Missions Association, 43
Evangelicals, 16, 20, 36, 46, 169
Evangelism, 44, 46, 169, 179
Evans, W. I., 50pl., 112, 121, 132, 133pl.
   on accreditation, 117, 223n.29
   dean of CBI, 116, 118
   on Pentecostals, 190
Executive Presbytery, 39, 96, 115
   on credentials for ministers, 189
   as Educational Committee of the A/G, 117–118, 122
   self-study of A/G, 166

Faith, 9, 156
Federal Council of Churches of Christ, 21, 26–27, 35, 36, 37, 38, 45, 88, 93
   Assemblies of God view of, 40, 44
   officers of, 99
   opposition to, 22–23
Ferrin, Howard, 21
Flattery, George, 148
Flower, J. Roswell, 34pl., 48, 49, 59, 61, 114, 135pl., 159pl., 166, 209n.24
   education, involvement with, 122
   integration, views on, 174, 175
   NAE, involvement with, 13, 24, 31, 41, 45, 212n.47
   PFNA, involvement with, 47
Flower, Joseph R., 194pl.
Foreign Missions Advisory Committee, 144
Foreign Missions Conference of North America, 43
Foreign Missions Department, 143–149
   personnel goals (1943) 143–144; (1957) 147
Fosdick, Harry Emerson, 36–37, 99
Freeman, William, 66, 70
Free Methodist Church, 26
Frodsham, Stanley, 18, 63
Fuller, Charles, 23
Full Gospel Business Men's Fellowship International, 78, 88, 89
Fundamentalism, 17, 18, 19, 24, 26, 35, 36, 208n.16
   definition of, 16, 20

Gannon, T. E., 193pl., 194pl.

Gardner, Velmer, 67, 71
Garlock, H. B., 144
Garlock, John, 177
Gee, Donald, 48, 88, 90
General Council sessions, (1949) 65,82pl.;(1964)194pl.;(1965) 178; (1967) 167
General Presbytery, 39, 47
  on ecumenism, 97
  on graduate training, 128
  on New Order, 65
Gerig, Jared F., 107pl.
Glad Tidings Tabernacle, 39
Global Conquest, 146–148
Global Conquest, 144, 147
Good News Crusades, 148
Good News Crusades, 144
Gordon, A. J., 17
Gordon, Ernest, 26, 27
Gospel Publishing House, 154–155, 173
Grable, Marcus, 41
Graham, Billy, 10
Graves, Arthur, 112, 113
Griffiths, H. McAllister, 22
Gundersen, Carl, 107pl.

Hagin, Kenneth, 78
Hardin, Ben, 31
Harrell, David Edwin, 75
Harrell, J. Otis, 151–152
Harris, Ralph, 42
Harrison, Bob, 193pl.
Hatch, Carl, 42
Hawtin, Ernest, 55, 58, 65
Hawtin, George, 55, 56, 58, 59–60, 65, 80pl., 87
Healing, physical, 18, 57, 69
Heard, R. D., 51pl.
Hearing impaired, 139
Herald of Faith, 58, 59
Hicks, Tommy, 75
Highlands Child Placement Services, 154
Hillcrest Children's Home, 153
Hinson, Gladys, 153
Hispanic (*see also*, Spanish-speaking, ministry to), 10, 48, 173
Hogan, J. Philip, 43, 193pl., 194pl.
Holsinger, J. Calvin, 149
Holt, Herrick, 55, 56, 80pl.
Holy Spirit, 14, 86, 98–99, 100–101
Home Missions, Department of, 137–141
Houghton, Will, 21
Hughes, Ray, 51pl.
Hunt, Percy G., 55, 56, 58, 80pl.

Independent Assemblies of God, 56, 58
International Church of the Foursquare Gospel, 55
International Correspondence Institute, 148
International Council of Religious Education, 41
International Media Ministries, 148
Isolationism of Pentecostals, 13–14

Jackson, Gayle, 71
Jagger, O. L., 71
Johnson, Torrey, 42
Jones, Bob, 35
Jones, Gwen, 50pl.
Jones, Rufus, 107pl.

Kamerer, J. z., 159pl.
Kendrick, Klaude, 121, 125
Kerr, Daniel, 57
Kinderman, Gustav, 144
Kinney, Seeley, 56, 61
Kuhlman, Kathryn, 78, 79

Laird, Harold, 22
Latin American Bible Institute, 192pl.
Latin American District, 192pl.
Latter rain, 12, 54–55, 86, 88, 112
Laying on of hands, 60, 64
Lewis, Gayle F., 51pl., 135pl., 182
Liberal arts education, Assem-

blies of God, 122, 124–125
LIFE Publishers, 173
Light-for-the Lost, 146, 147, 160pl.
Lindsay, Freda, 75, 79
Lindsay, Gordon, 67, 70, 71, 72, 74, 75–76, 79, 81pl.
Luce, Alice, 171
Lugo, Juan L., 172
Lutheran Hour, 40

Machen, J. Gresham, 20
Mackay, John, 91
Maier, Walter, 22, 40
Mallough, Don, 152
Manifest sons of God, 61–62
Maranatha Village, 153
Markstrom, Paul, 142–143
Marshall, Sunshine (Mrs. H. C. Ball), 171
Materialism, 11
Mattsson-Boze, Joseph, 56, 58, 59, 83pl.
McAlister, R. E., 61
McCarthy, Joseph, 99
McIntire, Carl, 26, 36, 37–38
  ACCC, formation of, 22–23
  Pentecostalism, view of, 44, 95, 209n.27
  views, 27, 28
McKay, John, 97, 98
McLean, Martha, 161pl.
McPherson, Rolf, 51pl.
Men's Ministries Department, 89, 146, 151–152
Menzies, William, 149
Minister's Benefit Association 152–153
Ministers
  rehabilitation of, 181–183, 188–189
  moral failure of, 76-77, 186, 190
Miracles (*see also* Healing), 68
Missionaries, home, 138
Missionettes, 150–151
Mobilization and Placement Service, 148–149, 160pl.
Modernism, 17, 18, 19, 21, 26, 45

Montgomery, Granville H., 76, 217n.46
Moody Bible Institute, 21
Moody, D. L., 17, 114
Moorhead, Max Wood, 56, 61–62, 215n.3
Morrison, Clayton, 92
Mountain Movers, 144

National Association of Evangelicals, 12, 24, 25, 36, 37, 88, 211n.45, 213n.4
  accrediting association, 114–115
  affiliates, 26, 28, 211n.44, 214n.17
  goals of, 29
  missions, 43–46
  officers, 107pl.
  opposition to, 26, 27
  origins, 16, 20–21, 23–24
  Pentecostal view of, 28–29
  radio time, 38, 40
  youth work, 42–43
National Commission for Christian Leadership, 29, 46
National Committee for Christian Leadership, 42
National Conference of Christians and Jews, 39
National Council of Churches of Christ, 45, 93
National Fellowship for Spiritual Awakening, 29, 6
National Fine Arts Festival, 150
National Religious Broadcasters, 40, 213n.18
National Royal Ranger Training Center, 151, 161pl.
National Sunday School Association, 41
National Vespers Hour, 36
National Youth Conference, 42
Netzel, Martin B., 193pl., 194pl.
New England Fellowship, 23, 27
New evangelicals, 22, 23, 35, 45, 46
New Order of the Latter Rain,

53, 57, 79, 80pl., 82pl., 216n.33
  meetings, 62
  Myrtle Beall's involvement
    with, 63
  origins of, 55–56
  practices of, 57–58
  spiritual gifts, use of, 60
  teachings of, 58
  in United States, 62–63
Nikoloff, Nicholas, 113
North American Association of
  Bible Institutes and Bible
  Colleges, 114
North Central Bible College, 131
  Deaf International Bible Col-
    lege, 139

Ockenga, Harold John, 20, 21,
  22, 23, 25, 26, 27, 28, 29, 30,
  31
Ohrnell, Arvid, 142–143, 157pl.
Olazabal, Francisco, 172
Old Fashioned Revival Hour, 22
Oneness, 14
Opperman, D. C. O., 116, 120
Organization, 15
  opposition to, 14, 58, 59
Osborn, T. L., 67, 71, 75
Osgood, Howard, 144
Osterberg, A. G., 42
Oxnam, G. Bromley, 99

Paine, Stephen, 40
Parham, Charles, 54, 59, 116
Peale, Normal Vincent, 11
Pearlman, Myer, 141
Pentecost, 48
Pentecostal Assemblies of Can-
  ada, 55
Pentecostal Digest, 139
Pentecostal Evangel, 11, 155,
  162pl.
Pentecostal Fellowship of North
  America, 46–48, 51pl.
Pentecostalism, 12, 31, 53, 56, 79,
  86, 99–100, 185–186, 190
Pentecostals, 48, 49, 58, 90

Pentecostal World Conference,
  88, 90
Perkin, Noel, 13, 24, 33pl., 43,
  143, 147, 159pl., 166
Peterson, Bartlett, 39, 116,
  159pl., 177, 193pl., 194pl.
Pethrus, Lewi, 48, 56
Pierce, Burton, 152
Position papers of the Assem-
  blies of God, 183, 196pl.
Positive confession, 78
Presbyterians, 17
Prison outreach (see Chaplains,
  institutional
Prophecy, 19, 64

Radio, 29, 36–40, 213n.12
  ethical standards, 39
  free air time, 23, 37, 38, 40
  NAE involvement with, 36
  purchased time, 39
Radio Department, Assemblies
  of God, 39
Rasmussen, A. W., 56, 63
Reneau, Kermit, 193pl.
Restoration, 54, 58, 62
Reveille, 141
Revival, 46, 54, 57, 166
Revivaltime, 39, 40, 50pl.
Rhema Bible Institute, 78
Rice, John R., 35
Richards, W. T. H., 194pl.
Richey, Raymond T., 15, 31, 70–
  71
Riggs, Ralph, 13, 24, 33pl., 41,
  112, 114,, 115 135pl., 151,
  159pl., 166
  education, involvement with,
    124
  segregation, views on, 175–176
Riley, William Bell, 26, 37
Robeck, Cecil, 101
Roberts, Oral, 68, 76, 78, 79, 88
Royal Rangers (see also Na-
  tional Royal Rangers
  Training Center), 151
Rusthoi, Howard, 51pl.
RV Volunteers, 149

Salvation/healing revival, 12, 53, 67–79, 88
Voice of Healing, 69
Sanctification, 56
Savell, James O., 74
Scandinavian Pentecostals *see also* Independent Assemblies of God), 56
Schmidgall, Robert, 190
School of Missions, 145
Scott, Charles W. H.,, 112, 125, 127, 193pl., 194pl.
Second Coming, 19
Separatism, 18
Sermons in Song, 39, 50pl.
Servicemen's Department, 141–142
Shakarian, Demos, 51pl., 88
Sharon School, 55–56, 80pl.
Sheen, Fulton, 11, 29
Short, Kenneth, 144
Shultz, Lee, 149
Signs of Life, 139
Society for Pentecostal Studies, 105
Southeastern College, 131
Spanish-speaking, ministry to, 170–173
Speed-the-Light, 145, 146, 158pl.
Spencer, Ivan, 56, 61, 62
Spiritual conflict, 14
Spiritual gifts, 86
Steelberg, Wesley, 39, 42, 51pl., 151pl.
Straton, John Roach, 18
Sumrall, Ernest, 113, 119
Sunday school, 10
conventions, 41, 52pl.
Department, A/G, 146
NAE involvement with, 41
Swaggart, Jimmy, 130, 186, 187–190

Talbot, Louis, 21
Taylor, Clyde, 43
Teen Challenge, 139–140
Teen Talent, 150
Televangelism, 186–187

Temporary Committee for United Action Among Evangelicals (*see also* National Association of Evangelicals,) 24
Tenzythoff, Gerrit, J., 134pl.
Third Force, 100–101
Tongues speaking, 57, 85, 89, 165, 229n.4
Torrey, R. A., 17, 18
Trinitarian, 47, 48

United Evangelical Action, 27
Utley, Uldine, 18

Van Dusen, Henry Pitney, 98, 100
Visually impared, 139
Vogler, Fred, 110, 159pl.
Voice of Faith, 63
Voice of Healing 71, 74, 87

Walker, J. H., 31
Ward, C. M., 39
Webb, Bert, 135pl, 159pl., 194pl.
Whipple, Edith, 161pl.
Whitney, Mrs. E. W., 139
Wilkerson, David, 140
Williams, Ernest S., 13, 24, 31, 34pl., 39, 48–49, 50pl., 51pl., 64
Woman's Touch, 150
Women in ministry, 216n.23
Women's Ministry Department, 147, 150, 161pl.
Women's Missionary Council, 161pl.
World Council of Churches, 37, 45, 90, 91, 92, 93, 94, 96, 219n.20
World Missions Plan, 146
World Pentecostal Conference, 48, 51pl., 176
World's Christian Fundamentals Association, 17, 18
World War I era, 48
World War II era, 151
affecting social change, 10

A/G support of war, 11
causing spiritual reawakening, 39, 77, 106
effect on education, 115, 124,
129
as sign of end times, 46
Wright, J. Elwin, 20, 21, 22, 23,
24, 25, 27, 28, 37, 94–95

Youth programs, 42–43

Ziese, Anna, 143
Zimmerman, Thomas F., 33pl.,
49, 50pl., 102, 134pl., 135pl.,
176 193pl., 194pl., 195pl.
NAE involvement, 24, 96
NRB involvement, 213n.13
Sermons in Song, narrator of,
39
women's movement, views of,
180

About the Author

Dr. Edith L. Blumhofer is the project director of the Institute for the Study of American Evangelicalism and assistant professor of history at Wheaton College, Wheaton, Illinois. She received her Ph.D. in American Religious History from Harvard University. She is a member of the American Society of Church History, the American Historical Association, and the Society for Pentecostal Studies. As Assemblies of God historian, Dr. Blumhofer wrote this two-volume work and an earlier, briefer work, *The Assemblies of God: A Popular History*. She has written articles for several periodicals as well as for the *Dictionary of Pentecostal and Charismatic Movements*.